Ghosts of Slavery

A LITERARY ARCHAEOLOGY
OF BLACK WOMEN'S LIVES

Jenny Sharpe

University of Minnesota Press
Minneapolis / London

The University of Minnesota Press gratefully acknowledges permission to reprint the following. Lines from "Nanny" (text version) by Jean "Binta" Breeze, from *Riddym Ravings and Other Poems* (London: Blackrose Press, 1988), copyright 1988, reprinted courtesy of Race Today Publications. Lines from "Nanny" by Lorna Goodison, from *I Am Becoming My Mother* (London: New Beacon Books, 1986), copyright 1986, reprinted courtesy of New Beacon Books. Lines from "mary prince bermuda. turks island. antigua. 1787" by Gale Jackson, in the *Kenyon Review* 14, no. 1 (1992): 48, copyright 1992, reprinted courtesy of the author.

An earlier version of chapter 4 appeared as "'Something Akin to Freedom': The Case of Mary Prince," *differences* 8, no. 1 (1996): 31–56; copyright 1996 by the Regents of Indiana University; reprinted with permission.

Published by the University of Minnesota Press
111 Third Avenue South, Suite 290
Minneapolis, MN 55401-2520
http://www.upress.umn.edu

Library of Congress Cataloging-in-Publication Data

Sharpe, Jenny.
    Ghosts of slavery : a literary archaeology of black women's lives / Jenny Sharpe.
        p.   cm.
    Includes bibliographical references and index.
    ISBN 0-8166-3722-9 (HC : alk. paper) — ISBN 0-8166-3723-7 (PB : alk. paper)
        1. West Indian literature (English)—History and criticism.   2. Slavery in literature.
    3. Stedman, John Gabriel, 1744–1797. Narrative of a five years' expedition against the revolted Negroes of Surinam.   4. Prince, Mary. History of Mary Prince, a West Indian slave.   5. Women, Black—West Indies—Biography—History and criticism.   6. Women slaves—West Indies—Biography—History and criticism.   7. Slave insurrections—West Indies—Historiography.   8. Slaves' writings—History and criticism.   9. Joanna, 18th cent.—In literature.   10. Women and literature—West Indies.   11. Prince, Mary—In literature.   12. West Indies—In literature.   13. Women, Black, in literature.   14. Nanny—In literature.   I. Title.
    PR9210.O5S47 2003
    810.9'353—dc21

                                                                                                    2002013315

Printed in the United States of America on acid-free paper

The University of Minnesota is an equal-opportunity educator and employer.

12 11 10 09 08 07 06 05 04 03   10 9 8 7 6 5 4 3 2 1

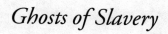

Ghosts of Slavery

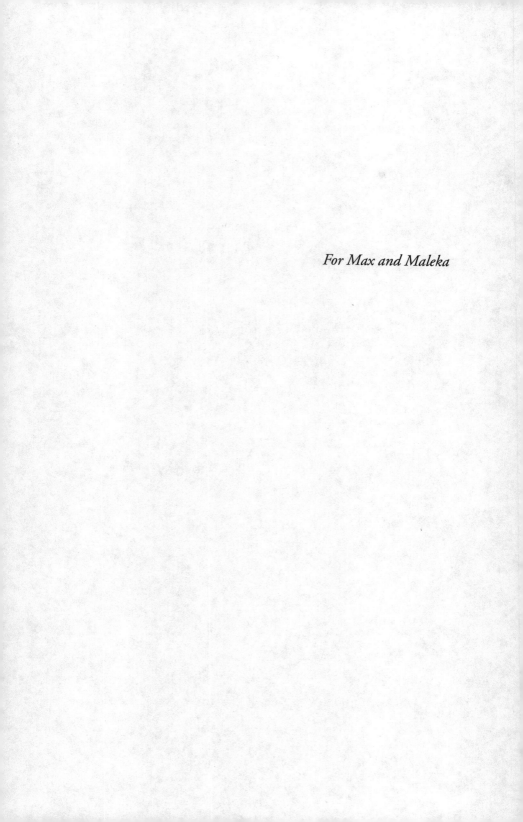

For Max and Maleka

Contents

Acknowledgments

This book was enabled by the financial support of the Center for the Study of Women at UCLA, the Council on Research of the Academic Senate of the Los Angeles Division of the University of California, the University of California Humanities Research Institute, and the University of California President's Research Fellowship in the Humanities. Sandra Harding and Kate Norberg at the Center for the Study of Women provided the enthusiasm and encouragement that were equally necessary for its completion. I was fortunate, during the period of the book's inception, to share a semester's residency at the Humanities Research Institute at Irvine in Spring 1995 with members of the "Feminism and Discourses of Power" research group—Wendy Brown, Judith Butler, Nancy Campbell, Rey Chow, Nancy Fraser, Angela Harris, Saidiya Hartman, Anne Norton, Jacqueline Siapno, and Irene Wei. The weekly arguments, debates, and discussions provided an invaluable forum for working through the questions of power and agency that this book addresses.

My study has benefited enormously from the critical input of Hazel Carby, Sangeeta Ray, Ellen Rooney, and Val Smith, who read chapters at different stages of their writing. Felicity Nussbaum, my most exacting reader, read the entire manuscript and shared with me her immense knowledge and love of the eighteenth century. The reports of the press readers, Abdul R. JanMohamed and Barbara Christian (in memory), were central to the revision of the manuscript, as were the encouraging responses to early drafts of the second chapter at the William Andrews Clark Memorial Library, the Center for Cultural Studies at the

University of California at Santa Cruz, the University of South Dakota, the University of Hawaii at Manoa, and the University of California at Riverside.

Since motherhood restricted my ability to travel, I have relied on the generosity of others for conducting library research. I would like to thank the staff at the James Ford Bell Library of the University of Minnesota for making a microfilm of Stedman's diaries available to me, and Eppie Edwards at the National Library of Jamaica for her help in my research of Nanny. The assistance of my graduate student Victoria Sams, who accompanied me to Kingston and visited the Public Records Office in London on my behalf, was especially welcomed, as were her companionship and sense of humor. I am also grateful to the UCLA graduate students who took my course "Caribbean Fictions of a Slave Past," in which I initially tested some of these ideas, and to those who served as my research assistants over the years, in particular Colette Brown, Vivian Halloran, Matt Titolo, Beth Wightman, and Laura Wyrick. The intellectual vitality and warm friendship of my colleagues at UCLA—Ali Behdad, King-Kok Cheung, Helen Deutsch, Bobby Hill, Rachel Lee, Françoise Lionnet, Arthur Little, Beth Marchant, Rafael Pérez-Torres, Shu-mei Shih, and Richard Yarborough—made the geographical distance of Los Angeles from the Caribbean easier to contend with. Carolyn Cooper's Jamaican hospitality and incisive critiques made my visit to Kingston particularly pleasurable.

The ideas reflected in this book would not have been possible without Jeff Decker, who served as a sounding board, read countless versions of the manuscript, and took the kids down to the playground and swimming pool so I could finish a book that was long overdue. He remains now, as always, my intellectual companion and partner in life. I also want to acknowledge my extended family—Cile, Max, Rosie, Russel, and Steve—for their wit and conversation, inspired meals and drunken revelries that nourished the body as well as the mind. The writing of this book has spanned times of sorrow and those of joy: the death of my parents and the birth of my children. For helping me see the world anew through the eyes of a child, I dedicate this book to Maleka and Max, with love.

Introduction

The Haunting of History

We live in a postmodern world, or so we are told, when narrative ceases to exist except as shadows of the past. Narrative functions less as a story to be told than as bits and pieces of stories we once knew but have forgotten because they no longer matter. But what if the story was not recorded from the start? What if the ghosts of the past are spirits that are doomed to wander precisely because their stories have not been told? Slaves believed that their earthly shadows lingered behind unless the appropriate burial rituals were performed. Their lost stories can be thought of as a violence analogous to the uprooting that denied New World Africans their burial rites. Slavery continues to haunt the present because its stories, particularly those of slave women, have been improperly buried. But an improper burial does not mean that they are irretrievably lost. Toni Morrison describes her historical novels as "a kind of literary archeology" of the life stories that are missing from the written records. She calls her imaginative recreation of the past an archaeology because she sees herself piecing together a world that exists only as fragments in the archives. At the same time she insists that just because the slave's world has to be imagined does not make it any less true (1987, 112–13). Alluding to the fictional narration of slaves' lives as a way of laying the past to rest, she speaks of the responsibility she feels for her characters, "these unburied, or at least unceremoniously buried, people made literate in art" (Naylor and Morrison 1985, 585).

Diasporic Caribbean writers have joined Morrison in resuscitating the lives of the dead by raising the painful memory of slavery.[1] Black

British novelists like Fred D'Aguiar, David Dabydeen, Beryl Gilroy, and Caryl Phillips engage the colonial records on slavery in order to find a place for the histories of black people those records exclude. Yet the story, unlike history, does not have to be faithful to the past. Jamaican American writer Michelle Cliff is not interested simply in recovering the lost stories of slaves who once lived; she also wants to unleash the imaginative force of what might have been. "As artists," she asserts, "Morrison has said it is our job to imagine the unimaginable" (1994, 198). This is what Cliff does when she identifies a powerful obeah woman mentioned briefly in an eighteenth-century West Indian history as a woman who derived her strength from loving other women. Her novels do not reconstruct the past so much as produce a memory that enables black women to act in the present. History matters to all of these writers because they consider a slave past to be intimately bound up with the present, as a point of departure for the African diaspora or a condition of existence for fractured identities. Slavery may be a thing of the past but that does not mean that its legacy is not still with us. "The past co-exists with the present," declares Cliff about the memory of slavery in the United States, "in this amnesiac country in this forgetful century" (1994, 198). By staging how a lost or forgotten past continues to exert its influence, active yet unseen, fiction makes the ghosts of slavery speak.

Ghosts of Slavery moves between past and present, history and fiction in order to narrate the everyday lives of slave women in the English-speaking Caribbean. The study centers on three singular Afro-Caribbean women: Nanny the maroon leader, Joanna the mulatto concubine, and Mary Prince the fugitive slave. Each woman lived during a different era of slavery: Nanny during the initial stages of Britain's acquisition of its West Indian colonies; Joanna at the beginning of the campaign to end the African slave trade; and Mary Prince on the cusp of the emancipation of slaves. And each one occupies a different place in the written records: Nanny appears as a name and not much else; Joanna is an object of desire in the travel narrative of a Scottish soldier; and Mary Prince is the narrator of the only known English-language testimony by a West Indian slave woman. The three women could not be more different. Nanny was the leader of a group of runaway slaves in Jamaica known as the windward maroons. Joanna belonged to an elite caste of Surinamese slave women who served white men as their concubines. And Mary Prince was a domestic slave who escaped from her Antiguan owners while accompanying them on a trip to England. I bring these three women together in a single study to tell a gendered story of slavery.

Although each woman was singular, she was not unique, and it is possible to trace a narrative path from each one to other, more anonymous slave women. The visibility of Nanny, Joanna, and Mary Prince can be used to address such questions as the conditions governing a slave woman's ability to act, the translation of their action into representation, and the complicity of our readings with the documents on which we rely for imagining what transpired in the past. Roland Barthes was one of the first critics to describe the problem of history as not simply one of writing but of reading as well. Since "the plain facts" or "raw data" are already embedded in discourse and narrative, the definition and determination of facts that prefigure the history to be written produces a tautology whereby "the noted issues from the notable, but the notable is . . . only what is worthy of memory" (1989, 138). In other words, what the author or, in the case of the slave narrative, sponsor of a particular document considered noteworthy to record often governs our effort to describe the past. There is very little archival evidence about Nanny's leadership role among maroons because, as a religious leader whose authority was derived from what the British regarded as "Negro superstition," she was considered inconsequential to the outcome of the first Jamaican maroon war. It is only due to the preservation of her memory in maroon oral histories that she is known to us today. All that we know about Joanna is what was recorded by John Gabriel Stedman, the soldier that she served in the capacity of wife. His *Narrative of a Five Years' Expedition against the Revolted Negroes of Surinam* (1796) presents her as a tragic victim of slavery but also as a woman capable of acting on her own. The animation of slave women's agency in colonial documents "acts" in the place of the women themselves, which is especially noticeable in a document like *The History of Mary Prince* (1831), which is the product of not only the slave woman who told her life story but also the abolitionists who recorded it. Although Prince is a speaking subject in her testimony, she does not speak freely. The information admissible as evidence of her life is governed by the kind of woman her middle-class English readers considered a reliable eyewitness to slavery.

This book disrupts the tautology of facts in the colonial documents that form the "raw materials" of the study with evidence from contemporary Caribbean fiction, poetry, and dramatic performances. "Where, if not in the imagination of the creative writers," inquires the Jamaican sociologist and novelist Erna Brodber about the problem of black history, "will we find the admissible data on the behavior of people who left no memoirs?" (1983, 7). Her observation is especially pertinent to an investigation of slavery. There has been such a proliferation of novels that tell the story of slavery from the perspective of slaves that this fiction has been designated as its own genre, "the neo-slave narrative" (Rushdy 1997). Some of the literature I include envisions a particular kind of slave woman in the interest of providing alternative genealogies from the present to the past. Other literature foregrounds the partial and subjective perspective of the document or else fills in the gaps with the information that is missing from the archives. Deborah E. McDowell observes that most of the African American novels on slavery are by black women because the majority of published slave narratives were written by men, who represented slave women primarily as the victims of sexual abuse. "These novels," she continues, "posit a female-gendered subjectivity, more complex in dimension, that dramatizes not what was done to slave women, but what they did with what was done to them" (1989, 146). McDowell's formulation of slave women's agency as "what they did with what was done to them" introduces agency into a site of subjugation. It raises the possibility of action without negating the unequal relations of power that restrict the ability to act. As such, it stages the problematic of this book—that is, the set of questions that delineates an object of investigation.

The objective of this study is to piece together a range of subjectivities from the fragmentary appearance of slave women in the historical records and, in doing so, complicate an equation of their agency with resistance. Slave women's participation in collective and individual acts of resistance has been extensively documented in a number of important Caribbean studies. Lucille Mathurin's *The Rebel Woman in the British West Indies during Slavery* (1975) was one of the earliest comprehensive histories to identify an opposition to slavery in slave women's satirical songs, insubordination, malingering, poisoning, and destruction of property. Since her pathbreaking work, other historians have shown how slave women's refusal to reproduce through individual acts of sexual abstinence, abortion, and infanticide constitute a more general attack on the system of slavery (Bush-Slimani 1993; Dadzie 1990; Hine and Wittenstein 1981). Major histories like Barbara Bush's *Slave Women in Caribbean Society, 1650–1838* and Hilary Beckles's *Natural Rebels: A Social History of Enslaved Black Women in Barbados* locate slave women at the center of a cultural resistance that strengthened their families and communities. "As non-violent protesters, as maroons, as the protectors of social culture and as mothers," concludes Beckles, "black women were critical to the forging of resistance strategies; and their anti-slavery consciousness is the core of the slave communities' survivalist culture" (1989, 172–73).

But the paradigm of resistance has also come under criticism for projecting onto the past a contemporary desire to identify an opposition to slavery. Marietta Morrissey argues that the relationship of slave families to the plantation economy was more contradictory than is suggested by the idea of family formation as a resistance strategy, and that the idea of slave women controlling their fertility is the product of a "European and North American fascination with African women's reputed sexual and healing powers" (96–98, 119). An uncritical celebration of slave resistance and resilience risks overlooking the conditions of subjugation and dehumanization that in many instances prevented an opposition to slavery, overt or otherwise. This is why Saidiya Hartman cautions against overestimating the subversiveness of everyday acts of resistance in the face of the terror and cruelty suffered by slaves and the constraints placed on their agency (54–56).

Several limitations exist to the idea of "resistance" as a category for analysis. To begin with, the term implies antislavery activity and, as such, cannot explain how slaves sought to improve their lives even if their actions did not attack slavery or lead to freedom. Second, the term is equated with an oppositional consciousness that is often difficult to demonstrate and, at best, can only be inferred. This critical move prevents an inquiry into the complexities of the master-slave relationship that produced more contradictory practices, ones that cannot be easily classified as "resistance," "accommodation," or even "resistance within accommodation." Third, the need to identify resistance in even the most accommodating of practices has resulted in the category becoming somewhat meaningless. As Haitian anthropologist Michel-Rolph Trouillot explains, "everything can become resistance to the point that we are not sure whether or not the word stands for an empirical generalization, an analytical category, or a vague yet fashionable label for unrelated situations" (cited by Mintz 1995, 14).

While "resistance" remains useful as an analytical category for collective agency, its value becomes less clear once it is expanded to include individual acts. Satirical songs offer concrete evidence of slaves challenging their masters' authority, but can one really say that these songs undermined slavery? And slave women's practice of abortion and infanticide may have diminished their owners' profits, but at what cost to the women themselves? In many instances, the decisions slaves made were life-or-death choices, especially when they were faced with the impossibility of escaping slavery. How are we to account for, on the one hand, the inordinate discrepancy of power between master and slave without demonstrating the slave's defeat and, on the other, an agency that contravened the master's will without bestowing on slaves a freedom they clearly did not have?

Chapter 1 begins to answer these questions by locating the historical recovery of the maroon as a heroic figure of resistance in an era of decolonization. An oppositional model of resistance, inasmuch as it belongs to a discourse of national liberation articulated through the Manichean opposition of colonizer and colonized, is inadequate for addressing the negotiated practices that existed under slavery. The chapter also demonstrates how periods of instability allowed for the more oppositional practices that we have come to identify with "resistance" in the narrow sense of the term. Although marronage is the clearest example of an escape from bondage, once the Jamaican maroons settled with the British, they pledged a loyalty to the colonial government that makes it difficult to define their existence strictly in terms of their early rebelliousness. Rather, the coexistence of the self-governing black communities with slaveholding plantations shifts the meaning of their significance away from its standard equation with resistance and introduces questions of negotiation and survival.

Nanny is a figure of resistance, whose significance as a rebel woman is bound up with Jamaican national independence. It is an indication of her symbolic value to national self-identity that she is the most celebrated woman from the era of slavery in Jamaica. Her powers have become legendary through their embellishment in oral histories, her literary embodiment in poems and novels, and her designation as a national hero. It is also a sign of the localized effects of knowledge production in decolonized nations that Nanny is relatively unknown in Great Britain and the United States. By contrast, the stories of her bubbling cauldron that caused British soldiers to tumble to their death, her magical pumpkin seeds that bore fruit overnight, and her amazing feat of catching bullets between her buttocks are well known to Jamaicans. Whether or not the feats attributed to Nanny actually occurred, these stories can be seen as dramatic reenactments of the female leader's domestic authority and the central roles early maroon women played in the survival of their communities. Nanny's authority is not simply the transportation of West African gender roles to the New World but also an outcome of the Middle Passage's disruption of tradition and the embattled conditions of maroon societies that allowed black women to assume new authoritative roles. Her hybrid and heterogeneous domestic authority is useful for rethinking the presumed domesticity of female household slaves, as we move from a woman who led a free, self-governing black community to one who was very much enslaved.

The case of Joanna tells the story of marronage from the perspective of slave women who did not escape to freedom, as she was the concubine of a mercenary soldier who was in Surinam to pacify its rebellious maroons. The women who served as "housekeepers" or "secondary wives," the discreet terms for concubines, occupied one of the more compromised positions within slavery. Colonial accounts characterize them as faithful and loyal slaves who emulated white culture and kept their masters informed of slave activities. There is no evidence in the records to prove that Joanna was not a loyal slave, as the only information available is what her white "husband" considered important to record. What we can determine with some certainty from his reports is that concubines were able to achieve a mobility of sorts by moving into the homes of white men who did not own them and extract from them favors for their extended families. When placed within the frame of a model of resistance, their action would be characterized as an accommodation to slavery. Yet, for the women to resist, they would have to refuse their sexual slavery, which begs the question of what such a refusal might look like. Because of the structures of slavery that sanctioned their sexual appropriation by white men, slave women had extremely limited options. They could be raped, paid a small sum for their outward "cooperation," or enter into more formal and long-term arrangements, but there was no position from which they could refuse. Within this dynamic of nonconsent, we are confronted with the contradictory practice of slave women subjecting themselves to sexual exploitation in order to remove themselves (if only provisionally) from the threat of rape or the control of their owners.

The signs of a slave woman's manipulation of her sexual availability to her own advantage can be detected in the well-known American slave narrative, Harriet Jacobs's *Incidents in the Life of a Slave Girl, Written by Herself* (1987 [1861]). Valerie Smith reminds us about important differences between a paradigmatic male testimony like *Narrative of the Life of Frederick Douglass, An American Slave, Written by Himself* (1987 [1845]) and Jacobs's female-gendered one. While Douglass's narrative plots "not only the journey from slavery to freedom, but also the journey from slavehood to manhood," Jacobs's journey passes through a sexual exploitation that denigrates black womanhood (Smith 1987, 34). This difference highlights the difficulty (if not impossibility) for a slave woman to claim her womanhood by acting for herself. Although Jacobs's narrative belongs to an African American rather than Caribbean tradition, it offers a model for understanding the problem of slave women's agency in general.

Harriet Jacobs, using the pseudonym Linda Brent in the autobiographical account of her life, describes how she prevented her master, Dr. Flint, from moving her into a private house "to make a lady" of her by taking on a "white unmarried gentleman," Mr. Sands, as a lover (384–85). The distinction Brent makes between the two men shows that she was exercising a choice of sorts, despite the limited options available to her. This choice, however, cannot be read as the expression of desire or self-autonomy. When invoked in an uncritical manner, slave women's agency can all too easily be articulated through notions of free will, self-autonomy, and self-making that are inappropriate for addressing the coerciveness of slavery.[2] Rather, her choice must be seen as an act of self-survival. For Flint to establish Brent as his concubine would be the culmination of a long history of sexual abuse and, as such, provide the circumstances for extending his power over her. As she bluntly declares: "He had an iron will, and was determined to keep me, and to conquer me" (373). By contrast, she presents Sands as a man who had no power of ownership over her and, as a result, was obliged to treat her well in order to win her affection:

To be an object of interest to a man who is not married, and who is not her master, is agreeable to the pride and feelings of a slave, if her miserable situation has left her any pride or sentiment. It seems less degrading to give one's self, than to submit to compulsion. There is something akin to freedom in having a lover who has no control over you, except that which he gains by kindness and attachment. (385)

Since Jacobs was writing for white middle-class Northern women, she drew on the language of the sentimental novel for describing the circumstances of concubinage. She invokes a scenario of seduction that her readers would recognize when she says that she was seduced by Sands's "kind words" that were "too eloquent, alas, for the poor slave girl who trusted him" and "by degrees, a more tender feeling crept into [her] heart" (385). Hartman correctly warns against reading these words as an expression of affection. Instead, she sees Brent deploying the language of seduction in a manner that foregrounds the restraints under which the slave woman had to operate (1997, 104). Although Brent presents Sands as a kinder man than her master, she also makes clear that he was not to be trusted. Indeed, he betrayed her in the end. While promising that he was going to send their daughter to freedom and safety in the North, he gave her to a female relative instead.

Still, the description of the white lover as one "who has no control over you, except that which he gains by kindness and attachment" suggests a relationship that is tangent to the one of owner and/or overseer, even if it is a relationship structured by slavery. Sands was not simply purchasing sexual favors but also earning social intimacy. The element of social intimacy in the relationship makes it a more contradictory practice than suggested by standard definitions of sexual abuse and exploitation. Brent identified her ability to make Sands earn her affection (rather than presume he already has it because she is a slave) as "something akin to freedom." This statement identifies the slave woman's subjectivity, not in terms of a self-autonomy, but as the assertion of a semi-autonomy through an action that both demanded from Sands a recognition of her humanity and sent a signal to Flint that he did not have total control over the body of his female slave. Brent gained her sense of freedom, then, not by asserting her selfhood but by removing herself from the immediate threat of her owner even if it meant attaching herself to another white man.

The expression "something akin to freedom" denotes the absence of a proper name for the contradictory practice of slave women achieving a degree of mobility through sexual subjugation. The absence of an appropriate term for describing the exact nature of Brent's action has presented a conundrum for critics who read this episode from her life. Is she a victim or agent or both? Smith notices that even when she "seems most vulnerable, she manipulates some degree of control" (1990, 216). At the same time, one cannot say that in offering herself to Sands Brent was opposing slavery. As Carla Kaplan argues, "by identifying Brent's agency solely with the rebelliousness of these acts the critic assumes that their liberatory meanings override their self-defeating or submissive ones" (1993, 102). And Hartman maintains that privileging "the force of determined will" over the constraints of agency reinscribes sexual exploitation within a discourse of seduction that presumes a relationship of reciprocity and exchange (1997, 111). Indeed, Brent's assertion of "pride and feelings" is qualified by "her miserable situation" that leaves her with no "pride or sentiment." Her characterization of the act as "less degrading" suggests that it was the lesser of an even more degrading situation, which makes it scarcely a choice at all. This is why Hartman explains the phrase "something akin to freedom" as presenting "the limited possibilities, constraint, despair, and duress that condition the giving of the self, not unlimited options, freedom, or unencumbered choice" (1997, 104). Unlike Hartman, however, who reads the phrase for its greater proximity to "nonconsent" and hence evidence of a sexual practice that is practically indistinguishable from rape, I am interested in the opening the phrase provides for considering slave women's manipulation of their sexual exploitation to their own advantage.

In order to understand how Jacobs deploys "something akin to freedom," we have to begin from the premise that slave women were not free to choose their partners, as Flint's refusal to allow Brent to marry the "respectable colored man" whom she loved makes clear. Brent's relationship with Sands thus cannot be seen as a substitute for a more meaningful relationship with a black man; the latter union is foreclosed by slavery. Rather, her action has to be placed in the context of a life in which, from the age of fourteen, a slave girl was, as she so dramatically portrays, the sexual prey of her master, his sons, and his overseer. Brent used the sexual availability of slave women to her own ends only inasmuch as she could not remove herself from a condition of exploitation. She manipulated a system in which slave women were sexual victims because she was not in a position to challenge it.

Brent's action belongs to what Michel de Certeau calls a tactic, which, as an "art of the weak," is to be distinguished from strategies that have the power of institutions behind them. In *The Practice of Everyday Life,* he explains everyday practices as the ability of people who are relatively disempowered to find a place for themselves within a system they are not free to oppose.[3] Rather than possessing a power of its own, a tactic inhabits the crevices of a power that is external to it:

> [A] *tactic* is a calculated action determined by the absence of a proper locus. . . . The space of a tactic is the space of the other. Thus it must play on and with a terrain imposed on it and organized by the law of a foreign power. . . . It operates in isolated actions, blow by blow. It takes advantage of "opportunities" and depends on them, being without any base where it could stockpile its winnings, build up its own position, and plan raids. What it wins it cannot keep. This nowhere gives a tactic mobility, to be sure, but a mobility that must accept the chance offerings of the moment, and seize on the wing the possibilities that offer themselves at any given moment. It must vigilantly make use of the cracks that particular conjunctions open in the surveillance of the proprietary powers. It poaches in them. It creates surprises in them. It can be where it is least expected. It is a guileful ruse. (1984, 36–37)

A tactic is not a planned strategy because it has no base from which to operate. The advantages of each move are not guaranteed but contingent on the circumstances of the moment. The tactic's power lies in its mobility, which allows for improvisation and the element of surprise. Tactics do not work through self-empowerment so much as they shift power from the dominating class to the dominated. Because it is drawing from a power that is external to it, a tactic is unable to build a power base of its own.

Since Brent's action is a tactic that insinuates itself into slave women's sexual subjugation, it is precariously balanced between having control and being dominated. She made use of her sexual exploitation when she became Sands's concubine in order to avoid becoming Flint's. And she describes the pleasure with which she told her owner that she was pregnant with another white man's child. Since Mrs. Flint refused to allow so immoral a woman as Brent in the house, her pregnancy removed her from the immediate threat of his sexual abuse. However, Flint refused to sell her and, as a result, she continued to be subjected to his physical, psychological, and emotional abuse. The episode nonetheless shows

Brent using the sexual competition between two white men to her advantage: Sands played his role of the favored lover as Flint did that of the
rejected one.

Although concubinage was not practiced as extensively in the United
States as it was in the Caribbean, there are sufficient resemblances between
the situation of Brent and Joanna to allow for a useful comparison. Both
were racially mixed women, the preferred choice for the domestic slaves
from whom concubines were selected, and both were the concubines
of unmarried white men. In describing the state of "something akin to
freedom," Brent makes a point of saying that Sands was an unmarried
man who was not her master (both of which Flint was not). The favors
that Brent won from Sands came to an end not when she disappeared
into hiding in her grandmother's garret, but when he married a white
woman. It is my contention that a slave woman's ability to manipulate
the place of her sexual exploitation was contingent on her performance
of the domestic function of the absent white wife.

Chapter 2 addresses slave women's performance of the domestic duties generally reserved for white women as a bid for greater autonomy.
Concubinage was not a sexual transgression against domestic life, which
is a reading we have inherited from the abolitionists and missionaries
who condemned the practice as immoral. Rather, it was part of a normative West Indian domesticity in which slave women served in such
intimate capacities as the surrogate mothers of white children, secondary wives of white men, and mothers of their mixed-race children. How,
then, are we to explain the action of women like Brent and Joanna who
empowered themselves through racial and gender hierarchies intended
to maintain their dependency and inferiority? To say that they assimilated into white culture or acquiesced to slavery constitutes too quick a dis-
missal of their enslaved condition. If, on the other hand, one considers
their assimilation in terms of de Certeau's notion of "the other within,"
then we can begin to unravel the seams of their apparent assimilation.
By shifting analysis from "competence" (knowledge) to a "performance"
(speech act) of rules, rituals, and laws imposed from the outside, de
Certeau describes how indigenous American people did not reject the
culture to which their Spanish conquerors subjected them so much as
they "deflected its power" (1984, xiii). Powerless to challenge the rituals and representations to which they were seemingly assimilated, they
could nonetheless manipulate them to their own ends. By showing how

the concubine's mimicry inhabited the fissures of white domesticity, I make a case for slave women's "deflection" of their sexual exploitation.

De Certeau derives his description of tactics from guerrilla warfare, which, operating from a position of weakness, uses surprise, ruse, and mobility to its advantage. The guerrilla warfare that the maroons perfected into an art is proof that they too did not operate from a position of power even though they were free.[4] The tactical nature of maroon warfare is evident in a story that the eighteenth-century historian Bryan Edwards tells about the second Jamaican maroon war of 1795, which took place after the pacification of the maroons. Introducing the story as "unquestionably true," he recounts how maroons, "in full cry," hunted down a battle-weary soldier and, after killing and cutting up his body, proceeded to eat the internal organs: "His savage pursuers, having decollated the body, in order to preserve the head as the trophy of victory, roasted and actually devoured the heart and entrails of the wretched victim" (1807, 544). Edwards authenticates the story he has heard from supposed eyewitnesses with testimonies from the maroons themselves. He reports that, rather than denying the incident, they boasted about it. Here we see maroons using a colonial representation of African savagery to their advantage in order to demoralize soldiers sent out to capture them. Their diversion of a racial stereotyping did not overturn the colonial image of maroon savagery but, rather, reconfirmed it.

Since tactics manipulate rather than challenge the rules of the dominant order, they are not self-evident in the records. As an action that poaches on the power of the dominating class, they do not constitute oppositional practices. Within this critical framework, slave women's agency can be read as a performance that exceeds strictly defined roles assigned to them and as an action through which they reappropriated the place of their subjugation. By considering agency as tactical moves, we see that slave women empowered themselves through a subjugation to sexual exploitation or assertion of their status as property. These forms of agency contravene a discourse of emancipation belonging to the antislavery movement, the objective of which was to demonstrate that slaves were precisely not chattel to be bought and sold.

Although antislavery offers a powerful language of liberation, its language can also inhibit a reading of the day-to-day existence of slaves. Chapter 3 introduces the limitations of antislavery discourse and establishes a continuity between the antislavery and postcolonial model of slave women's agency. The chapter examines two Black British novels—Beryl Gilroy's *Stedman and Joanna* (1991) and Caryl Phillips's *Cambridge* (1991)—that rewrite existing documents on slavery in order to expose the unequal power relations that structure them. Through these novels, I investigate the continued efficacy of antislavery as a grand narrative of emancipation that asserts the slave's humanity by extending the subjectivity of the free individual to him or her. While *Stedman and Joanna* brings Joanna's story closer to an abolitionist paradigm, *Cambridge* stages the difficulty in deriving an authentic black voice from the testimony. Both novels establish connections between the West Indies and an English nation that disassociated itself from the slavery of its colonies. The Black British fiction shows that, instead of finding freedom in England, the runaway slave who was called upon to give his or her testimony was in fact "bound" to the abolitionist cause.

The last chapter, which addresses the life story of Mary Prince, examines the slave narrative as an expression of not only the slave woman, but also her abolitionist sponsors and middle-class English readers. To recover an autobiographical voice from the testimony involves locating its meaning in the intentions of its narrator. This move conceals the critic as agent of "a black female voice." Thus treating the document as generative of meaning, it is a strategy of reading that locates meaning in the past. To understand how meaning emerges from the writing of the slave narrative, its reception among its Victorian readers, and our reading of it today involves separating an academic agenda from the political intentions of the antislavery document.

The political objective of the slave testimony was to demonstrate the subjectivity of a human being whose humanity had been negated and to produce its narrator as a reliable eyewitness to the horrors of slavery. In order to fulfill this objective, it was obliged to privilege the Christianized, morally upright, and obedient worker over the Africanized, ungovernable, and troublesome slave. Its teleological narrative necessarily placed the slave on a path toward Christianity and freedom. What kinds of slave women are excluded from the socioethical being that is the speaking subject of the slave narrative? How does the moral agency favored by British abolitionists act in the place of other kinds of practices? How does the abolitionist presentation of the slave's journey toward freedom prevent an inquiry into the more equivocal means by which slave women negotiated greater autonomy from their owners, even if they did not (or could not) achieve freedom?

This book is organized around the two "ends" of slavery, beginning with an African-born woman who lived in a free maroon community during the early period of British colonialism in the West Indies and ending with a slave woman who ran away from her owners in England shortly prior to the emancipation of slaves. Between them is a woman who was purchased by a kind mistress and, as a result, was believed by abolitionists to have been free. The discrete moment of each woman's state of "freedom" allows us to consider the historical conditions governing their ability to act. I examine different kinds of documents—government papers, planter journals, travel literature, private diaries, proslavery propaganda, and antislavery pamphlets—for the limited repertoire of power and agency they present. The slave woman is the evil Obeah Woman or loyal Mammy, the Sable Venus or Noble Slave, the foul-mouthed whore or high-minded Christian. Yet it is possible to draw a line from such stereotypical images to the women they represent. In order to do so, I derive a critical matrix from contemporary Caribbean literature that engages the problem in representing a slave past. I also turn to oral histories as the site of a countermemory. Finally, I read slave songs as satirical commentaries on the colonial stereotypes they apparently reproduce. The veiled signification of the songs points to gendered subjectivities that do not negate or overturn the racial stereotyping of black women so much as rework them from within.

Even as contemporary literature, oral histories, slave songs, and slave narratives provide alternative models for reading the past, they do not always present a language for naming the power slave women might have exercised. Jacobs's use of the phrase "something akin to freedom" for a relationship that was oblique to the master/slave relation dramatizes the absence of a term that is adequate to the more negotiated instances of slavery. The language of freedom is so bound up with large narratives of emancipation like feminism, Marxism, and nationalism that it is often difficult for us to think outside of their terms of "self-determination," "self-making," and "consciousness." The use of such phrases in this book as "a certain degree of autonomy" but not self-autonomy, "the semblance of freedom" instead of freedom, and "restricted choice" rather than the exercise of a free will is intended to describe an agency that was precariously balanced between acting and being acted upon.

A black female subjectivity has been even more difficult to identify. I resort to such terms as "wild femininity," "mimicry," and "differential identities" for describing gendered subjectivities that cannot with any degree of certainty be established. Rather than equating a black female subjectivity with individual consciousness or modes of self-expression like songs and testimonies, I locate it between written and oral histories, first-person and third-person accounts, pro- and antislavery writings, and at the point where the unspoken narratives of everyday life intersect with the known stories of slavery. In noting the inadequacy of language, I also denote the limits of this study as an effort to describe the everyday lives of female slaves, about which we have much to learn but can never fully know.

1.

"The Rebels Old Obeah Woman"
History as Spirit Possession

This study begins with Nanny because she is emblematic of slave women's resistance to slavery (see, for instance, Mathurin 1975). By beginning with Nanny, however, we are confronted with a paradox. As the leader of a group of rebellious maroons, she is the most prominent of the three women in this study, but she is also the most invisible in the archives. Her name appears but three times in the official records on the first Jamaican maroon war and once more on a patent assigning a parcel of land. Even then, we cannot establish with any certainty if the woman mentioned on the land deed was the maroon leader. Nanny's exploits *are* well documented in maroon oral histories, but these stories did not endow her with a historical reality prior to Jamaican independence. As a woman leader whose memory was preserved in oral form alone, she was relegated to the fictitious world of folklore. As historian Lucille Mathurin Mair remarks, "for as long as [she] can remember, she [Nanny] has been in the Jamaican consciousness but without acquiring solid flesh and blood" (52–53). Today Nanny appears in more fiction, plays, and poems than any other Afro-Caribbean woman who lived during the era of slavery. There are even drawings based on maroon descriptions of her. To consider Nanny as a historical agent, then, is to test the limits of what we traditionally consider to be history. In this regard, beginning with her serves another purpose—to open up the kinds of texts that form the basis for writing about the everyday lives of women slaves.

I am interested in the stories that circulate around the figure of Nanny. Who tells them? How are they told, and which ones do not get told? What accounts for her appearance or disappearance in the colonial archives? What kinds of narratives become attached to her life at different moments in the history of slavery, colonialism, and national independence? What interests do these narratives express?

The story of Nanny is the story of contending forms of knowledge: written versus oral histories, colonial versus national cultures, institutional versus popular ways of knowing. She exists as a ghostly presence in colonial narratives that address her more as the product of myth and superstition. In a newspaper story written in the early 1950s by mountaineer, historian, naturalist, and retired headmaster Reginald Murray, her intangible body signifies the unreality of oral history. Maroon lore of Nanny's spirit guarding the ruined site of Nanny Town—a maroon stronghold that was virtually impregnable—appears under the section heading of "Haunted," while colonial accounts of the men who "penetrated the deep recesses" of Jamaica's Blue Mountains to defeat the rebels are presented as "History" (Murray 1951). Michel de Certeau characterizes the modern social sciences to which history belongs as "'heterologies' (discourses on the other) [that] are built upon a division between the body of knowledge that utters a discourse and the mute body that nourishes it" (1988, 3). As a scientific form of knowledge, historiography gains authority over the temporal unknown—a past that is irretrievably lost—by conquering the primitive space of folklore, magic, and superstition. This discourse of conquest is visible in Murray's need to relegate Nanny to the realm of fiction in order to authorize his own exploration of her land.

The newspaper story is an account of Murray's journey into maroon country to the inaccessible site of Nanny Town. He tells of his visit to the place known as Nanny's Pot, where Nanny was reputed to have defeated the British and where he mockingly imitates the action maroons attribute to her supernatural powers. "Here, according to tradition," he writes, "Nanny had concocted devil's brew to bemuse her pursuers, had stood and caught the bullets hurled from their muskets, hurling them back with unseemly gesture and imprecation. My comrades and I spent pleasant moments skirring flat stones across the crystal surface in series of ricochets." Murray's description of Nanny displays the colonial perception of African-based religious practices as witchcraft. He also cites the maroon story that her spirit will not allow straight-haired men to enter her town in order to banish women from the adventure tale he is

telling. "No woman," he reports, "has crossed Stony River within two
centuries. Nanny would not tolerate that intrusion." I consider the appearance of a black female leader in this seemingly innocuous piece of
journalism to be paradigmatic of the place of black women's power and
orality, figured as feminine, in colonial narratives. Nanny is not simply
absent as a historical actor. Her name is invoked, if only as legend, to
exclude black women as historical agents. The only references to a powerful woman leader like her in colonial accounts of the early maroons
occur in exploration narratives like Murray's.

By contrast, Nanny lives large in oral histories, where factual evidence
merges with myths and legends. While the British records on the first
maroon war derogatorily refer to her as "the rebels old obeah woman,"
maroons respectfully remember her as "da great scientist." Obeah or
Obi, from the perspective of Europeans, was "a term of African origin,
signifying sorcery or witchcraft" and involving the practice of "diabolic
arts" (Edwards 1807, 2:106). Maroons, however, do not consider Nanny
an obeah woman, preferring to use the term *science* for designating the
ability to command and communicate with dead ancestors, and to draw
on their powers for healing the sick and for determining the outcome of
events (Martin 1973, 69). They credit her, and the power of her science,
with no lesser feat than a defeat of the British in 1739. "It was miracu-
lous to know how it happens but it did happen in truth," claims one
maroon. "Nanny scientifically works her way out and the British has got
to subdue by asking for a peace treaty to be signed betwixt the maroons
and the British government" (Miller 1979). While de Certeau describes
Western historiography as a writing that conquers the primitive body,
a maroon use of the term *science* for their African-based powers shows
the signs of a body that exists more as a parasite, feeding off a colonial
discourse of power.

Maroon historians have an intimate knowledge of all the written
records that affect their communities and incorporate these documents
into their histories in order to further legitimate their version of the past.
In view of the parasitical relationship of orality to writing, I locate the
story of Nanny neither wholly within the oral histories nor within the
written records, but in an interspace between the two, what Mary Louise
Pratt calls "contact zones," which are "social spaces where disparate cultures meet, clash, grapple with each other, often in highly asymmetrical
relations of domination and subordination" (4). One outcome of a

contact zone is the appearance of the colonial classification of maroons as "wild Negroes" in maroon histories as the source of their unique identity as free people.

This chapter tracks stories about Nanny not only in oral histories and exploration narratives, but also in postindependence historiography and contemporary Caribbean literature. Different "Nannys" were envisioned depending on the kind of "imagined community" (to use Benedict Anderson's term for the nation) that was invoked. Her significance as a rebel woman is bound up with decolonization and the emergence of Jamaica as an independent nation. Her symbolic value lies in her ability to represent both the buried tradition of an African culture and the long history of anticolonial struggles so central to the identity of emergent nations in the Caribbean. This chapter makes a case for the diasporic experience of slavery that allowed black women to assume an authority they did not have in Africa. And it foregrounds the constraints of colonization that produced the contradictory scenario of maroons inspiring the slave rebellions they helped suppress. Jamaican women performers, poets, and writers recreate from the maroon and national histories of Nanny's powers new myths that redefine her significance more strongly in terms of black women's self-sufficiency. Their poetic renditions of Nanny's life are nonetheless grounded in an authority that the historical woman possessed.

THE SORCERY OF HISTORY

The term *maroon* is believed to be derived from *cimarrón,* a Spanish term for "wild" or "untamed" originally used for domestic cattle that had escaped into the bush.[1] That a term for runaway cattle should be extended to slaves is not accidental. Planters inventoried slaves along with domesticated animals as "stock"—a classification that was visible in such practices as using the same names for cattle and slaves and the belief that dark-colored cattle, like dark-skinned people, were better equipped to labor under the hot sun (Morgan 1995). According to this system of classification, plantation slaves were to the maroons what domestic animals were to those in the wild, which is why maroons were also known as "Wild Negroes" (Long 1774, 1:124).

The original maroons were Spanish-owned slaves who escaped to the inaccessible recesses of Jamaica when England captured the island from Spain in 1655. They inhabited two regions that were separated from each other by a strip of white settlements: the Cockpit Country on the leeward side of the island and the Blue Mountains on the windward side. The two major settlements of the leeward maroons were Cudjoe Town and Accompong Town, named after their two leaders, while the major settlement of the windward maroons was Nanny Town, named after Nanny. The Cockpit Country, a limestone plateau pockmarked with sinkholes, and the Blue Mountains, with their deep folds of thickly forested slopes that ascend rapidly to the Grand Ridge, provided ideal terrain for guerrilla warfare. Existing as autonomous pockets of resistance, the maroons conducted raids on the surrounding plantations, ever increasing their numbers with new runaways.

The colonial classification of Negroes as "wild" or "domestic" stock was intended to establish a clear division between rebellious and docile slaves that did not in reality exist. The presence of the self-governing black towns encouraged plantation slaves to plot uprisings, and Cudjoe (Kojo), leader of the leeward maroons, was himself the son of the chief conspirator of a plantation rebellion in 1690 (Campbell 1988, 46). During the 1720s, the British began an aggressive military campaign to pacify the maroons, who responded by burning and looting, stealing slaves, and even taking hostages. Rebels stole into plantations under the cover of dark and secreted away slaves. They mingled in broad daylight with free blacks in the marketplace so that the British could no longer tell who was a loyal and who was a rebel slave. The maroon rebels made significant advances by the latter half of 1733. In February 1734 the Assembly appealed to the British government for assistance, claiming that "the evil is daily increasing, and their [the rebels'] success has had such influences on our other slaves, that they are continually deserting to them in great numbers: and the insolent behaviour of others gives us but too much cause to fear a general defection."[2] The rebelliousness of the maroons cut at the heart of the plantation system, for it proved that even a presumably loyal slave could suddenly become "wild."

The difficulty in drawing a clear line between rebellious and loyal slaves is crucial to a nationalist discourse in which maroons represent the incipient rebelliousness of all slaves. Maroon identity, on the other hand, is rooted in the knowledge that, unlike other Jamaicans, they fought for their freedom and thus never were slaves. As Colonel Henry Rowe of Accompong Town told the American folklorist Martha Warren Beckwith in the late 1920s, maroons have "always been free and were

the earliest settlers on the island" (1929).[3] Traces of the colonial cate-
gories of the "wild" and "domestic"—with their new values of free
and enslaved—are visible in an oral story that presents Nanny as an
originary ancestress of the maroon people. The story tells of two sisters,
Nanny and Sekesu, who were captured and brought to the New World
as slaves. Although there are several versions to the story, they all speak
of how Nanny, unlike her sister, decided to fight for her freedom. The
maroons are Nanny's *yoyo* or children, while the rest of Jamaicans are
the descendants of Sekesu, who remained a slave until *backra* (the white
man) decided to free her. The maroon's struggle for freedom in the story
simultaneously embodies the docility of slaves. As the retired Colonel
C. L. G. Harris of Moore Town reports, "had the maroons submitted
tamely to bondage, the noble-minded emancipators might have thought
that the slaves welcomed their lot, and then slavery might have remained
unto this day" (emphasis added) (1967a).[4]

Whereas folklorists identify in the story of Nanny and Sekesu the
fragments of a myth belonging to West Africa (Bilby 1984, 458; Dalby
1971, 49–50), I am interested in how the African myth has been recon-
figured so as to account for the formation of free maroon societies in
Jamaica. A replacement of the negative connotations of "wild" with the
positive value of being free constitutes one of the first interventions into
a colonial discourse on the maroons. This reevaluation of colonial values
can be detected in Colonel Harris's letter to the *Daily Gleaner* protest-
ing Murray's characterization of Nanny as "notorious." Harris reclaims
maroon history in the act of declaring the colonial educator's ignorance
when he writes that "those of us who have intimate knowledge of the
history of the Maroons assert that Nanny was a liberator of no mean
repute" (1951). Control over the past is crucial to maroon identity because, as anthropologist Leann Thomas Martin explains, Moore Town
maroons do not simply think of Nanny and her contemporaries as their
ancestors but also as spirits that protect and guide them (68).[5] These
spirits are invoked whenever their traditions and the terms of their treaty are threatened. Martin describes the maroon past as a "useable history" inasmuch as it forms the basis for group identity, can be changed
and reinterpreted to benefit its users, and has heroes that appeal to the
imagination (184). No single person embodies these aspects of a usable
history more than Nanny, which is why oral historians like Harris have
been vigilant about defending her name. Maroon histories of the war of

1734–39 center on the powerful nature of Nanny's science, and all of the stories of her powers are testimony to the maroons' own cunning and bravery that won them their freedom.

Colonel Harris popularized the maroon stories of Nanny in a three-part series that appeared in the *Daily Gleaner* (the same Kingston newspaper in which Murray in a colonial era published *his* story) shortly after Jamaican independence. He describes how Nanny placed sentinels on a hill to watch out for approaching British soldiers and claims that it was her idea for maroons to disguise themselves as bushes and trees. The hill is now called Watch Hill, and the guerrilla tactic of camouflage came to be know as "ambush" (Harris 1967b, 11–12). Although Nanny is never described as a warrior, her science is inextricably bound up with her skills in waging war. "If Nanny's ingenuity was proverbial," declares Harris, "the extra-physical powers with which she is credited are certainly beyond belief" (11). He proceeds to tell the story of Nanny's Pot, which was a cauldron of boiling water she placed on a pathway so narrow that British soldiers were forced to pass by in single file. Since there was no fire under the pot, each soldier felt compelled to peer into it and, in doing so, fell down the precipice. The life of the last one was spared so that he could tell the others of the fate that awaited them at Nanny Town. Harris also recounts how Pumpkin Hill got its name. During a food shortage, Nanny was ready to submit to the British because her people were starving. But she heard a voice tell her to plant pumpkin seeds, which she did, and they miraculously bore fruit in a few days. Finally, he tells the story of Nanny's skills in bullet-catching. On the day of the signing of the treaty, she asked a British officer to order his men to fire their muskets at her. The officer thought it was a ploy to renew the war. As round after round of bullets was fired, she half-turned her back and, catching them, returned them to the soldiers (12).

Nanny's powers are both real and legendary: They are instances of an authority that the historical woman possessed and what she has come to represent in the popular imagination. Both the historical and legendary aspects of the stories reveal the existence of a heterogenous female-gendered authority: Nanny is responsible for planning and implementing guerrilla tactics and feeding her people; she is remembered as a symbolic fighter as well as a symbolic mother. The colonial transliteration of the oral stories as "folklore" performs what Gayatri Chakravorty Spivak calls an "epistemic violence" by making their polymorphous structure conform to the binary logic of a Western system of meaning (1988, 281). This epistemic violence can be detected in Herbert T. Thomas's *Untrodden Jamaica* (1890), an account of the author's journey through the Blue Mountains to Nanny Town that is also one of the earliest written records of maroon oral histories.

It is no accident that the maroon tradition was first recorded in the late nineteenth century, when Western interest in those societies on the brink of disappearance due to increased travel and communication was high. American anthropology was established in the 1890s through the "salvage ethnography" of Indians, at the same time that British anthropology attempted to legitimate itself as a "new science" for the colonial civilizing mission (Fabian 1985; Stauder 1974). The beginning of an ethnographic interest in the Jamaican maroons can be traced to the 1891 Exhibition at Kingston for which Herbert Thomas was commissioned to journey to Nanny Town. The objective of the Exhibition was to introduce Jamaica to tourism by dispelling the perception of it as a disease-ridden place whose prosperous estates had been ruined by emancipation.

The 1891 Exhibition was a testimony to the successes of the colonial civilizing mission and the wonders of industrialization, while also demonstrating the quaintness of indigenous crafts and knowledge. Raw materials from the West Indies, such as coffee, sugar, and cocoa, the machines and processes for manufacturing them into finished products, and the advances in Western education, fine arts, literature, and science, were displayed. Large coconut and fruit trees were transplanted to the Exhibition site, which involved the joint harnessing of fossil power and human labor in a marvel of Industry and Empire. The surrounding grounds, with its fountains, gardens carefully planted with tropical trees, ornamental walkways, and a bandstand, also featured a model Jamaican village (Booth 1985, 42). Jamaicans from rural areas were encouraged to exhibit their handicrafts, and a maroon was invited to demonstrate the use of medicinal herbs and roots for treating wounds and curing sicknesses. In the words of one organizer, "the poorest person need not say he had nothing to send" (*Jamaica Exhibition Bulletin* 1890, 6). The idea was to appeal to the tourist's desire for the unknown, while showing that Jamaica had all the comforts of civilization. The island was promoted as a health resort, which meant that its mountains rather than its beaches were the main attraction. Subsequent travel guides featured maroon towns as quaint spots to visit on motoring tours of the island (see Figure 1).

An inspector in the Jamaican constabulary, Thomas was instructed to bring back for the Exhibition evidence of the pacification of the leeward maroons in 1734 when the British army destroyed Nanny Town. He hoped to collect old muskets and other paraphernalia left by departing soldiers, and any fragment of the portable swivel guns Captain William Stoddart was reported to have used to defeat the maroons. Such trophies were to play a strategic role in demonstrating the longevity of the British conquest of the island. Although new roads and settlements were built after the destruction of Nanny Town, the stronghold was never resettled. It became so overgrown with bush that it was virtually impossible to distinguish the town from the surrounding terrain. The dense undergrowth, steep slopes, and heavy rains of the Blue Mountains prevented outsiders from exploring the area without a guide, and it was difficult to find a maroon who would serve as one.

To maroons, Nanny Town was a sacred site presided over by Nanny and haunted by the spirits of those killed in the battles. Prospective guides did their best to keep strangers away by telling stories of what would happen to anyone who dared to trespass the sacred land. They spoke of strange noises and a speckled bird with a red tail that alighted on a hut and set it aflame. A member of an exploration group that spent the night on the site in 1860 claims to have been awakened in the middle of the night by terrifying birdlike sounds (Tuelon 1973, 25).

Thomas published an account of his visit to Nanny Town as proof that the wild terrain of maroon country had been made safe for civilization. He informs his readers that, after hearing of his intentions to visit Nanny Town, a maroon guide told his party that no white man had seen it and lived to tell what he saw. The guide proceeded to recount all the terrible things that would happen to them, punctuating each story with the phrase—"Inspector can't go deh" (Thomas 1890, 36). The inspector was determined to prove him wrong. As a means of combating the maroons who might try to discourage him from visiting their sacred site, Thomas decided to gather their "folk-lore," which is the term he uses for their oral tradition. Since his reason for collecting the stories was to acquaint himself with a knowledge he feared maroons might use against him, they exist in his book as a talisman for self-protection:

a

b

Figure 1. (a) *Maroon Town* and (b) *Surrender of the Maroons* from *Stark's Jamaica Guide* (1902). The maroons were romanticized in travel books as noble savages. This depiction of the pacification of the maroons highlights their savagery even as it presents a domesticated image of them for tourist consumption.

The notorious Nanny was a woman, and the wife of the leader Cudjoe,—or, I presume, one of his wives—and, like all unsexed women who have led a freebooter's life, ten times more ferocious and blood-thirsty than any man among the Maroons. She was possessed of supernatural powers, and spirited away the best and finest of the slaves from the outlying estates. She never went into battle armed like the rest, but received the bullets of the enemy that were aimed at her, and returned them with fatal effect, in a manner of which decency forbids a nearer description. She kept at the junction of the Nanny and Stony rivers, at the foot of the precipice on whose brink Nanny Town stood, a huge cauldron boiling, without any fire underneath; and when the soldiers and militia drew near to inspect this marvellous phenomenon, they fell headlong into it and were suffocated. (36)

This is clearly a degraded form of the oral histories, as Thomas depicts a powerful black woman as "unsexed" and even more savage than the men. He has embellished the stories he heard, for maroons would scarcely call Nanny a "ferocious and blood-thirsty" woman. He also labels her the Maroon Amazon, a title that not only belies the mythological light in which he saw her but also confirms, like the classical stories he invokes, the abnormality of women warriors. Scholars who have attempted to establish the historical existence of Amazons now believe it to be a story that Greeks told to reinforce normative gender roles (Tyrrell 1984).

Thomas's account is nonetheless useful as a record of the existence in the nineteenth century of the same stories told today. His Victorian sensibility does not permit him to say exactly how Nanny caught and returned the bullets that were aimed at her. This has not prevented scholars from being more explicit in their reports of her catching bullets between her buttocks and firing them back at her enemies (Craton 1982, 81; Kopytoff 1973, 84).[6] Edward Kamau Brathwaite takes academics and maroons to task for repeating "this ridiculous story," which he thinks may have originated in Thomas's *Untrodden Jamaica* (1977, 5, 33n; 1994, 121). Since the shaking of the backside (sometimes accompanied by raising the skirt) is a sexual gesture Afro-Caribbean women use to gain the upper hand, he makes a case for this gesture—or rather, what it symbolizes in the popular imagination—being taken literally by a culturally biased European like Thomas.[7] Or else, he explains, it is possible that Nanny was in fact a bullet catcher and may have shown the British a gesture of contempt and the two actions were conflated through rumors and half-truths into "the fabrication that has reached us" (1977, 33–34n).[8] What concerns Brathwaite is that, in the absence of exploring the symbolic function of the buttocks in Jamaican culture, scholars simply reduce Nanny to her body, thereby enacting a racial stereotyping that disempowers her (1994, 126).

Jamaican literary critics counter colonial stereotyping of black women by explaining the bullet-catching story as the popular expression of a specifically female form of defiance. In *Noises in the Blood,* Carolyn Cooper reevaluates the scatology of the story by locating it within the "vulgar body" of an oral culture that has historically been devalued. She calls the story a "legendary instance of female 'bottom power,'" the echoes of which appear in women's dance-hall culture (1995, x–xi). Honor Ford-Smith considers the stories of Nanny's bullet-catching ability and her magical pumpkin seeds to be the sign of a female autonomy that European missionaries attempted to eradicate through marriage and Christian conversion:

> Female warrior leaders such as Nanny for example had based their legitimacy on their powers as priestesses. Their femaleness—in particular their sexuality and their religious power were important parts of their tactics against the British. Witness for example the famous legend of Nanny bouncing the bullets off her bottom, her ability to make the pumpkin vine grow miraculously to save her people from defeat and starvation and her powers as a healer. In the Caribbean context the African religious practice seemed not to have laid down rigid codes for the conduct of male/female relations in the seventeenth and eighteenth centuries. The arrival of the missionaries challenged both female autonomy and its religious/aesthetic base. It accelerated the process of conversion of the image of woman as warrior/priestess as epitomised by Nanny to the domesticated Nanny, black Mammy of the Great House by insisting that drums and dancing were to be outlawed, by insisting on an end to "concubinage" and by insisting on virginity and marriage. (Ford-Smith 1986, 14–15)

Ford-Smith's description of Nanny's legitimacy as a maroon leader focuses on what could be called her "wild femininity," which is to be distinguished from the domesticated kind endorsed by missionaries. This heterogeneous femininity includes a defiant sexuality capable of returning the violence directed against black women as well as a nurturing domesticity through which women were healers and cultivators. As Ford-Smith points out, Nanny's authority does not adhere to the terms of the public/private division belonging to the Victorian ideal of womanhood. Through religious conversion, missionaries domesticated black womanhood in a manner that replaced the image of Nanny, mother of the "wild Negroes," with that of the loyal Mammy, the nursemaid or nanny to the planter's children. This is one kind of epistemic violence enacted against the female-gendered agency presented in the oral tradition.

Still, it is difficult to fix the origins of the bullet-catching story as Brathwaite attempts to do. As a living memory, oral histories do not exist in a fixed form but change across time, often bringing into their narratives new evidence, published sources, and more recent events. Brathwaite's suggestion that maroon historians integrated Thomas's version of the bullet-catching story into their histories after encountering it in his book also means that maroon historians had (and continue to have) a knowledge of colonial narratives, which they weave into their own accounts. But if oral stories incorporate writing into them, how are we to distinguish authentic accounts from their corrupt or inauthentic versions? The maroons have had too much contact with outsiders and been the subject of too much scrutiny for their stories to exist in a pure, unmediated form. Although Thomas potentially distorts the oral version of the bullet-catching story, the act of writing does not negate its prior existence. But even if the story were the product of a miscommunication between maroon storytellers and their white interlocutors, since history is also an act of possession, it belongs to the maroons once they claim it as their own. Conversely, as much as colonial writing attempts to separate itself from the maroon culture it classifies as magic and superstition, orality reenters its textual web. Like a disturbing ghost, Nanny haunts Thomas's story of the triumph of science over superstition, history over myth and legend, and Western civilization over maroon savagery.

Thomas's purpose in writing *Untrodden Jamaica* was to demystify a region associated with the uncertain history of those early years when the island was first settled. Exploring the Blue Mountains constituted the act of claiming the wilderness, rescuing it, so to speak, from the wildness of the maroons. "Should you ask me what the Maroons are like," Thomas instructs his readers, "I should reply:— 'Just like other negroes.' I saw no stately savages of stalwart frame and martial appearance armed with gun and cutlass, but simply a peaceable and contented peasantry following their customary occupations" (18). In the course of retracing the steps of the British soldiers that preceded him, he imagines the battles that took place. He reconstructs for his readers images of runaway slaves being pursued by bloodhounds and maroons hiding in the undergrowth waiting to ambush unsuspecting soldiers. Yet, his desire to relive the excitement of the past would have to wait, as a storm forced him to turn back, confirming in the minds of the maroons, he suspects, that "Nanny's obeah had been too strong" (38). Two months later, he started out again and this time he was more successful. He embarked on his trip with a group of five policemen, including a rural policeman called Hibbert who served as his guide. Hibbert claimed he was the descendant of a free man who made his living hunting down runaway slaves. Although he was no maroon himself, he told Thomas that he was friendly with them and that "they told him many of their secrets" (38, 49).

Untrodden Jamaica records the police inspector's journey over the Cuna-Cuna Pass to Nanny Town as a narrative of colonial conquest. The group had to trek a narrow, winding path that climbed to a height of approximately 5,500 feet, then cross a ridge before descending to the site of Nanny Town. Along the way, Thomas christened an unnamed spring he chanced upon "Police Spring." And, like the Spanish conquistadores who built churches on top of leveled Amerindian temples, he insisted on setting up camp on the abandoned site of the old maroon town: "'This,' I said, 'is the precipice down which the affrighted Maroons hurled themselves in their terror at the bombardment, and here is the site of Nanny Town. On this spot and no other shall we encamp'" (46). Thomas describes how his men cut down saplings with which to build a hut or, as they called it, "the Police Barrack." "And soon the shades of Nanny and Captain Cudjoe, if they were hovering near," he declares, "were scared by the sound of axe and hatchet and cutlass among their ancient forest trees" (46). But Nanny's ghost may have gotten the better of him. According to a surveyor who has worked extensively in the region with maroon guides, the place Thomas visited was located several hundred feet above the actual site of Nanny Town (Tuelon 1973, 26n).

Thomas returned to Nanny Town on at least two other occasions in the hopes of recovering the much-coveted trophy of the swivel guns to which historians generally attribute the capture of Nanny Town. He did not find them. Beverly Carey, a trained historian of maroon descent who is also a member of the Moore Town council, introduces the possibility that the famous swivel guns did not exist (1997, 280–81).[9] There is a record of Captain Stoddart requesting the guns but no evidence of his receiving them. She concludes that the "legend of the swivel gun" was possibly perpetrated by the planter-historians Edward Long and Bryan Edwards, and repeated by subsequent historians. Long's *The History of Jamaica* (1774) and Edwards's *History, Civil and Commercial, of the West Indies* (1794) are instances of what Ranajit Guha identifies as a "secondary discourse" of historical writings. Being temporally removed from the raw materials it reworks while belonging to the same system of power, a secondary discourse legitimates the official version of "what happened" by transforming records into events (50–53). Edwards's account of the first maroon war is, in fact, extracted from Long's report "because," he claims, he has "nothing to add, concerning the origin of the Maroons, to what Mr. Long has so distinctly related; and secondly, because its adoption exempts [him] from all suspicion of having fabricated a tale" (1:535). Historiography may well have its own set of myths and legends, which are transformed into fact through the magical operation of writing.

But it is maroon sorcery that Thomas is intent on exposing. He proves Nanny's cauldron of boiling water to be a rocky basin into which the frothy and foaming waters of two merging rivers fell and which was known as Nanny's Pot. He then describes how he used the instruments of Western science to tame the fear-provoking site, recording that he "measured the dimensions of 'Nanny's Pot'; and took a delicious draught of water from its icy depths" (51). Since this is the same water that, according to maroon tradition, vanquished British soldiers, he presents his actions as science's defeat of maroon superstition. The natural explanation for a supernatural phenomenon suggests that Nanny was not a historical person but rather a symbolic and mythic manifestation of nature. In maroon histories, however, Nanny is not simply identified with nature through her skills in camouflage and fertile pumpkin seeds. She is also identified as a woman who had power *over* nature.

Thomas's natural explanation for a supernatural phenomenon performs a different kind of epistemic violence than the one of making black womanhood conform to a Victorian domestic ideal. In this instance, a female-gendered agency is reduced to nature so that a powerful black woman can be made to represent an unconquered land that needed to be tamed for tourism. By providing a lens through which to view the maroon oral tradition, Thomas disembodies Nanny even in the oral narratives in which her memory is preserved. His *Untrodden Jamaica* may be an inconsequential book, but it served as an authoritative source on Nanny's legendary status among maroons for the first half of the twentieth century. The terms that subsequently became associated with her name—"the notorious Nanny" and "the Maroon Amazon"—are derived from this work. It was not until after Jamaica gained independence that a maroon oral tradition was taken seriously as history and Nanny's leadership role in the maroon war of 1734–39 was officially recognized.[10]

REBEL WOMAN, ASANTE QUEEN

The prominence of Nanny today is inseparable from her designation as a National Hero of Jamaica, and it is of some consequence to this designation that she was a maroon. As Barbara Lalla explains in her study of the figure of the maroon in Jamaican literature, "a compelling character in the story of Jamaica itself is that of the Maroon" (1). The historical recovery of slave resistance at the moment of national independence was integral to dislodging a colonialism responsible for statements like V. S. Naipaul's infamous indictment of the Caribbean for having created nothing of its own, and for living off a borrowed culture (29, 68). As a people who exhibit the strongest residual elements of African culture, maroon societies are living proof of a resistance to European hegemony.[11] During the era of decolonization, marronage became a popular metaphor among Caribbean writers for characterizing their own escape from the European culture that had colonized them (Gikandi 1992, 20–24; Silenieks 1984; Webb 1992, 58).

How Nanny came to be a National Heroine of Jamaica is a story of its own. The United Nations declared 1975 International Women's Year, and Michael Manley's socialist government was looking for a heroic woman to serve as a role model for Jamaican women. In the meantime, maroons had been campaigning for three years for recognition of their Grandee Nanny, as she is affectionately known ("A Maroon Celebration" 1976).[12] Here is how Moore Town council member Beverly Carey presented the case:

> Take Granny Nanny for example, there is no Jamaican woman as distinguished as she was. An African by birth, she led over 800 Maroons for 50 years, planning strategy after strategy to avoid slavery. . . . By her excellent understanding of *bush chemistry,* she cured her fellowers' illnesses, by her deep study of the power of the mind, she could mystify the soldiers. Yet she is not acknowledged. (1973)

With courage, vision and purpose she led her people in the struggle against oppression. NANNY of the Maroons

Self-awareness· Self-confidence· Self-reliance

a

b

Figure 2. This artistic impression of Nanny has been reproduced in numerous places, including (a) a publication of the National Library of Jamaica and (b) a McDonald's cup celebrating Jamaica's national heroes. The sketch is based on maroon descriptions of her as "a small, wiry woman with piercing eyes." Maroons were consulted as to the accuracy in the depiction of her head-tie. Figure 2a courtesy of the National Library of Jamaica.

As the African-born leader of rebel slaves, Nanny embodied the aspirations of a new Jamaica that was emerging from the yoke of colonization.[13] Yet, the choice was not without controversy. Residents of St. Thomas parish (home to Paul Bogle, who led the Morant Bay rebellion and was believed to have been betrayed by a maroon) objected to the recognition of maroons as freedom-fighters. And middle-class Jamaicans, unimpressed by stories of Nanny's extraordinary powers, thought Mary Seacole, the famous Victorian "yellow doctress" who was skilled in herbal cures and folk medicine, to be a more suitable choice (Aub 1989).

In order to dispel rumors that one of its national heroes was simply a folkloric character, the Jamaican government commissioned Brathwaite to prove her historical existence. An artist was also assigned to sketch a portrait based on maroon descriptions of her. This sketch, along with others that followed, gave tangible reality to the woman that many considered to be a myth (see Figures 2 and 3). In *Wars of Respect* (1977), the carefully documented book that was the outcome of his research, Brathwaite explains the difficulty in conducting a historical recovery of Nanny. Since she belonged to what he calls the "pre-recorded period" of Jamaican history (5), the written records provide few details of her life. The paucity of the archives has to do with the maroons being visible only when their actions affect the lives of white settlers. "But even these reports," Brathwaite goes on to explain, "no matter how valuable, are still . . . fragmentary in nature, and suffer, in any case, from the censorship of European cultural prejudice and ignorance; so that a report will often contain what it thinks it sees or hears (or what it wishes to see or hear), rather than what was" (5). He cites the bullet-catching story in Thomas's *Untrodden Jamaica* as one instance of such an imaginary report.

Because the written records and eyewitness accounts are untrustworthy, Brathwaite does not use them to explain Nanny's role as a maroon leader. Rather, he treats the archives as secondary and subservient to the oral tradition. At the same time, her historical existence cannot be established except by corroborating maroon stories with evidence from the colonial archives.

Before Nanny could be declared a National Hero, Brathwaite had to demonstrate that she contributed to the freedom of slaves and served as a symbolic force in the national liberation of Jamaica. He sees her fulfilling both criteria inasmuch as maroons were examples to slaves of the possibility for their own liberation and they practiced an Afro-Creole

Figure 3. A sketch of Nanny by Wilfred Limonious for a small booklet published by JAMAL Foundation, an adult literacy program. She is shown carrying an abeng (the cow's horn maroons used for transmitting messages), a large knife, and a staff, and she is leading her people into freedom. This sketch more accurately represents Nanny's age (she was believed to have been in her sixties) than the standard depiction of her. Courtesy of JAMAL Foundation.

culture so crucial to national self-definition (1977, 17). Since the British classification of maroons as "Wild Negroes" carried with it the stereotyping of African people as a savage and barbaric race, postindependence studies like Brathwaite's show that, rather than returning to the wild, maroons returned to the African culture that plantation owners, through a process known as "seasoning," had attempted to eradicate.

It is now widely recognized that the early maroon settlements were complex and hierarchical societies based on the social order of the Akan-speaking nations to which many of their inhabitants belonged. The Akan appear in the colonial records as "Coromantes," "Koromantee," or "Coro-mantine," a label that refers to the Fante town on the Gold Coast (now Ghana) from which they were transported to the Americas.

Although menstrual taboos prevented Asante women from serving in the state army, the matrilineal structure of Asante society provides a possible explanation for Nanny's prominence as a maroon leader. Since *Nana* is an Akan term of respect for ancestors and spiritual leaders and *ni* means "mother," folklorists suggest that her name is a corrupt New World version of these terms (Barret 1976, 16, 117; Dalby 1971, 48). Brathwaite takes the meaning of Nanny's name beyond its Akan roots of "ancestress" and "mother" to include a range of Asante words that encompass what he calls the "total complex" of her roles as a female leader: "woman, mother, ancestor, leader, priestess, judge and legislator, healer of the breach and revolutionary: the nommo of many forces" (1977, 42n). He also establishes a link between her judicial, political, and spiritual powers and those of the *ohemaa* or queen mother, which is the most powerful political office for an Asante woman (1977, 14–15; 1994, 122–23). The queen mother co-ruled with her son or brother and only in the absence of an heir ruled alone. The more famous of the ohemaas were women like Ama Seewaa, who fought alongside her sons in the 1830s, and Yaa Asantewaa, who led her troops in battle in the Asante war of 1900.[14] In assigning Nanny the title of ohemaa, Brathwaite places her within the tradition of these African warrior queens.

Nanny-Town (1983) by Vic Reid, Jamaica's leading novelist, gives literary representation to the historical recovery of Nanny. Reid presents the story of the first maroon war as a lesson given by the community's griot, Kishee, to an apprentice griot, Kwame Oduduwa, who in turn passes it on his apprentice. Since a griot is a West African storyteller whose role is to preserve the histories of his clan, the naming of Kishee and Kwame as griots identifies the West African structure to maroon oral histories.[15] The chain of narrations follows that of maroon storytelling, except that the story's ultimate recipient is Jamaican rather than maroon. Nanny appears in the novel wearing a "high-winged turban" (49) and full-length robe made from the blue, green, and bronze feathers of the mountain turkey, all of which denote her high rank among maroons. Her wrist and ankle bracelets of copper, silver, and gold speak to the skill of the Akan in metallurgy. This image embellishes her simple clothing in a manner that emphasizes its royal African origins.

The griot's characterization of Nanny as "the Mother of mothers" extends the maroon identification of her as their foremother to all Jamaicans. "It is a way towards the understanding that we are children of the one womb, the womb of the nation," declares Kwame (49). The term *nation* here refers to maroons who are united in their shared New World experience despite divisions back in Africa. But *Nanny-Town* also suggests a direct lineage from a nation of free maroons to the free nation of Jamaica. Nanny's spirit is passed on to Li' Nan, who was born on a plantation but now lives among the maroons (100). And, the apprentice-griot to whom Kwame is telling the story of Nanny-Town notices that the two leaders who signed the peace treaties, Cudjoe and Quao, were not old maroons but former slaves who began their lives on plantations. "'True-true word, pikni-Griot,' Kwame comments on the truth to his observation. 'And it is this that makes all our people one, Bell-People and Mountain People. Maroons and those not Maroons. We all fought for, and won, together, our freedom'" (266). The exchange between veteran and apprentice storyteller is a lesson to Jamaicans of their unity in a free nation. While maroons jealously guard their unique identity as freedom-fighters, cultural nationalists demonstrate that the line separating maroon from nonmaroon is practically nonexistent.

Inasmuch as cultural nationalists trace a maroon identity back to West Africa, they perform what Stuart Hall calls an "act of imaginative rediscovery," which does not recover the past so much as retell it in a manner that centers the fragmentation of the diaspora in Africa (1990, 224). While acknowledging the importance of this recentering as a means of overturning the colonial ideology of England as mother country, he also makes a case for articulating the idea of Africa as mother country with a diasporic notion of what Africa has become in the New World rather than what it was prior to the point of departure. To consider the maroons as a diasporic African culture is to see that the Akan basis to their social organization exists only in a hybrid and translated form. This hybridity is evident in the early maroons' use of the English term "Kramanti" for their culture and the title of "Grandee" or "Granny" for Nanny (Carey 1997, 433).[16]

I want to argue that Nanny's ability to lead was derived not only from the matrilineal structure of Asante society but also a transatlantic crossing that disrupted such traditions, allowing for women to acquire an authority that was unique to the experience of slavery. There exists a difference in the authority of the ohemaa, whose legitimacy is based on her royal lineage rather than proficiency in government, and that of the science-woman.[17] Since the stories of Nanny's science speak so strongly of her skill in survival, from ambushing soldiers to feeding her people, they potentially represent the central role maroon women played in their communities at the time. "What myth could better symbolize the vital role of women," inquire Kenneth Bilby and Filomina Chioma Steady about the story of Nanny's magic pumpkin seeds, "in ensuring regeneration and continuity to a fledgling society struggling for survival?" (1981, 458–59). The Asante queen mother played no symbolic role in representing female power since her high-ranking position was inherited rather than earned (Aidoo 1981, 76). As a means of locating Nanny's skills as a leader within the frame of colonial relations that existed at the time, I now turn to her appearance in the written records on the first maroon war.

THE GENDERED BODY OF THE ARCHIVES

The difficulty in reading the archives for evidence of slave women's agency is that they do not provide information about what existed so much as what the colonial government considered important to record. If Nanny does not appear as a significant leader, it is because the British were not interested in learning about a woman whose authority was based on what they considered to be the superstitious beliefs of Africans. But information is also scarce because maroon warriors took an oath of secrecy and, if captured, were silent about the social organization of their towns or any other information they thought the British might use against them (Campbell 1988, 5). The written records are so fragmentary and incomplete that Nanny appears in them as a puzzle with mostly missing pieces. The holes in the archives have forced historians to fill in the gaps with conjectures about events that may have transpired and to turn to the oral histories for explaining the silences.

Yet, there exists a certain conformity between the maroon histories and colonial archives in their characterization of Nanny as a spiritual leader or what the British called an "obeah woman." It is perhaps telling that the only colonial statement designating her high status among the windward maroons is made in the context of recording her death. Cuffee, "a very good party negro," was commended for "having killed Nanny, the rebels old obeah woman" during a successful raid on Nanny Town in March 1732.[18] This appears to be the end of Nanny, except that she is later recorded as being alive. On January 31, 1734, Cupid, an Ibo slave who escaped from the maroons, testified "that he saw three white men . . . carried to the Negro Town [the British term for Nanny Town] and there putt to Death by Nanny." It is possible that Cupid witnessed Nanny ordering these deaths prior to the raid in which Cuffee killed her. However, he also identifies her as belonging to a group that escaped the raid: "That Adou keeps still to windward . . . with a great party and amongst them is Orgills Scipio Cesar and Adubal. Also Nanny and her Husband who is a greater man than Adou but never went in their Battles."[19] Since Nanny rather than her husband is referred to by name, the statement "who is a greater man than Adou" potentially designates her status as a female leader. In patois, the male pronoun is used to designate both men and women, and an English transcriber would presume "he" to mean a man.

The fact that Nanny ordered British soldiers to be put to death suggests that she was in command of the Negro Town. This reading would confirm Cupid's reference to her as "a greater man" than Adou, who was the leader of the group that escaped. Despite the male-gendering of the statement, it preserves the female-gendering of Nanny's authority. While the authority of male leaders was derived from their skills as warriors, a female leader did not have to prove herself in battle. As a woman, Nanny could not function as leader or "head man," but that does not mean that she was a lesser "man" (to invoke the characterization of her as a "greater man"). The female-gendering of her authority is also preserved in the oral histories, as Thomas's record of stories claiming that "she never went into battle armed like the rest" echoes Cupid's assertion that Nanny "never went into their battles." However, because such references are unsolicited and accidental, there is no context for interpreting them.

As fragmentary and unreliable as the archives may be, they show that Nanny was considered dangerous enough for the British to offer a reward for her death or capture, and that she had the power to order the execution of enemy soldiers. For most historians, however, the indisputable proof of her high rank among the windward maroons was the existence of Nanny Town. "We may safely assert," declares Mavis Campbell, "that no mediocre person, within the context of Maroon tradition, could give his or her name to a town" (176). The settlement consisted of a cluster of villages that appear in the colonial records as one of the "Chief Towns," the "Great Negro Town," or simply the "Negro Town." Yet, it is difficult to fix the exact date when the site went by the name of Nanny Town, not only because the records reflect what the British knew, but also because the names of maroon towns changed according to their leaders. The earliest record of the "Negro Town" going by the name of Nanny Town is in the testimony of Sarra, a maroon who was captured during the 1732 raid. It is clear from his report, coupled with that of Cupid, that Nanny had considerable authority in the maroon settlement even if she was not its head man. Sarra also provides one of the more detailed accounts of the gendered division of labor in the maroon towns:

> [T]hat the old Town, formerly taken by the Soldiers goes now by the Name of Nanny Town, that there are now, or were when he was there three hundred men, all armed with Guns or Launces, that they have more fire Arms than they use, that the number of the Women and Children far exceed those of the Men, that the Rebels have one head Man [Cuffee] who orders everything. . . . the Women . . . and such of the Men as are least noted for their Courage perform all such work as is necessary for the raising of Provisions. . . . they have a Guard Night and Day over the Women who for their Defens carry about them each two or three Knives.[20]

Sarra's testimony describes maroon women's survival skills that range from providing food for the entire community to carrying knives with which to protect themselves. Although the women performed the "womanly" task of subsistence farming, which was also done by the men who were not warriors, the embattled conditions of maroon existence forced them to carry weapons for self-defense. While a West African division of labor continued to exist in the maroon towns, those divisions were also eroded due to the necessity of men and women to assume multiple tasks for the community's survival. The female-gender roles that appear in Sarra's description of Nanny Town mirror the oral stories of Nanny providing food for her people and being able to defend herself by rendering British bullets harmless.

Nanny exists in the colonial archives, then, as a phantom figure behind the naming of Nanny Town and a mysterious woman who was seen with a group that escaped its fall after she had supposedly been killed. A far more dramatic portrait appears in Philip Thicknesse's *Memoirs and Anecdotes* (1790), even though we cannot say with any certainty that the woman he describes was indeed Nanny. Thicknesse was the lieutenant sent in search of the windward maroons shortly after Cudjoe signed a peace treaty with the British. He was one of the first officers to enter Quao's Town, where he discovered that a soldier who had been sent on ahead with news of Cudjoe's treaty had been beheaded. Thicknesse reports that Quao claimed he wanted to spare the soldier's life, but their obeah woman opposed his decision, saying, "him bring becara for take the town, so cut him head off" (74). Thicknesse proceeds to describe the obeah woman in the following manner: "The old Hagg, who passed sentence of death upon this unfortunate man, had a girdle round her waste, with (I speak within compass) nine or ten different knives hanging in sheaths to it, many of which I have no doubt, had been plunged in human flesh and blood." Thicknesse also expresses how, throughout their stay, he and his men feared that at any moment "that horrid wretch, their Obea woman would demand their deaths" (77). He characterizes this authoritative woman as a malevolent and blood-thirsty hag who was not to be trusted. Besides being prone to exaggeration, his description reflects the European stereotyping of powerful women as witches and African-based religious practices as witchcraft.

Most scholars presume the obeah woman in Thicknesse's memoirs to be Nanny and are puzzled as to why Quao's name and not hers appears on the treaty. They suggest one of two possibilities—either the British were unwilling to negotiate with a woman or Nanny refused to settle with them.[21] The latter explanation is derived from maroon oral histories. According to maroons, Nanny did not trust the British and had removed the women and children to concealed settlements known as Woman's Town and Young Gal Town (Carey 1997, 388). She then negotiated a parcel of land for her own people, the evidence of which is a patent signed by the governor on August 5, 1740, granting 500 acres of land to "a certain Negro woman called Nanny and the people residing with her." The wording of the land patent—which claims that Nanny and her people "have Transported themselves and their Servants and Slaves into our said Island in pursuance of a Proclamation made in the Reign of his late Majesty King Charles the Second of Blessed memory and for their encouragement to become our planters there" (cited by Campbell 1988, 175)—has encouraged some maroons to believe that she never was a slave.[22] Campbell notes, however, that the language belongs to the standard deeds used for populating the area with white settlers as a means of controlling maroon activity. This leads her to entertain the possibility that the Nanny of the land deed was not the famous maroon leader at all but rather a free black woman (Nanny was a common name at the time), concluding that "if the Nanny who received the land grant is the historical Nanny, then ironically, she would thus have availed herself of an act for which she and her kind were responsible" (179).

Brathwaite, on the other hand, thinks that the implication of there being more than one Nanny diminishes the famous maroon leader's achievements. He considers it ludicrous that Campbell should even raise the possibility "that this parcel of land which we thought had been granted to Grandee Nanny in recognition of her Honourable Opposition/her Valiant Warriorship (resulting of course in the PEACE TREATY) could really have been intended for some faithful Nancyperson who had done oddjobs for the Plantation" (1994, 137n). Brathwaite's defense maintains the symbolic value of Nanny as liberator by devaluing the labor of the domestic ex-slave: one receives her freedom through armed struggle, while the other receives it as a gift in return for faithful services. The statement reveals that even as a discourse of cultural nationalism extends maroon resistance to those who were enslaved, it simultaneously maintains an opposition between the rebellious and the loyal slave. Since the category of resistance classifies slaves as either rebellious or loyal (which parallels the British classification of "wild" or "domestic"), it cannot account for tactical and negotiated practices except as the sign of the slave's loyalty or accommodation to slavery.

Yet, the possibility that Nanny's victory for her people was achieved through an act intended to restrict maroon mobility points to the more contradictory effects of her negotiation. It is difficult to define the maroons simply in terms of the early years of their rebelliousness after they signed treaties with the British in 1739. According to the terms of the two treaties, the colonial administration granted the maroons land and agreed not to interfere in their government on condition they returned runaway slaves to their owners, defended the island against an invasion, and allowed colonial civil servants to reside in their towns (Campbell 1988, 126–41). The treaties thus endowed maroons with self-autonomy within a larger colonial system, whose laws they had to respect and obey. The existence of a self-autonomy derived from the re-enslavement of future runaways is less an indication of maroon accommodation than a freedom structured by the system of slavery.

Maroons rebelled in 1790 when the terms of their treaty were threatened, but thirty years earlier they helped subdue a widespread slave revolt led by an Akan slave and obeah man called Tacky.[23] Thomas Thistlewood, an English overseer and small landowner, recorded in his diary that "Col Cudjoe's Negroes behaved with great bravery" in putting down the rebellion (Hall 1989, 101). But he also recorded that the maroons were a source of inspiration for the rebellious slaves, who were reported to have said they were going to burn down all the plantations to "force the whites to give them free like Cudjoe's Negroes" (110). The contradictory status of the maroons as ones who inspired the rebellions they helped quell demonstrates the difficulty in establishing a clear line between rebelliousness against and loyalty to the British. It is a contradiction I want to hold on to as I turn now to imaginative journeys into the past and mythic recreations of Nanny's life.

THE SCIENCE-WOMAN'S DOMESTIC AUTHORITY

Nanny belonged to a period of Caribbean history that presented the possibility for a black woman to have greater authority than even male warriors and to assume a leadership role. It is not surprising that such a woman should seize the imagination of Jamaican women novelists, poets, and performers who take poetic license in their literary renditions of her life. Despite the fictional nature of such representations, they are grounded in what I would like to call a "domestic authority" that the historical Nanny possessed. Literary reenactments of Nanny's life show that she was not simply a powerful leader who happened to be a woman or that she was able to command authority despite being a woman. Rather, she led as a woman. Her powers—which encompassed the ability to order executions and to heal, to bear weapons for self-defense and to feed her people, to make political decisions and to predict the future—embody a domestic authority that was not restricted to the domestic sphere. Writers and performers use this authority to redefine slave women's agency in general. Jean "Binta" Breeze, Sistren Theatre, Lorna Goodison, and Michelle Cliff not only celebrate Nanny as a maroon leader but extend her agency to all black women. By indicating the obeah women and fighters that existed among ordinary slaves, they reevaluate slave women's presumed docility. In this manner, they pry the term *domestic* loose from its colonial equation with the "domesticated Negro." These works belong to a cultural nationalism that demonstrates black women's participation in anticolonial struggles. A second set of works by Honor Ford-Smith and Maryse Condé stage how a mythologizing of resistance also fetters the nation to the past through its refusal to address a more ignoble history that accounts for today's color-class divisions in the Caribbean.[24] Taken together, these literary representations of Nanny show the power of the resistance paradigm while also indicating its limitations.

Since Jamaican culture is largely oral, women's performance poetry and dramatic performances of Nanny's life give greater visibility to her female-gendered authority. In "soun de abeng fi nanny," dub-poet Jean "Binta" Breeze calls on the maroon leader to lead the way for all Jamaicans in their fight for freedom, while claiming her specifically for Jamaican women. "Dis a fi we lan," she proclaims, "a yah we mek wi stan" (Breeze 1988, 45–47). But, as one who lives the life of a guerrilla fighter and wears "er savage pride," Nanny is also the foremother of a new kind of woman, one who always existed but was not necessarily recognized. The phrase "er savage pride" identifies a wild femininity that is missing from the romantic musings of patriot and journalist Walter Adolphe Roberts, in a sonnet he wrote (while Jamaica was still a colony) to capture his feelings about the maroon's love of freedom. The sonnet, "Maroon Girl," describe her as a "figure of savage beauty, figure of pride" (1955, 196). In Breeze's poem, Nanny is not simply a figure for the nation; rather, "er savage pride" represents the pride of Jamaican womanhood.

As a female dub-poet in a largely male-dominated field, Breeze extends Nanny's wild femininity to the present through her performance. The abeng was a cow horn that the maroons used to transmit messages to each other and to warn of approaching soldiers. Its long wailing sounds, which the British found "hideous and terrible," had the same effect on them as African "tom-toms" (Campbell 1988, 48). Echoes of the abeng can be heard in the "noise" of dub poetry, which is usually performed to the back-beat of a heavy bass reggae rhythm. But in her musical rendition of "Nanny" (1991), Breeze breaks the standard reggae beat of dub poetry with the polyvocality of multiple rhythms.[25] As it echoes in the refrain, her broken dub rhythm announces the dirty tough ("dutty tuff") women who are breaking new ground by fighting for what is rightfully theirs:

> we sey wi nah tun back
> we a bus a new track
> dutty tuff
> but is enuff
> fi a bite
> fi wi fight

Breeze's poem traces a direct lineage from Nanny to contemporary Jamaican women who are pathbreakers.

The 1980 Kingston production of *Nana-Yah* by Sistren, a theater collective for and by working women, challenges maroon stories that Nanny never went into battle.[26] As the play's storyteller explains: "Talk bout warrior, dat deh woman was a warrior fe true. . . . She betta dan any man. As a matta ov fack we doan even bodda talk bout she husband fa him doan feature at all." These words separate Nanny's high rank from its association with her husband, while making her authority conform more closely to the standards of male warriorhood. Sistren's dramatic reenactment of Nanny's life explicitly shows her engaging in hand-to-hand combat. The scene opens with Nanny having escaped from a plantation and meeting up with the windward maroons. When she tells them that she has been sent by Cudjoe to join them, the group's leader laughs at her, saying, "Mountain fighting a man business. Women fe look afta de pickney dem an cook de food. Guerrilla mean *man*. Me no talk to no woman." Nanny draws out her knife, and as the colonel sends one after another of his best men to fight her, she wins each battle until he finally concedes: "Alright. Me see you can fight." It is of some significance to a postindependence culture that Nanny is shown doing battle with maroon men rather than their British enemies.

As the dialogue between Nanny and the maroon leader indicates, what is being staged (and overturned through its dramatization) is the more strictly defined gender roles that supplanted the heterogeneous femininity existing in the early years of slavery. I have identified this latter femininity as belonging to a diasporic African identity, one that is derived not only from the gender roles that existed in West African societies but also the embattled conditions of maroon life. Out of necessity, maroon women had to know how to use weapons, despite the menstrual taboos that prohibited their Asante counterparts from doing the same. Yet, other African societies used women in their armies, which is why Lorna Goodison traces the figure of the warrior woman back to Africa.

Goodison's poem "Nanny" (1986, 44–45) characterizes the black female body as a weapon capable of combating the violence of slavery. In the poem, Nanny speaks of how she was groomed in Africa to become a fighter and sent to the New World as a slave. Her womb was sealed with wax to induce "the state of perpetual siege/the condition of the warrior" and her breasts bound tightly against her chest. Yet, this process does not make her into the monstrous "unsexed" woman that Thicknesse and Thomas describe. Rather, Goodison takes the "unsexing" of Nanny in colonial narratives and turns it on its head. The process of unsexing the warrior woman extends her maternal feelings beyond her birth children: "From then my whole body would quicken/at the birth of everyone of my people's children." Once her breasts are fastened, Nanny is all the more one with nature, sensing its rhythms, sounds, and scents. The removal of the warrior woman's primary and secondary sex organs heightens her maternal and survival instincts. Her gender roles cut across the boundary that an ideology of separate spheres enforces: Nanny is mother and warrior in one; her training consists of learning the arts of herbal healing and of waging war.

Goodison's portrait of Nanny invokes a more pervasive culture of African women fighters, whose existence was documented in Europe. One of the earliest literary representation of a "Coromantine" woman is that of Imoinda in Aphra Behn's novel *Oroonoko* (1688), which shows her, while pregnant with Oroonoko's child, fighting off their pursuers with a bow and arrow. The former slave Olaudah Equiano reports in his *Interesting Narrative* that in his Igbo village "even [their] women are warriors, and march boldly out to fight along with the men" and describes a battle in which he saw his mother wielding a "broad sword" against her attackers (1987 [1789], 18–19).[27] Equiano was perhaps appealing to his reader's knowledge of the famed women soldiers of the West African kingdom of Dahomey, whose existence was first documented in the early eighteenth century. Travelers to Dahomey believed they had found the legendary Amazons in the king's all-female army. However, even as the warrior women were recognized, they were perceived not to be true soldiers but simply an elaborate masquerade (see Figure 4).

Figure 4. *Armed Women, with King at Their Head, Going to War,* from Archibald Dalzel, *The History of Dahomy, an Inland Kingdom of Africa* (1793). The engraving demonstrates how the king had the royal women dressed as soldiers in order to deceive his enemies into thinking his army was larger than it was. Courtesy of Department of Special Collections, Charles E. Young Research Library, University of California at Los Angeles.

The British Guyanese poet Grace Nichols has spoken of the need for new myths about black women with which to break "the slave stereotype of the dumb victim of circumstance" (1990, 288), and "Nanny" offers a myth of this sort. Drawing on maroon stories that claim the leaders of the first maroon war were sent to start the revolts, Goodison's poem depicts Nanny being sold into slavery, not out of betrayal, but as a Trojan horse filled with weapons to be unleashed on the other side:

> And when my training was over
> they circled my waist with pumpkin seeds
> and dried okra, a traveller's jigida
> and sold me to the traders

all my weapons within me
I was sent, tell that to history.

When your sorrow obscures the skies
Other women like me will rise. (45)

Nanny is singular but not unique. Other fighters are concealed among
ordinary slave women awaiting the right moment to make themselves
known. Both Sistren and Goodison depict Nanny as a slave who escaped to join the maroons rather than a woman who always lived in a
free maroon society. Her lowly existence as a slave is proof that other
women like her existed, even if their actions went unrecorded. By demonstrating how Nanny represents the potential for rebelliousness that
existed in other slave women, these works adhere to the logic of a cultural nationalism that extends maroon resistance to all slaves.

Ford-Smith, who was artistic director of the Sistren Theatre Collective between 1977 and 1989, also suggests that Nanny differed little from
other slave women but by demythologizing the warrior woman. "Message from Ni" opens with Nanny saying, "They write so much about
me now/that sometimes I read about myself. . . . I never recognize that
woman they describe" (Ford-Smith 1996, 15). The poem emphasizes the
warrior woman's all-too-human body over the human shield that can
repel bullets. Nanny proceeds to explain that her "body shook in battle,"
she vomited from the sight of the dead and felt faint from the smell of
blood. The maroon leader appears less as a fearless warrior than a fearful
slave marooned in a strange land. Nanny confesses that the stories of her
supernatural powers were "invented dreams to fill the hollow/sleepless
nights" (16) that she repeated so often that she began to believe them
herself. The stories give her the strength to go on until she becomes the
woman she dreamed herself to be.

According to Nanny's admission, the stories of her feats precede her
enactment of them, a move that reverses agency and representation. This
reversal shows that heroism is not an essential part of her being but contingent on the circumstances that produced a woman like her. Nanny
claims that she was driven by terror, but "they never mention that, or/
how close courage is to fear" (16). Is an action less valid because one is
acting out of terror rather than courage? The question not only com-
plicates the idea of maroon heroism but also forces an inquiry into the
equation of "domesticated" with the tame or docile slave. The possibility
for other warrior women to rise from slavery exists not because they are

equally heroic, but because Nanny might have been less extraordinary. Ford-Smith's poem, published ten years after Goodison's, belongs to an era of growing disillusionment with the early utopian vision of national independence, which might explain its mixed sentiments about the mythologizing of Nanny as a warrior woman. Both poets, however, bring the singular maroon leader into an economy of slavery in order to force a consideration of the women who remained slaves.

The black mammy or nursemaid who supposedly valued her owner's children above her own is a domesticated image of Nanny as the mother of free slaves. Yet, the nursemaid that planter-turned-abolitionist John Riland describes in his memoirs appears to have the secret identity of an obeah woman:

> Much as I despised and abused the mass of the Black population, there were, nevertheless, two of our domestic slaves, who possessed over me an amazing, and one of them an awful, influence. The first of these was my nurse, called Mahali . . . [who] was an extraordinary favourite with my parents; and, having been imported from Africa at the age of sixteen, was well acquainted with all the customs and mythology of her native country. . . . The power of my nurse on my infant mind partook, as already intimated, of something supernatural. I was indeed, at times, insolent even to *her;* but I kept all her secrets; and they were such secrets as children ought never to know, much less to keep. But a kind of mysterious terror, which she had the power of inspiring, obliged me to be silent. She had filled my mind with terrible stories of witchcraft and sorcery: and I would do and suffer any thing for her, if she would promise to sit by me at night when I went to bed, and not let in to me the evil spirits. She used to tell me, that the dark shadows of the bushes on the lawn, when the moon shone, were spirits. In fact, she, on some occasions, almost *put me into obi.* (1827, 3–4)[28]

Riland invokes the actual power of obeah in his use of words like "amazing," "awful," "supernatural," and "mysterious terror," to emphasize the power of suggestion Mahali had on his "infant mind." Reversing the master-slave relationship, she extracts from him a loyalty in the assurance that he "kept all her secrets." Here is an apparently devoted slave who as a "favourite" had the trust and confidence of her owners but who was also able to make the young master fear her as she indeed must have feared his more powerful father.

Mahali's secret actions constitute what James C. Scott calls the "hidden transcript" of the public records, which are acts of everyday resistance that take place behind the master's back. These acts, which he characterizes as "an acting out in fantasy—and occasionally in secretive practice—of the anger and reciprocal aggression denied by the presence of domination" (1990, 37–38), do not have the same effect as more overt acts of resistance. An "acting out in fantasy" is done for the purposes of self-satisfaction rather than self-empowerment. For this reason, my interest in the idea of a hidden transcript concealed within the official records lies less in demonstrating acts of everyday resistance. Rather, the significance of the double identity of the slave is that it prevents us from establishing with any certainty her loyalty to her owners and devotion to her charge. To her master and mistress, Mahali was a loyal mammy; to their son, she was a much-feared obeah woman. This double identity is not the same as the trickster figure, whom Scott locates between the official record and its hidden transcript. "This is a politics of disguise and anonymity," he explains about the trickster, "that takes place in public view but is designed to have a double meaning or to shield the identity of the actors" (19). Although the secret lives of slaves inflect the information that appears in the public transcript, their action is more likely to remain a secret. The mammy appears as a loyal and faithful slave in the colonial records because that is the public role she played.

In *Abeng* (1984), Michelle Cliff traces a direct line from the slave's need for secrecy to the problem of overturning the master's discourse. Set in late-1950s Jamaica, just a few years before national independence, the novel is a coming-of-age story that is precisely not a Bildungsroman because the development of its light-skinned, middle-class protagonist, Clare Savage, is stalled by her failure to learn the truth of her family's history.[29] The novel's narrative is fragmented and disjointed like Jamaican history; its linear development interrupted by a slave past that the present is doomed to repeat, as the signs of neocolonialism are evident even before the British leave. The double origin of Clare's first name is emblematic of the problem of history the novel addresses. Her mother, Kitty, led her husband to believe that their daughter was named after the Cambridge University college his grandfather had attended. The name actually commemorated a simpleminded country girl called Clary, who had cared for her through an illness. Kitty does not tell her daughter that she was named after a Jamaican peasant woman rather than an elite institution for the education of English men. By failing to pass the stories of black women on to her daughter, she is complicit with her husband's emulation of English culture and the raising of Clare as a domesticated colonial.

Members of Jamaica's educated class to which Clare and her family belong are ignorant of their own history because they have been raised to think of England as the mother country. This ignorance allows a domestic worker to stand in the place of the fierce warrior: "Some of them were called Nanny, because they cared for the children of other women, but they did not know who Nanny had been" (21). Cliff shows how the ghost of Nanny haunts the activities of these civilized colonials because the power of the fearless maroon leader has been tamed. Clare's mixed-raced grandmother, Miss Mattie, "wasn't a sorceress, just a woman who led Sunday services" (14). And Kitty possesses the same knowledge of bush medicine as the maroons, except that she does not know how to turn her knowledge into a source of strength. Despite the characters belonging to a world that is governed by an ignorance about slavery, maroon resistance, and Afro-Creole culture, the reader learns about this repressed past through a series of history lessons that serve as the novel's unconscious.

Cliff's literary project is to claim sorcery as a figure for black women's history by privileging those forms of knowledge—myth, legend, magic, dreams, and superstition—traditionally excluded from factual evidence. She sees Nanny's supernatural powers as capable of not only vanquishing her enemies but also reversing a colonial version of the past and the value system that is its legacy. "The extent to which you can believe in the powers of Nanny, that they are literal examples of her Africanness and strength," Cliff explains, "represents the extent to which you have decolonized your mind" (1991, 47). In *Abeng,* she gives the maroon leader a slave counterpart in the character of Mma Alli, an elderly obeah woman who derives her strength from her love of other women. The similarity between Mma Alli and an old slave woman whom Edwards describes as the evil practitioner of obeah suggests that Cliff is rewriting her character (Edwards 1807, 2:115–17). In Cliff's novel, the obeah woman is characterized as "a one-breasted warrior woman" (34), which alludes to the legendary Amazons and stories linking them to an all-female colony on the island of Lesbos.[30] Although Mma Alli is not explicitly identified as maroon, she is in possession of an abeng, their instrument for transmitting secret messages.

Mma Alli is a spiritually powerful woman who instructs black women in the art of sexual pleasure, from which they derive their own power and strength. She shows them how "to keep their bodies as their own" (35) even when raped by their owner, Judge Savage (Clare's white ancestor), and his slave-drivers. Inez, a captured maroon woman whom Judge Savage forcibly takes as his concubine, comes to Mma Alli for help in getting rid of her mixed-raced baby. In what constitutes a highly eroticized ritual of an abortion, the obeah woman massages the fetus out of Inez's body.[31] As Farah Jasmine Griffin explains in her reading of the scene, the "erotic ritual [that] is performed in the service of resistance . . . is not an act that ensures heterosexual reproduction, but instead, because it is an act of abortion, it challenges heterosexuality and male control over female sexuality and reproduction" (1996, 522). By showing how Mma Alli's opposition to the sexual and reproductive exploitation of slave women is inseparable from her lesbianism, Cliff disrupts the heterosexual norm in Jamaican nationalist and maroon discourses. By locating lesbianism in African culture, she disputes the perception in the Caribbean that homosexuality is an aberrant sexual practice introduced by Europeans.

Another character, that of Mad Hannah, represents what a powerful obeah woman like Nanny has become in a world that is intolerant of homosexuality. Hannah is an herbal healer whose mind became unhinged after her son, Clinton, was allowed to drown in the local swimming hole to the taunts of "battyman, battyman," the derogatory term in Jamaica for homosexual men. Clinton was given an "incomplete and dangerous burial" (66), as the men Hannah paid to ensure that he received the proper rites ignored her instructions. On the third night after his funeral, she saw his duppy emerge from the grave. Hannah is considered mad because she spends her days looking for her son's duppy so that she might perform the rituals that would allow his spirit to return to its grave.

In *Abeng,* the ghost that haunts a Caribbean present is not only a slave past but also the open secret of the region's homophobia.[32] This homophobia makes it difficult to address whether same-sex relationships existed among slaves. By making the lesbian body into a site of resistance, Cliff does not introduce a sexuality that is repressed in the archives but rather one that is foreclosed—that is, cut off with no possibility of representation. The character of Mma Alli serves as a reminder of slave women's secret sexual practices, the details of which we cannot possibly know. In representing slave women as being able to keep their bodies their own even when raped by their white masters, Cliff proposes an "unsexing"—that is, a disengagement of sexual pleasure from heterosexual intercourse—in the interest of sexual autonomy. Her critical intervention disrupts the economy of slavery by suggesting another economy that exceeded it. To invoke Luce Irigaray's characterization of female homosexuality, when the goods get together there is nothing to take to market (1985, 192–97).

Since Cliff emigrated to the United States when she was three years old and has not returned to Jamaica since 1975, she has been criticized in the Caribbean for having the perspective of an outsider (see, for instance, Mordecai and Wilson 1989, xvii). Cliff, on the other hand, sees herself maintaining the dual perspective of a Jamaican and American, while existing as an outsider to Caribbean society (Raiskin 1993, 57–60). The duality of her perspective is reflected in the memory about Nanny her novel produces. The maroon history that exists as the subterranean text to the Savage family's Anglicized existence aligns *Abeng* with a cultural nationalism that recenters the Caribbean around Africa and privileges oral histories. This alignment, however, is asserted from the perspective of an outsider, as the maroons represent an oppositional consciousness that the novel's light-skinned protagonist cannot hope to approximate.

The separation of her heroine from the revolutionary action that the maroons have come to represent is more evident in Cliff's second novel, *No Telephone to Heaven* (1987), which follows the life of Clare Savage after her family emigrates to the United States. Here, the historical unconscious of a heroic maroon past gives way to a postmodern recession of the real. Magic in a neocolonial era lies less in the power of Nanny's science than that of media images to generate reality. Clare returns to Jamaica during the 1980s to join a group of revolutionaries whose desire to act as freedom-fighters is mediated through revolutionary films like *Burn!* and *Viva Zapata!*[33] The world has become so saturated with images of the past that history is one among many stories and action can only imitate art. As Foucault remarks about the media images that have taken the place of the past, people are shown as not what they once were but what they must remembered as having been (1989). Although the revolutionaries see themselves as acting in the memory of Nanny, they are wearing American army surplus uniforms that suggest a B-movie:

The camouflage jackets, names and all, added a further awareness, a touch of realism, cinematic verité, that anyone who eyed them would believe they were faced with *real* soldiers. True soldiers—though no government had ordered them into battle—far from it. But this is how the camouflage made them feel. As the gold and green and black knit-ted caps some wore—a danger because the bright gold would sing out in the bush—made them feel like real freedom-fighters, like their com-rades in the ANC—a cliché, almost screenplayed to death, *Viva Zapata!* and all that—but that *is* what they were, what they *felt* they were, what they *were* in fact. Their reason emblazoned in the colors of their skulls. *Burn!* (7)

The actions of the would-be revolutionaries are implicated in the U.S. imperialism they seek to overthrow. Their uniforms are stolen from stoned American kids, and they have acquired their weapons from the American black market in exchange for the ganja they have grown. With the increasing globalization of culture, there is no longer the possibility for heroic oppositional practices.

The problem of revolutionary action today is not one of historical forgetting, as it was during the era of decolonization, but of a global cul-ture that has manufactured a plethora of images for popular consump-tion. In Cliff's novel, an American film company in Jamaica to make a movie about the early maroons recasts their story within the frame of a formulaic Hollywood script. Clare and her fellow revolutionaries are hiding in the bush preparing to attack the film crew that is shooting a scene in which Cudjoe saves Nanny from an attack by the fire-breathing demon Sasabonsam. Ironically, they are waging a war against the same Western image-making machine that has inspired their own revolution-ary action. The American film's romantic dramatization of the maroons is evident in its representation of Nanny as a beautiful young heroine wearing breeches and a billowy silk shirt, and Cudjoe, who appears in the colonial records as a short hunchback, as a strapping athlete. Yet Cliff does not go so far as to suggest a connection between the heroic image of maroon resistance in her novel and the filmmaker's imagina-tive reconstruction of the past. Rather, she holds on to the oppositional practices of the maroons as a pure form of resistance that is lost to a present contaminated by globalization.

Maryse Condé, who as a Guadeloupean is even more of an outsider to Jamaican culture than Cliff, is more critical of the notion of an un-

contaminated past in her novella *Nanna-ya* (1999). Its story, which like
Abeng is set in the period shortly before national independence, features
a respected and much-feared maroon woman and healer, Jane, who is a
direct descendant of Nanny. When the maroons at Moore Town, Corn-
wall Barracks, and Comfort Castle hear that Jane has given birth to
a light-skinned baby girl, they think, "How awful. The Koromantyn
ancestors were surely turning over in their graves! As for fearless Nanny,
had she fought to the death just so a white man could plant a child out
of wedlock in her descendant's womb?" (80). Modern maroons invoke
the name of their foremother not in the interest of preserving her wild
femininity, but in order to condemn the transgressive sexual practice of
a maroon woman. Jane's child, whose name is Grace, is nonetheless em-
braced by her grandmother, Maddah Louise, a maroon from Seaman's
Valley. As the reader soon learns, Maddah Louise, like all of the maroons
in Seaman's Valley, has "some of the blood of the Englishman George
Fuller . . . in her veins" (82).[34] She is lighter-skinned than even her own
children, especially Jane, who is described as "dark" and "statuesque."
The fact that a racially mixed but dark-skinned woman like Jane could
be a respected healer shifts the signification of science-woman closer to
a diasporic notion of "Africa," while complicating the equation of rebelliousness with the African slave and accommodation with the mulatto.

Due to the other maroons' refusal to acknowledge the existence of
racial mixing in their people, Grace grows up hating Moore Town and
maroon pride. Whenever she hears the children singing the popular
song honoring Nanny, "Nanna Ya," she is reminded that, as a racially
mixed woman, she is excluded from the lineage of her famous ancestor:
"That story was not hers, she knew it. Somewhere along the line, and
just for her, the family tree had broken and a shoot of unknown origin
had appeared. Her golden skin and her long braided hair swinging on
her shoulders were a constant reminder of it" (81). The irony in these
words is that the family tree was already broken long before Grace came
along, and it is the earlier trace of white blood that accounts for her
golden skin and straight hair.

Grace marries a man whose own claim to pure African ancestry is
equally suspect but who attempts to disavow it through an invented
past. George is the bastard child of a sugarcane worker and a wealthy
merchant, who is characterized as "a crossbreed of Indian, Chinese, and
white" (85), but who says he is descended from the Spaniards who came

over from Cuba to help the British pacify the maroons. George's family story, one in which a planter impregnates a sugarcane worker, is a scenario that has been repeated countless times during and since the days of slavery. In order to compensate for his dubious and ignoble origins, he invents a more illustrious genealogy for himself by tracing his mother's lineage to Tacky, leader of the 1760 slave revolt. His marriage to a maroon woman is a constant reminder that Tacky was killed by a maroon. He begins to write a "History of Tacky" to show how "slaves are the invisible agents of history" (94) and to destroy the idea of maroons as heroic freedom fighters. George becomes so obsessed with his history that he begins to neglect his family. He has an affair with a mixed-race British Jamaican woman, who steals his manuscript, turns it into a first-person narration, and declares it to be an oral history that she recorded. She is awarded the Norman Manley prize for history. Grace, aware of the affair that George was having, believes her mother had a hand in returning him to her by having his mistress steal his prized history. In this instance, the name of the dead mother is invoked in a manner that heals the wounds of the past. "Only when he [George] was free of the mythical past," explains Condé, "did he begin to learn to live in the present" (Pfaff 1996, 57).

Condé's plotting of *Nanna-ya* can be read as an allegory of the nation. The union of slave and maroon in the Jamaican nation, as represented by the marriage of George and Jane, breaks down due to the need for one side to identify their ancestors as the "true rebels" at the other side's expense. Within this scenario, it is perhaps appropriate that a mixed-race diasporic Jamaican, who is in Jamaica out of a desire to find her roots, claims authorship over the oral history she has stolen. Yet, because the history is based on an invented genealogy, there is no true proprietor to its story.

The need for a different narrative of a slave past becomes apparent if one considers that George creates a heroic ancestry for himself in order to disavow a scene of gender oppression. He traces his family history to a male hero of a slave revolt so as to erase the knowledge of his mother's sexual appropriation by a culturally white merchant. A parallel erasure is enacted through the female character of Inez in Cliff's novel *Abeng*. Inez is a maroon woman whom Judge Savage takes as his concubine and repeatedly rapes, but she manages to abort her mixed-race child and escape to freedom. The unspoken story behind Inez's abortion is how Judge Savage came to be Clare's ancestor, a story that the novel hints at but does not tell. After all, white men did keep slave women as concubines, often for years, and the existence of their mixed-race slave children prevents their stories from being written under the sign of an abortion. In both acts of narration—that of George and Cliff—a figure of resistance covers over a scene of sexual exploitation and, in doing so, leaves unanswered questions about the historical possibilities of oppositional practices. For, even as the maroon has come to represent rebelliousness and an African belief system, the mulatto signifies assimilation into European culture. How can we describe the agency of women who did not resist the white men who sexually appropriated them but appear to have "willingly" given themselves to them? Is it possible to use the terms *resistance* and *submission* to talk about women who were so disempowered that they had little choice in the matter?

2.

"An Incomparable Nurse"
The Obi of Domesticity

Possessing a knowledge of herbal cures for the tropical diseases to which European men were susceptible, the mulatto concubine appears in colonial narratives as the domesticated and slavish counterpart to the maroon obeah woman. Yet it is possible to pry the concubine's domesticity away from the colonial signification of "domesticated" by introducing questions of female agency to a site of subjugation. Doing so does not suggest that concubines were essentially rebellious. Rather than focusing on acts of resistance, this chapter considers the tactics through which they negotiated some power without necessarily challenging the system of slavery. While a study of West Indian concubinage will reveal little about the culture of resistance among slaves, it can tell us something about how slave women achieved a certain degree of autonomy from their owners through a form of domesticity that was unique to West Indian slave culture. This autonomy was, of course, contradictory, for it was acquired through a dependency on white men, and a woman was often placed at greater risk of physical violence, particularly if her keeper (as they were known) was a jealous man. However, the existence of sexual exploitation does not diminish the mobility black and racially mixed women were able to acquire for themselves within the coercive relations of slavery.

The concubine's performance of the role of a white man's wife gave her access to privileges that were otherwise denied slave women, and it was this domestic role that was the source of her unique status. In order to make this argument, we must distinguish the concubines of unmarried white men from those who served married men, especially if they were also their owners. In *Slavery and Social Death,* Orlando Patterson explains how slaves who lived away from their masters had greater autonomy or what he calls "partial 'freedom'" (1982, 175). This is in fact what slave women were able to achieve through a manipulation of their sexual exploitation, as their ability to establish conjugal relationships with white men who were not their owners allowed them to move out of the households to which they belonged.

It is difficult to detect the signs of the women's tactical use of their sexual exploitation, as images of their power are so phantasmagoric that they halt an inquiry into the validity of the claims. What is curious about colonial accounts is that white men are perceived as being under the power of their concubines rather than the other way around. Lady Nugent, who was in Jamaica from 1802 to 1807, expressed the common perception of the time when she recorded that high-ranking men were "almost entirely under the dominion of their mulatto favourites" (Cundall 1907, 131). The term *mulatto* here refers to a class of racially mixed free women who served as the mistresses of wealthy white men, and Lady Nugent follows the practice of using "mulatto" as a generic term for concubines, whether they were black or racially mixed, slave or free. This practice might have to do with the greater visibility of the free colored women, who tended to live in the towns, and their predominance in the nineteenth century. In rural areas, however, concubines were commonly drawn from slave women (Parliamentary Papers 1831–32, 70–71). As missionary Richard Bickell observes, some seven or eight thousand white men had concubines in Jamaica alone, and while merchants, shopkeepers, and overseers kept free mixed-raced women, book-keepers (deputies to the overseers) made use of black or mulatto slaves (1825, 104–6).

The colonial practice of using *mulatto* as a convenient shorthand can be considered ideological, for it identifies the power that slave women negotiated for themselves *within* slavery with the concubine's status of having white blood and being free, as well as with the rank of the men who were their "keepers." It also allows for the argument that concubinage was a practice in which racially mixed women, out of an identification with the white race, preferred white men to those of their own kind. This argument presumes that slave women had the license to exercise a sexual preference, which they did not. In this manner, a unique story of sexual relations across the master-slave divide is subsumed within that of the free colored woman. The eighteenth century is useful for examining the ambivalences in the position of concubines, as it was an era before a class of free mulatto women was established and, hence, when most of the women who served white men in this capacity were slaves.

Perhaps the most visible of these slave women was the one known simply as Joanna, who has been immortalized in John Gabriel Stedman's *Narrative of a Five Years' Expedition against the Revolted Negroes of Surinam* (1806 [1796]). Stedman was a professional soldier who in 1772 volunteered to join a military expedition against rebellious maroons who were threatening the security of Surinam, on the northeast coast of South America.[1] He kept a daily log of events during those four and a half years with the intention of publishing a travel narrative. A two-quarto volume with eighty-one illustrations by prominent engravers (among them William Blake) was published in 1796 by Joseph Johnson, a radical London publisher whose circle included Thomas Paine, William Godwin, and Mary Wollstonecraft (Tyson 1979).[2] The first-person narrative wove descriptions of Surinam's flora and fauna, along with social sketches of Amerindian and plantation life, into reports on the military campaigns against the maroons. In this regard, the book followed the literary form of the numerous travelogues that were so popular at the time. But Stedman's *Narrative* was also unique in its vivid portraits of the inhumane treatment of slaves and the author's declaration of his devotion to his mulatto concubine.

My chapter tracks the changing representation of Joanna in Stedman's private and published writings, particularly the editorial changes made to his *Narrative* as it became adopted as an antislavery tract. I am interested in how abolitionists perpetrated a myth that was initiated in Stedman's *Narrative*—namely, that a slave woman could be capable of exercising free choice. In the antislavery literature, Joanna served as a model for the tragic mulatta, a figure that would eventually displace an earlier stereotyping of mulatto women as vain, arrogant, and sexually promiscuous. Stedman represents Joanna as a mixed-race version of the noble black slave and domestic white woman, an image that particularly appealed to abolitionists. In doing so, however, he eliminates contradictions in the practice of concubinage that slave women were able to exploit. I hope to unravel these contradictions by weaving Stedman's *Narrative* into other colonial texts from the same era.

THE ENCHANTMENT OF THE SABLE VENUS

One of the more startling colonial representations of slave women's agency concerns the almost magical power concubines were believed to have had over their keepers. Consider J. B. Moreton's *Manners and Customs in the West India Islands* (1790), in which he recorded the five years he spent in Jamaica as a book-keeper, which was a deputy to the overseer. He speaks disapprovingly of how the "elevation" of slave women to the status of concubine licensed their insubordination:

> It is quite common for an attorney to keep a favourite black or mulatta girl on every estate, which the managers are obliged to pamper and indulge like goddesses. . . . The vanity of female slaves is raised to unbounded degree to be chosen objects of their master, (for they call an attorney their master) on which account they are often intolerable insolent to subordinate white men: woe betide a poor overseer if he affronts one of them! (77)

Attorneys were hired by absentee owners to manage their plantations, and Moreton is clearly indignant that, as a low-ranking book-keeper who often had to serve years of apprenticeship before becoming an overseer, he had to follow a higher-ranking official's directions. Moreover, as an English man who is arguing against the slave trade in his book, he wants to expose the decadence of West Indian culture. Yet, there appears to be an underlying discourse governing his characterization of slave women being "indulged like goddesses," for his choice of phrase is not an isolated case.

Bryan Edwards, considered the most liberal of the West Indian historians, includes in his *History, Civil and Commercial, of the British Colonies in the West Indies* (1807 [1793]) an anonymous poem that addresses the concubine as a "sable Queen" and "playful Goddess."[3] Alluding to Botticelli's Venus who ascends from the sea in a giant scallop shell, "The Sable Venus; An Ode" creates a myth of origins for the New World African woman. The Black Goddess of Love is depicted as traveling from Africa to the shores of Jamaica in an ivory chariot inlaid with shells and amber and pulled by flying fish. As a sign of her regal status, she is seated in a gold throne decked with ostrich and peacock feathers; her feet rest on a coral footstool. She arrives in the New World as conqueror rather than slave. The poem ends with the observation that traces of this

African beauty are to be seen in the smile of one slave woman, the look of another, and the pout of a third. All of these coquettes bear African names: Phibia, Benneba, Mimba, Cuba, Quasheba.

Although the poet attempts to locate the origins of the women's beauty in Africa, hence their African names, the Sable Venus herself is not Africanized. With the exception of her skin, she bears no distinctive racial mark such as hair texture, facial features, and body type. In the place of racial characteristics, the poem presents the fragrance of her breath, brightness of her eye, softness of her lip, and mildness of her appearance. The Sable Venus is a more exotic version of her European counterpart, who serves as a universal standard of beauty:

> Her skin excell'd the raven plume,
> Her breath the fragrant orange bloom,
>   Her eye the tropick beam:
> Soft was her lip as silken down,
> And mild her look as ev'ning sun
>   That gilds the COBRE stream.
>
> The loveliest limbs her form compose,
> Such as her sister VENUS chose,
>   In FLORENCE, where she's seen;
> Both just alike, except the white,
> No difference, no—none at night,
>   The beauteous dames between.
>   (Edwards 1807, 2:35)

Barbara Bush correctly identifies the poem as "part of white male mythology [that] reflected a common and often near-obsessional interest in the 'exotic charms' of African womanhood" (11). But it also exhibits a West Indian inflection to this popular mythology. The dark-skinned woman with Europeanized features belongs to a white male fantasy of the mixed-race woman as an object of desire, which might explain why Edwards includes the poem at the end of his chapter "People of Colour."[4]

Edwards introduces the poem with the statement that it is intended to expose "the character of the sable *and saffron* beauties of the West Indies, and the folly of their paramours" (emphasis mine; 2:31). The poem's mocking tone makes it less a tribute to black women's beauty

than a satire of the white men who have become their sex slaves. This is
the opening stanza, delivered in the voice of one such man:

> O sable Queen! Thy mild domain
> I seek, and court thy gentle reign,
>   So soothing, soft and sweet;
> Where meeting love, sincere delight,
> Fond pleasure, ready joys invite,
>   And unbought raptures meet. (2:33)

The poem's reversal of the master-slave relation offers one possible explanation for why it gives no inkling of the woman's status as slave or of
her Atlantic crossing as anything but a pleasant sea journey. The reversal
belongs to what Mary Louise Pratt identifies as a narrative of the anticonquest, which represents imperial relations as reciprocity and mutual
exchange (78–85). This is a narrative of the anticonquest with a ven-
geance. It is not simply the case that the white man does not appear as
colonizer; rather, the African woman is represented as conqueror of the
New World. The poem not only eliminates the violence of slavery from
the picture, it also animates female agency in a manner that binds black
women to a racial stereotyping of their sexual promiscuity.

Thomas Stothard's painting *The Voyage of the Sable Venus from Angola
to the West Indies,* which was included as a black-and-white engraving
in the second edition of Edwards's *History of the West Indies,* also depicts
the black woman's beauty as inextricably bound up with her sexuality
(see Figure 5). However, in the visual image of the Sable Venus her
body is more explicitly racialized. Whereas Botticelli's Venus is slim and
long-limbed with arms draped across her front in feminine modesty,
Stothard's Venus stands with outstretched arms to display her squat,
muscular body and large, fleshy thighs. She is no graceful image of
classical beauty; her blackness represents a dark sexuality. In contrast
to the poem's mythological rendition of the journey from Africa to the
New World, the painting provides an iconography of Britain's marine
power in the allegorical figure of Neptune holding a Union Jack. Hints
of shackles are visible in the necklace, bracelets, and anklets the Sable
Venus wears. The black woman's sexual power is framed by the even
greater power of a colonial allegory of imperial masculinity.

"The Sable Venus; An Ode" is unusual as a cultural artifact inasmuch
as black women were not admired for their beauty, a quality associated

Figure 5. *The Voyage of the Sable Venus, from Angola to the West Indies,* from Bryan Edwards, *History, Civil and Commercial, of the West Indies* (1794). Courtesy of Department of Special Collections, Charles E. Young Research Library, University of California at Los Angeles.

more with the mulatto woman. The mixed-race woman, however, was perceived to be in possession of not only a great sensual beauty but also superior nursing skills. Colonial eyewitnesses considered the doctoring of mulatto women to be superior even to Western medicine, as is evident in this planter's observation about the free colored woman who served his attorney: "She is perpetually in the hospital, nurses the children, can bleed, and mix up medicines, and (as I am assured) she is of more service to the sick than all the doctors" (Lewis 1929, 142). The power of the mulatto woman lies in both "the magical art"—which is how Moreton characterizes her sexual knowledge—and the art of healing, which was an actual skill handed down from one generation of concubines to the next.[5] Stedman justifies the constant references to Joanna in his travel book with a confession of the enormous debt he owed her for saving his life. He describes her as "an incomparable nurse," a "Heavenly Young Woman, to whom alone [he] owed [his] life," and "so Good a Nurse as Joana . . . Who had now Once more Literally Saved [his] Life" (Price and Price 1988, 262, 278–79, 377). Pratt identifies Joanna as belonging to a more sentimental vision of the anticonquest, "the beneficent female figure of the 'nurturing native,' who tends to the suffering European out of pity, spontaneous kindness, or erotic passion" (96). The inequalities between white men and their concubines are mystified through a discourse of exchange and reciprocity, as is the case with the Sable Venus, except that in this instance the relationship is not only sexual but also social.

While Pratt reads the transracial romance of Stedman and Joanna as an allegory of colonial relations in which Joanna's refusal to assimilate into European culture figures the emergence of a postcolonial creolized society, I am interested in "the nurturing native" as a sign of the unique position concubines occupied within slavery. If we consider the obeah woman and nurturing native in terms of what Peter Hulme identifies as the polarized stereotyping of Amerindians as "good" and "bad" natives (65), then the concubine is the "good" counterpart to the rebel woman, which is why she is generally imagined as racially mixed just as her "wild" sister is figured as African. It is no coincidence that the mixed-race woman comes to represent the image of the concubine as nurse and nurturer, for the latter's spirit of self-sacrifice and dedication to white men overlaps with that of the domestic (white) woman.

In his *Narrative,* Stedman presents Joanna as a woman who embodies both the Sable Venus's exotic beauty and a late-eighteenth-century European ideal of femininity. The feminine virtues of "innocent modesty" and "native Simplicity" (cited by Poovey 1984, 22) from a late-eighteenth-century conduct book could just as easily apply to her. Throughout his *Narrative,* Joanna appears as a sentimental heroine who always speaks with downcast eyes and tears falling on her heaving bosom. Stedman's description of his first sighting of Joanna is a more sentimental image than that of the Sable Venus, alluding not only to her outer beauty but also the inner beauty of her sweetness, modesty, and innocence (see Figure 6).

> She was perfectly streight with the most elegant Shapes that can be view'd in nature moving her well-form'd Limbs as when a Goddess walk'd—Her face was full of Native Modesty and the most distinguished Sweetness—Her Eyes as black as Ebony were large and full of expression, bespeaking the Goodness of her heart. With Cheeks through which glow'd/in spite of her olive Complexion/a beautiful tinge of vermillion when gazed upon—her nose was perfectly well formed rather small, her lips a little prominent which when she spoke discovered two regular rows of pearls as white as Mountain Snow—her hair was a dark brown—next to black, forming a beauteous Globe of small ringlets, ornamented with flowers and Gold Spangles—round her neck her Arms and her ancles she wore Gold Chain rings and Medals—while a Shaul of finest indian Muslin the end of which was negligently thrown over her polished Shoulder gracefully covered part of her lovely bosom—a petticoat of richest Chints alone made out the rest bare headed and bare footed she shone with double lustre carrying in her delicate hand a bever hat the crown trim'd rown[d] with Silver.[6]

Elements of the Sable Venus are visible in Stedman's description of Joanna's well-shaped limbs that allowed her to move like a goddess and the exotic touch of adjectives like "ebony." But her eyes are both an indication of her dark beauty and a window into the goodness of her heart. Stedman's choice of words implicitly contrasts Joanna's appearance to that of the Negro, emphasizing her "olive" over a black complexion, her small and well-shaped nose to be distinguished from a large and flat one, and dark brown ringlets as opposed to woolly black hair.[7] Existing halfway between the European and African, she is a domesticated Other

Figure 6. *Joanna,* from Stedman's *Narrative of a Five Years' Expedition against the Revolted Negroes of Surinam* (1796). Courtesy of Special Collections and Archives, University of California at Irvine Libraries.

who appears more white than black, the only betrayal of her race being her brown skin, slightly prominent lips, curly hair, and exotic clothing.

What Joanna really looked like, one cannot say with any certainty, for Stedman's description more aptly fits the quadroon or octoroon woman, who was the ideal of mixed-race beauty, than a mulatto, whose features white men considered too "negroid." In fact, Stedman begins his description of Joanna with a characteristic generally attributed to the quadroon—namely, her "well-form'd limbs"—as is evident in his own description of quadroon women as being "mostly tall, Streight, and gracefully form'd, though generally rather more Slender than the Mulattos" (Price and Price 1988, 242). The plate representing a "Female Quadroon Slave" so resembles Holloway's engraving of Joanna that Richard and Sally Price believe it to have been modeled after her (see Figure 7) (xxxix).

Despite her feminine virtues, Joanna is also not a domestic woman, who is too pure and too modest to exist as a sexual object of desire. Unlike the portraits of English wives, the one of Joanna is done in an ethnographic style. The engraving, which was executed by T. Holloway from a sketch by Stedman, depicts her at different stages of her life: when Stedman first saw her in the foreground; and several years later with their son John in the background. The ethnographic rendition of the engraving, a style already implied by the details of Joanna's manner of dress, accounts in part for its more ambivalent portrayal of her femininity than the text. Her facial features are, following Stedman's description, Europeanized, but her body is far too muscular to conform to a classical ideal of feminine beauty. Joanna stands, like Botticelli's Venus, with one arm bent and the other extended, but her pose—with hand on hip and thrust-out breasts—and clothing—half-naked with a clinging, transparent skirt—makes her a more sexualized being than the woman of Stedman's sentimental description.[8] Holloway's engraving portrays the mulatto woman as a sexual object of desire. Although Joanna is depicted as a mother in the background, the viewer's eyes are drawn to her well-formed and nubile body in the foreground frozen as an image of youth and beauty. She was but fifteen years old when Stedman first met her, which was around the age slave girls tended to be initiated into concubinage.

The image of Joanna presented by Stedman in his *Narrative* exists outside the harsh conditions of slavery and plantation life. The right breast,

Figure 7. *Female Quadroon Slave,* from Stedman's *Narrative of a Five Years' Expedition against the Revolted Negroes of Surinam* (1796). Courtesy of Special Collections and Archives, University of California at Irvine Libraries.

so perfectly exposed to voyeuristic effect, is the same breast that he records in his private diary as having "a large hole" and "a most painful sore" from fevers that almost killed her (Thompson 1962, 161, 165). Visually, her body must be unmarred by the overseer's whip or the ravages of illness and disease, for only then can she exist as a desirable woman. As Tassie Gwilliam observes, Joanna is set apart in Stedman's *Narrative* as "modest, fair-skinned and physically unmarked by torture" from black slave women who "are positioned either as uncontrollably sexual or as silenced (but erotic) symbols of pain" (658). The light-skinned body that is unmarked by the whips of slavery belongs to a woman who served in the domestic capacity as wife and mother of Stedman's child. Whereas the Sable Venus exists outside of the domestic sphere in a sensual world of sexual pleasures, the mulatto wife escapes the torments of slavery by participating in West Indian family life.

A mocking Jonkonnu song (transcribed by colonial observers as John Canoe) sung by Jamaican slaves during Christmas masquerades deploys the colonial image of the "nurturing native" in a manner that exploits its ambivalence.[9] The song appeared in Michael Scott's *Tom Cringle's Log* (1833), a fictional diary of a midshipman based on the Scottish author's own stay in the West Indies between 1789 and 1822. It opens with an image of the Jonkonnu players dancing for the amusement of the white man ("Massa Buccra"). Thus seducing his audience with the comforting image of the capering slave, the singer proceeds to describe how the master, having eyes for his white love alone, ignores and even mistreats brown and black women. But then there is a dramatic reversal in the song. After spending a few years in the colony, the white man begins to think that the white woman is too demanding ("Him tink white lady wery great boder"). And, when he catches a fever, the mulatto woman who nurses him back to health appears sweet and desirable ("In sickroom, nurse voice like music—/ From him [patois for "her"] hand taste sweet de physic"), at which point he realizes that the "brown girl" to whom he was scarcely civil ("barely shivil") in fact makes a better wife:

> Massa Buccra lob for see
> Bullock caper like monkee—
> Dance, and shump and poke him toe,
> Like one humane person—just so.

> But Massa Buccra have white love,
> Soft and silken like one dove,
> To brown girl—him barely shivil—
> To black girl—oh, Lord, de Devil!

> But when him once two tree year here,
> Him tink white lady wery great boder;

De coloured peoples, never fear,
Ah, him lob him de morest nor any oder.

But top—one time bad fever catch him,
Coloured peoples kindly watch him—
In sick-room, nurse voice like music—
From him hand taste sweet de physic.

So always come—in two tree year,
And so wid you massa—never fear;
Brown girl for cook—for wife—for nurse,
Buccra lady—poo—no wort a curse. (243)

Whereas nursing and doctoring became disassociated from housework in seventeenth-century Europe, it was very much a part of domestic duties in the West Indies. This explains why the "brown girl" is better even than the white lady at nursing white men through their illnesses. The Jonkonnu song is a direct affront to the white man's professed devotion to white womanhood; it not only assumes the master's voice to declare the mulatta a better woman but also "makes" him abuse his wife: "Brown girl for cook—for wife—for nurse, / Buccra lady—poo—no wort a curse." For this reason, the singer elicits from the white man observing the performance (at least within the framework of the narrator's presentation of the scene) a response that indicates his disapproval: "Get away, you scandalous scoundrel . . . away with you, sir!" (243).

The Jonkonnu song, in true trickster style, inhabits a racial stereotype in a manner that exploits the anxiety that the stereotype was intended to alleviate. Unlike "The Sable Venus; An Ode," which positions the concubine outside of the domestic sphere thus leaving the white-on-white relationship intact, this versification shows her displacing the white woman in her performance of domestic duties. The singer is implying that the brown-skinned woman does not exist outside of white domesticity so much as she threatens to take over its sacred space. And it was through her ability to occupy the place of the domestic woman that the concubine was able to acquire some mobility within slavery.

THE POWER OF DOMESTIC MIMICRY

The polite title that was used in the West Indies for concubines— "housekeeper" or "secondary wife"—speaks to a more formal arrangement in which the women assumed white women's domestic roles. As one English visitor observed, "They embrace all the duties of a wife, except presiding at table; so far decorum is maintained, and a distinction made" (Bolingbroke 1807, 43–44).[10] Due to the shortage of white women, concubinage was so widespread that, as one West Indian explained, "it was the greatest disgrace for a White man not to cohabit with some woman or other" (Parliamentary Papers 1791–92, 97).[11] Stedman provided one of the more detailed descriptions of the practice known in Surinam as marriages "Surinam-style," but his description was deleted from the Johnson edition of his *Narrative*. In the book manuscript he explains that all unmarried men had female slaves, "sometimes Indians sometime Mulattos and often negroes," to prepare their food, do laundry, knit and sew, and nurse them when they were ill (Price and Price 1988, 47–48). He asserts that the women who served white men in this capacity were "generally as faithfull as if he were their lawfull Husband," concluding that the relationship was as close to a legal marriage as the women could possibly have, since they could not have Christian weddings. But there were noticeable differences as far as Dutch society was concerned. The men could abandon their Surinam wives when they tired of them or considered them too old, and had no obligation toward the women or their families. And one Dutch owner observed, "A white woman will never degrade herself by entering into a marriage Surinam-style—only mulattoes and slaves do" (cited by Van Lier 1971, 78).

There existed fine but crucial distinctions between secondary and Christian marriages: a secular rather than religious ceremony; a monetary payment to the woman's family; its availability to men who were already married; and the absence of a lifetime bond (Price and Price 1988, xxxv). The arrangement was convenient for white men lower down in the plantation hierarchy, such as book-keepers and overseers, who were discouraged from marrying. Others, who were in the West Indies for a short time to make money and return to Europe, did not consider it economically feasible to bring a wife (Atwood 1791, 210). Owners often hired out their female slaves to these men, who paid the bride's mother a small sum for arranging the "marriage" (Stewart 1823, 126; Waller 1820, 20). Secondary marriages were desirable for slave and free women alike. Lacking the artisanal skills that permitted the men to hire themselves out in exchange for cash, black and racially mixed women had limited options for acquiring money of their own (Morrissey 1989, 67–68). They could raise some money doing laundry, a poorly paid domestic chore, or sewing, which was the only female equivalent to the male occupational skills. As secondary wives, the women were given command over house- holds and an intimacy with European men from whom they could exact favors. The entire family benefited from such marriages in the form of money, gifts, and prestige. As a result, mothers exercised considerable control over choosing a prospective "husband" for their daughters and negotiating the price of the transaction. The concubines also tried to get their keepers to purchase them and their children from their owners, although colonial observers have overestimated the number of women and children who were manumitted in this way (Brana-Shute 1989; Higman 1984, 141; Mathurin 1974, 407).[12]

The system of concubinage reproduced itself as the daughters from such relations were primed to become concubines themselves. Since racially mixed women were the daughters of women who had children by their white "husbands," they were inevitably placed within the economy of secondary marriages either as daughters or future "wives." These women, being more successful than black women in extracting favors from white men, built a culture of privilege around themselves (Beckles 1989, 147). The privilege this class of mulatto women enjoyed accounts for the perception of them as ones who accommodated (rather than resisted) the oppressive structures of slavery.[13] Yet this image does not present the whole picture.

One can easily say that Joanna belonged to a privileged class of racially mixed women who were complicit with the class of masters. She appears in Stedman's *Narrative* as a loyal slave who was devoted to the white man she married. Her mother, Cery, was a black slave woman who was married to a Dutch man and who negotiated Surinam-style marriages for her daughters. Yet Stedman's text also reveals that Joanna's family had intimate connections with the maroon rebels, a point that is easy to overlook in the face of the overwhelming evidence of their loyalty. Jolycoeur, a sambo from the same plantation as Joanna, served as her family's protector before running away to join the maroons.[14] He was promoted to the rank of captain and, as Stedman indicates, was noted for being "one of the fiercest Rebels in the forest" (Price and Price 1988, 90, 271). Stedman describes meeting Jolycoeur's daughter Tamera, who was the charge of Joanna's uncle Cojo, a loyal slave who voluntarily fought against the rebels before his fellow slaves joined them but who still wore an armband declaring him to be "true to Europeans" (Price and Price 1988, 271). Would a fierce rebel like Jolycoeur entrust his daughter to a man who declared himself to be loyal to his enemies, or had he abandoned her when he fled to join the maroons? Are we to read the silver armband Cojo wore as a ruse to allow him to spy for the maroons, or was he actually a loyal slave? It was common for slave families to have some members who lived with the rebels, while others held trusted domestic positions in the homes of the plantocracy—a situation that allowed maroons to be informed of the planters' activities.[15] Slave women in particular played more hidden roles in rebellions, as spies and conspirators rather than fighters and leaders (Morrissey 1989, 154). What this relationship demonstrates is the difficulty in determining with any certainty, particularly during times of unrest, who was a loyal and who a rebel slave.

The perception of the concubine's loyalty to the white men she served is derived from white Creoles who defended their practice of secondary marriages against their European critics.[16] In his *History of the British West Indies,* Edwards presents secondary wives as respectable women who are faithful to their husbands:

> In their dress and carriage they are modest, and in conversation reserved; and they frequently manifest a fidelity and attachment towards their keepers, which, if it be not virtue, is something very like it. The terms and manner of their compliance too are commonly as decent, though perhaps not as solemn, as those of marriage; and the agreement they consider equally innocent; giving themselves up to the husband (for so he is called) with faith, plighted, with sentiment, and with affection. (2:27)

Since the women are not lawful wives (an illegitimacy that is also the sign of racial difference), Edwards cannot extend domestic virtues to them. Yet, his statement that their "fidelity and attachment" to their husbands is "something very like" a virtue is a reverse image of Brent's claim that "there is something akin to freedom in having a lover who has no control over you, except that which he gains by kindness and attachment."[17] Both writers are searching for words to describe a relationship that conventional language cannot name because it breaks with the conventions of slavery and freedom, on the one hand, and marriage and morality on the other. After all, what slave other than a concubine would be permitted to dine at the same table as a white man?

Although concubinage was tacitly condoned in the West Indies, it was a scandal for most Europeans. The practice brought black women

*reading family
[?]tt[?]s of 1900
back into time*

and the exploitation of slavery into the most intimate of sanctuaries, the home, at a time when romantic love was becoming the dominant code for middle-class marriages. Nowhere is the threat that secondary wives posed to middle-class domesticity and white femininity more evident than in the writings of European visitors to the islands, particularly missionaries and abolitionists. They record disbelief at the knowledge of white Creole women's complicity with their men's adulterous practices and express horror at the thought of respectable ladies serving as godmothers for racially mixed children or else openly receiving the colored companions of their male friends and family members into their homes (Bickell 1825, 105; Stewart 1823, 175; Waller 1820, 20). Bickell envisions the transformation that would take place if overseers were allowed to marry:

> [T]he poor degraded and shunned mistress, who is thrust into a back-room with her unfortunate offsprings, and must not appear at the break-fast or dinner-table, would give place to the respectable, and acknowl-edged, and unobtrusive wife, who would adorn her husband's board, and at the same time that she gave birth and life to harmless and pleas-ant chat, and encouraged virtuous love and admiration by her smiles and agreeable demeanor, and the proud exhibition and fond caresses of legitimate children, would also repress any indelicate sallies or obscene allusions from the mouths of her husband's guests; whilst the gross expressions, repeated oaths, and other lamentable effects, which must result from the now frequent Bachanalian orgies, would be abolished. (109–10)

Bickell's argument works through a series of oppositions intended to distinguish the true form of domesticity from its corrupt West Indian form, with the latter being characterized by illegitimate half-cast off-spring and verbal and sexual excesses. Yet the need to draw so sharp an opposition between the lawful Christian wife and her illicit dark-skinned counterpart betrays their proximity.

The concubine inhabits what Homi K. Bhabha characterizes as the ambivalent world of "the not quite/not white," which is the space of the colonial production of "a reformed, recognizable Other" (85–92). This ambivalence, he goes on to argue, oscillates between resemblance and difference producing a split representation in which mimicry turns to menace. Mimicry involves a disavowal of difference that simultaneously invokes difference through the recognition that the copy can only approximate the original. The ambivalence of the concubine is visible in the play between her resemblance to respectable white women and the threat she poses to the sanctity of marriage.

Bhabha's theory of colonial mimicry, however, makes the slippages internal to the discourse itself, thereby leaving little room to account for human agency. Luce Irigaray, by contrast, describes mimicry as the performance of gender identities through which women assume the feminine role "deliberately" in order to undermine their subordination. "To play with mimesis is thus," writes Irigaray, "for a woman to try to recover the place of her exploitation by discourse, without allowing herself to be simply reduced to it" (76). The concubine is menacing because she performs her domestic roles so well that she threatens to usurp the place of white women. As the Jonkonnu song mockingly proclaims, she is to be distinguished from a lawful wife perhaps only through the nursing skills that her white counterpart lacks.

Despite the missionary perception of concubinage as an inferior copy of Christian marriages, it was the most blatant manifestation of a normative West Indian domesticity. Bickell's vision of the respectable home did not exist and could not exist so long as slavery was implicated in West Indian family life. In managing their household, white women spent more time with their domestic slaves than they did with their own husbands. This social mingling is visible in Lady Nugent's journal entry that complains about Creole women speaking "a sort of broken English, with an indolent drawling out of their words, that is very tiresome if not disgusting" (Cundall 1907, 132). Several decades before Lady Nugent visited the West Indies, Edward Long lamented the difficulty in preventing Creole women from adopting the speech patterns and mannerisms of their domestic slaves (2:278–79). Other visitors were shocked to witness half-naked black men waiting on delicate young ladies, who appeared oblivious to the men's state of nakedness. And there were not only real kinship ties between white men and their slave children but fictive ones between black women and white children as well. Mammies served as surrogate mothers and wet-nurses to white children, often raising them alongside their own. It was the structure of the Creole household itself— one in which a strict division of the races was difficult to maintain—that licensed secondary marriages. This license allowed slave women to manipulate their sexual exploitation even if they could not escape it.

The signs of the unique status of slave women who occupied the domestic role of "housekeeper" or "favorite" can be detected in the private
diaries of Thomas Thistlewood, who assumed the duties of overseer on
a Jamaican sugar estate in 1751.[18] The diaries document in great detail his
work routines, punishment of slaves, sexual activity with slave women,
diseases, and medical knowledge at the time. Thistlewood was perhaps
not any more cruel an overseer than his peers or less indifferent to the
plight of slaves, as indicated by the matter-of-fact way he records the
sadistic punishments he designed and executed to break the will of intractable slaves. He is prolific in his sexual relations with slave women
and meticulous in recording the time of day, place—the cane field, the
curing house, the boiling house, the parlor—and position, the latter in
pig Latin to add a touch of decency. In his thirteen years as overseer of
the Egypt estate, he recorded 1,774 separate sexual acts with 109 different slave women (Burnard 1998, 171).[19] These acts follow what Angela Y.
Davis calls "the institutionalized pattern of rape": they are less the sign
of a man acting on his sexual urges than controlling his labor force (7,
23–24). If the women complied, Thistlewood gave them a small sum of
money; if they resisted, he raped them. We cannot say that the women
who complied consented to sex, for consent suggests its opposite—the
right to refuse—and, as is evident from his treatment of women who
refused his sexual advances, they did not have this right without the
consequence of rape.

Thistlewood's diaries show a man for whom sexual intercourse was
a way of exercising power over his female slaves and displaying the masculinity on which his authority as overseer depended. Yet they also offer
evidence of at least one slave woman who was able to refuse his sexual
advances and not suffer the routine consequences:

Saturday, 4th January 1755: p.m. *Cum* Phib. At night Phibbah slept in
the hammock in the hall; would not come to bed. She was rather too
saucy. . . .

Saturday, 1st February 1755: About 2 p.m. *Cum* Phib. At night she
slept in the cook-room.

Sunday 2nd: Phibbah did not speak to me all day.

Monday 3rd: About midnight last night I fetched Phibbah from her
house. Had words with her again in the evening. At night *Cum* Phibbah.

Friday 7th: Phibbah denied me. (Hall 1989, 67)

These entries were made less than a year after Thistlewood moved Phibbah into his home, and it appears that the change in status allowed her to exercise a refusal that was previously denied her.

By indicating that Phibbah could turn down the sexual demand of an overseer, I do not mean to suggest that their relationship escaped the conditions of sexual exploitation or the day-to-day violence of slavery. To say that Thistlewood did not rape Phibbah because he loved her gives him far more credit than what is apparent from his diaries. As Davis explains in response to the argument that love may have existed between white men and their concubines, "there could hardly be a basis for 'delight, affection and love' as long as white men, by virtue of their economic position, had unlimited access to Black women's bodies" (1983, 25–26). What I am suggesting is that there is a third way of explaining sexual relations between master and slave other than the proslavery narrative of seduction and the antislavery one of rape. And only by considering this third possibility can we introduce questions of slave women's agency.

In Thistlewood's records of Phibbah's sauciness, her refusal to come to bed or speak to him, and her withholding of sex (which is quite different than offering sexual pleasure), we can read the signs of a domestic arrangement that cannot be explained as either black women's seduction of white men or white men's rape of slave women. Rather, they show a struggle for power that extended over a period of time. In the entries of January 4 and February 1, Phibbah refuses to spend the night in Thistlewood's bed. On February 4, he asserts his power over her by "fetching" her in the middle of the night and forcing her to stay until the following night. But he does not have the final word, for on February 7 there appears the simple but definitive statement, "Phibbah denied me." Four years after this incident, Thistlewood records her staying away from his bed for weeks and being "very saucy and impudent" when she did see him (Hall 1989, 88–89). He records that he believes her to be spending her time with the master but does not appear to act on these suspicions. Long after their relationship was well established and Phibbah was living with him, he suspected her of having an affair with a fellow slave. What is it about this slave woman that can account for her being able to negotiate power through a withholding of sex and risk an overseer's wrath and jealousy by entering into sexual relations with other men? Identified simply as a Creole, that is, an island-born slave, Phibbah ran the cook room at the Egypt sugar estate, where Thistlewood was employed between 1751 and 1767. She served as his wife for thirty-three years. Before his death in 1786, he made arrangements to purchase her freedom and a small plot of land, and left her an annual allowance effective after his death. Thistlewood had tried to buy or hire Phibbah from her owner, John Cope, in June 1757, when he left Egypt to work on another estate, but Mrs. Cope refused to sell her (Hall 1989, 79). Phibbah gave Thistlewood a gold ring when they parted, which could be interpreted as the sign of a growing intimacy and/or her effort to maintain her position as a favorite while he was gone. During their separation, they visited each other and exchanged gifts. On one occasion, when she sent him a land turtle, dried turtle eggs, biscuits, a pineapple, and cashew nuts in return for the plantains he sent her, he recorded three simple words— "God bless her!"—to express his gratitude (80). Philip D. Morgan, who has examined Thistlewood's diary for the year he spent at a livestock pen prior to working at Egypt, observes a similar pattern of gift-giving with his favorite there, Marina, who was an African slave. He also notices that she "once spurned his advances, at no apparent cost" (1995, 67). Morgan locates these transactions within a larger economy of bartering and gift-giving between Thistlewood and slaves, which allowed the latter to acquire some property (67).[20] Trevor Burnard argues that a blurring of the boundaries separating whites and blacks, the propertied and non-propertied, allowed the women to exercise limited power (178–79). It is evident that the ability to give or loan an overseer goods and money, as Phibbah so often did, made it harder for him to perceive her as property herself.[21] In this regard, slaves' gifts to the men who ran their lives can be seen as an act of self-empowerment rather than the sign of subservience and acquiescence.

Did Thistlewood's social intimacy with slave women spill over into his job as overseer or did favorites gain their privileges at the expense of their fellow slaves? Based on his reading of the diaries, Douglas Hall believes that Thistlewood's close relationship with Phibbah and her extended family tempered his cruel treatment of slaves (215). However, since concubinage introduced trauma and divisions to the slave community at large, Burnard makes a case for the difficulty in arguing that such relationships improved the lives of slaves in general. Rather, he argues, one needs to examine how the men's social and sexual intimacies with slave women created "a fissure in the brick wall of white dominance" (180). The signs of this fissure are visible in Phibbah's questioning of Thistlewood's handling of his slaves. In 1760, while at Egypt, Thistlewood records that he "reprimanded Phibbah for intermeddling with the field Negroes business with me, & c." (Hall 1989, 94). She also expressed disapproval when he had Sally, a particularly rebellious African slave, and another male slave flogged (199). The slave had been sent after Sally, who had run away, but he let her go when she told him that Thistlewood had raped her.

Sally's unfortunate life story provides all-too-painful evidence of how individual acts of rebellion were not necessarily the best course of action for survival. Thistlewood bought her when she was nine or ten years old to work as a seamstress and began sexually abusing her once she reached puberty. Her noncompliance is evident in his recording each and every encounter as being *sed non bene,* that is, unsatisfactory (Hall 1989, 150). Thistlewood then tried to match her with another slave, but she did not want to be coupled. Six weeks later, she failed to return from an errand. When she was found, she was branded and placed in leg stocks with a collar and chain around her neck. It was later discovered that she had been brutally raped by a sailor while away (150). This incident shows that slave women faced the constant risk of rape and that running away was not necessarily an escape from sexual abuse. Nor was a relationship with a black man a more suitable option when it was the overseer who made the match. Sally continued to run away and each time was captured or else returned herself. Thistlewood continued to use violence as an instrument for control, as he kept raping her despite his lack of sexual enjoyment. Sally's pain and trauma needs to be acknowledged, if we are to admire her for her resistance. In view of the absence of sexual choice slave women had, the question of whether concubines accommodated to slavery—a formulation that suggests choice—also has to be reevaluated.

John Stedman's private diaries (as opposed to his published *Narrative*) reveal such similarities between his relationship to Joanna and the one Thistlewood had with Phibbah that it suggests a larger social structure governing secondary marriages in the Caribbean.[22] The resemblances are all the more uncanny if one considers that Stedman was an altogether different kind of man. Unlike Thistlewood, he was not responsible for running a plantation and protests rather than executes the cruel treatment of slaves. On one occasion, for instance, Stedman records that he paid to replace five plates a slave girl had broken in order to save her from being whipped. As a Scotsman, he had no national affiliation to the Dutch colony he was defending against the rebel slaves. Yet, he also found himself thrust into a slave economy in which he willingly participated. In his *Narrative,* he describes how shortly after his arrival at Paramaribo, the capital of Surinam, an elderly black woman entered his room with her daughter, whom she offered to be his wife. Conveying to his readers his astonishment at the proposal, he says he promptly but politely refused. The woman's offer is recorded more bluntly in his diary as a monetary proposition: "A negro woman offers me the use of her daughter, while here, for a sertain soom. We don't agree about the price" (February 22, 1773). Unlike the more ambiguous term *wife,* these words leave no doubt as to the terms of the marriage. While his *Narrative* suggests that he refused the offer out of moral prudery, his diary denotes that the only disagreement was one of price.

Whereas Stedman's manuscript emphasizes the domestic roles of secondary wives and their faithfulness to their "husbands," his private diaries reveal a practice that blurred the distinction between sexual exploitation and social intimacy. During the first few months of his stay, Stedman records having spent the night with several women, sometimes two or three at a time. Among the women vying for his attention was Joanna (referred to as "a mallato girl"), who sent him cordial and oranges when he was ill:

Feb 25: soop in me room with two mallato girls.
Mar 1: Receive a cordial and two fine oranges from a mallato girl.
Mar 12: 3 girls pass the night in me room.
Mar 26: B——e comes to me and stays the whole night.
April 7: A discovery concerning B——e
April 8: I have a remarkable discovery B——e
April 11: J——a, her mother, and Q—— mother, come to close a bargain with me. We put it of for reasons I gave them.
April 12: B——e and J——a both breakfast with me. I call meself Mister.
April 13: B——e sleeps with me.
April 23: J——a comes to stay with me. I give her presents to the value of about ten pounds sterling, and am perfectly happy.
May 8: Give me wedding.

The diary entries indicate that Joanna and B——e were competing for the role of Stedman's concubine, an arrangement that was not only contingent on the man's preference but also the ability of the girl's mother to negotiate a fair price.

When Stedman explains in his *Narrative* that Joanna sent him cordial and oranges out of sympathy for his condition, he deploys the trope of the "nurturing native" in order to conceal the sexual competition between her and other slave women. Once all signs of a monetary exchange are banished from the text, there is no logical explanation for Joanna's actions other than her concern for his pain and suffering. In this regard, the trope of the "nurturing native" not only represents exploitation as an exchange between equals, it is also a figure that acts in the place of the historical woman. Recounting the time when he returned from a campaign crippled, Stedman writes in his *Narrative* that the "inestimable *Joana* . . . burst in tears" out of sympathy for his "distress'd Situation" (Price and Price 1988, 231). His diary entries for the same episode offer a brief glimpse into the woman behind the literary conventions that govern her appearance in the public discourse, and she appears not to be quite so nurturing:

> Jan 15 1774: Go to La Marre's to lodge, barefooted, and in rags. Send for me girl, dear girl, who had heard that I was dead, and whom I gave a hearty welcome.
>
> Jan 16: I've come home lame being no more used to shews. J—— a good for nothing. Was sod crippel last night.

Stedman's diary entry for January 15 centers on his pleasure in seeing Joanna rather than the other way around, as is the case in his *Narrative*. His anger at Joanna for being "a good for nothing" suggests that she was unable to alleviate his misery. The feminine virtues of empathy and self-sacrifice are nowhere present in the mulatto wife who appears in his diary. One can infer that Joanna may well have been more self-interested than the public discourse on her suggests. She must have been practicing some form of birth control, as she did not become pregnant again after giving birth to their son, John. Since sons were more likely to be manumitted than daughters (as John eventually was), it is possible that her pregnancy was calculated rather than accidental.

Stedman's diary entries reveal that the marriage ceremony, although not legally binding, had social signification for him and that the exis-

tence of a child made a difference to the terms of his relationship with
Joanna. On receiving news a month after the wedding that his corps was
to return to Holland because the rebellions had subsided, he decided
to refrain from having sexual intercourse with her. He also gave her as
a remembrance the gold medal his father gave his mother on the occasion of his birth, a gesture indicating the close bond he had formed with
her in a very short time. (In his *Narrative*, he claims he gave Joanna his
father's medal on the occasion of their son's birth, which was a year and
a half later than the date recorded in his diary.) Stedman did not leave
Surinam just then, as the maroons renewed their war on the plantations.
Joanna subsequently assumed the duties of wife, sending food, drink,
provisions, and letters to him when he was away fighting the rebels.
He, in turn, responded as a dutiful husband. Near the end of one of his
campaigns, after learning that she was pregnant, he forged a pass to take
food and supplies to her "at a desperate risk" (April 25, 1774). He also
presented her family with food, money, and livestock.

This gift-giving does not represent the paternalistic act of a master
rewarding his loyal slave but rather a familial gesture that was recipro-
cated, or even initiated, by Joanna and members of her family. Stedman
records receiving bananas and cassava from her uncle Cojo, a cock and
two hens from Joanna for his thirtieth birthday, half a dozen chickens
from her grandfather, and a dozen chickens and ducks from her aunt,
Lucretia. Familial ties were established through such exchanges, as is evident in Stedman's diary entry that Lamarre, who was married to Joanna's
sister, treated him like a brother-in-law, and his reference to Joanna's
uncle as "my uncle Cojo."

The diaries reveal that, through their domestic roles, slave women
acted in the capacity of the absent white wife—an action that gave
them greater liberties than what would normally be granted slaves. But
secondary wives were also slaves and not exempt from being treated as
such. Stedman records getting into a fight with a sailor over Joanna
who, as a slave woman, was potentially available to all white men. He
also notes that he made sure Colonel Fourgeoud, an arrogant and dis-
agreeable officer who commanded the Corps of Marines to which he
belonged, treat her with respect. "When Fourgeoud was here yesterday,
I let him see my house, and told him of my girl in such a way that, by
God! he was obliged to approve both, and behaved civilly" (Thompson
1962, 151). The demand that his officer be civil is a contradictory one,

for it shows that Stedman knew Joanna did not escape her status as slave outside of the domestic space he built around her. Yet it also reveals that he needed to police the space to keep it intact—at least for the duration of his stay in Surinam.

Once his duty ended, Stedman returned to Europe without Joanna, although he maintained contact with her for at least a year and a half after he left Surinam. He also married Adriana Coehron nine months before Joanna died, a marriage that underscores the temporary nature of his conjugal relationship with his slave wife. After his mother's death, Johnny went to live with his father and was educated at the Soho Academy in London (Thompson 1962, 242). He went on to serve in the British navy and died at sea off the coast of Jamaica shortly before the first edition of Stedman's *Narrative* appeared in print. The circumstances of Joanna's death are unclear, as the diary entries for that period of Stedman's life are missing. All that exists is a letter from his cousin stating that he was "sorry for the melancholy end of the poor mulatto girl" (237). In his *Narrative*, Stedman reports that some believed Joanna had been poisoned by slaves who were jealous of her wealth and status, while others contend that she died of a broken heart (Price and Price 1988, 624). Narratively speaking, her death by poisoning confirms that she was a loyal slave, for poison was more likely to be used against slaves who were traitors. The two explanations could potentially be literary inventions, as they reinforce the teleology Stedman provides for her life—namely, that he ensured that she was free before leaving Surinam and that she remained faithful to him until the end.

In his *Narrative*, Stedman memorializes the commitment to Joanna that he was unable to give her in life. His slave wife may have died young, but he gave her a literary life through which he could demonstrate his devotion to her. It is a sentimentalized image, however, that exists in the absence of the historical woman and of the social norms that governed their relationship. The next section examines the public discourse of Stedman's life with Joanna in order to demonstrate how his elimination of sexual exploitation from their relationship produces her as a subject capable of exercising her free will. Since the woman in Stedman's *Narrative* is the one that readers most closely identify as his slave wife, this public discourse is responsible for the common perception that the decision to remain in Surinam was hers alone.

AN ANGELIC AND VIRTUOUS SLAVE

Stedman's *Narrative* tells a story of mutual love and self-sacrifice with all the emotive drama of a sentimental novel. The hero, a young captain, falls in love with a beautiful mulatto girl the first time he sees her and succumbs to a fever out of sympathy for her pitiable condition. She in turn risks her own life by tending to his illness. He would have died if not for the virtuous slave; she would have been sold to a tyrannical master if not for the noble soldier. He makes a lifetime commitment by marrying and educating her and offering to take her to Europe. She refuses to return to Europe with him because she does not want society to shun him for being married to a slave. Slavery is the villain responsible for their tragic parting, and Mrs. Godefrooy, the woman who lends him money to purchase his slave family's freedom, the angel who saves them from bondage. The interracial love story must have appealed to Stedman's readers, for the reviewer for the *British Critic* assessed "the tale in particular of Joanna, and of the author's attachment to her, [to be] highly honourable to both parties" ("Stedman's Surinam" 1796, 539).

Stedman undoubtedly did his best to convince his readers of his undying love and devotion to Joanna. In order to do so, however, he can admit no evidence of sexual exploitation into his *Narrative*. He leaves out the details of his initial sexual encounters with Joanna, before she became his "wife," as well as all economic transactions between himself and her family. He makes no mention of negotiating a fair price with her mother, and he goes so far as to have Joanna return his gifts with the explanation that they devalue her commitment to him. Thus do her actions elevate her to the status of a woman introduced to his readers as "a Gentlemans Daughter Reduced to the Situation of a humble Slave" (Price and Price 1988, 8). This phrasing asserts Joanna's patrilineal heritage that is white and free, over a matrilineal one that establishes her as a slave, since by law children inherited the status of their slave mothers. Stedman's *Narrative* perpetrates the fiction that Joanna freely chose him to be her husband. However, not only could she be bought and sold, a reality that continuously disrupts the domestic tranquility Stedman constructed around her, but he also had to pay her owner for her services. The existence of a monetary transaction does not mean that they could not, or did not, have an intimate relationship. Rather, Stedman's purchase of sexual and domestic services from Joanna suggests that their relationship was implicated in the slave society from which he, through his connection to her, attempted to disassociate himself.

It is important to remember that Stedman was in Surinam to subdue slave rebellions he believed to be justified. Not only was he a mercenary soldier defending a slave colony that he intellectually found indefensible, but he also had to do so under extremely harsh conditions. While on patrol his regiment was exposed to blistering heat, heavy rain, tropical diseases, stinging insects, poisonous snakes, and attacks from wild animals. The soldiers suffered food and water shortages, at times having to eat raw meat and drink disease-infested creek water, and were forced to march barefooted through swamps because their poorly constructed boots had disintegrated. Stedman lost many of his men to sickness and disease. Those who survived encountered the dismembered and decapitated remains of fellow soldiers, which the rebels left as a warning for them. The small groups of raiding maroons were much better adapted to the tropical rainforests and used guerrilla warfare to its best effects.

Joanna, and the domestic space she occupied, served as a point of stability during Stedman's long military campaigns against the rebels. The knowledge that he had a wife awaiting his return helped him to survive the despairing conditions of life in the bush. While away on his first campaign, he recorded in his diary: "I often think on the fort, where I had me wife, and riding horse, 2 servants, white and black, free bed and board, wine in my cellar, and money in me pocket" (July 20, 1773). Here, Joanna leads the list of property that made the hardships he suffered worthwhile. However, his possessive use of the phrase "me wife" does not denote her status as slave so much as domestic partner (most of the time her refers to her as "my girl"). He also calls her "wife," something that he never does in his published *Narrative*. A diary entry made a couple of months after they first parted reveals that Joanna was often in his thoughts: "I pas me time making baskets for the girl I love" (December 18, 1773). His *Narrative* presents this episode in terms of his effort to learn basket-weaving from Amerindians and sending the finished products to his friends. In hindsight, the idea of weaving baskets for the slave girl he loved must have seemed too unmanly, even for a man with Stedman's sentimentality. His diaries demonstrate that the public declarations of his love for Joanna were as sincere as one might expect, given the circumstances of their relationship. However, the form they take in his published and private writings are quite different.

Whereas Stedman's diary reveals a defensiveness about his slave wife, his *Narrative* suggests that their love transcended the oppressive conditions of slavery. In the published text Stedman likens his life with Joanna at the Hope, the sugar plantation where he was stationed, to that of Adam and Eve, as represented in Milton's *Paradise Lost.* This is no mere literary allusion, as the blissful innocence of the primal couple represented domestic love in eighteenth-century sentimental literature. As the Prices explain, "in denying that his relationship with Joanna was the product of its colonial time and place, Stedman drew on then-current European sentimental ideals to elevate it, in retrospect, to an example of pure and faithful love" (xxxvi). The purity of their love hinges on the innocent femininity of Joanna. Here is how Stedman reports the episode in which the colonel whom he loathes visited his home:

And at last arrived about 10 O Clock, Colonel Fourgeoud with one of his Officers, and with the very Devil painted in his Countenance, which alarmed me much, however I instantly introduced him to my Cottage, where he no sooner saw my mate, that the Clouds /like a vapour by the Sun/ were dispeld from his gloomy forehead, while I Confess that I never saw him behave with more Civility—

—Her heavenly form,
Angelic but more Soft & feminine,
Her Graceful innocense, her ev'ry Air
Of Gesture, or least Action, over aw'd
His Malice, and with rapine Sweet bereav'd
His fierceness of the fierce intent it brought— (271–72)

Like Eve whose sweetness and innocence dispels the Serpent's evil intents, Joanna has a calming effect on Fourgeoud's rage. She, rather than Stedman himself as he records in his diary, has the power to enforce civility in the angry colonel. However, it is an empty agency emanating from a feminine ideal behind which the slave woman disappears.

In erasing all signs of sexual exploitation in his relationship with Joanna, Stedman simultaneously effaces a site of her agency. The ability of concubines to elevate their status above that of slaves hinged on their assumption of white women's domestic duties. In Stedman's *Narrative,* there is no indication of Joanna performing in the capacity of wife; rather, she is the embodiment of the domestic woman. His diaries, on the other hand, give some indication of her manipulating the Surinamese dress code in order to be perceived as a (potentially) free woman. Stedman notes approvingly that she wore a wool suit as "proof of her sense, and modesty" when she was invited to dine with the executor of the Faukenberg estate (Thompson 1962, 170). Despite the entry being coded in terms of the domestic virtue of feminine modesty, it nonetheless shows Joanna's initiative in Stedman's efforts to purchase his slave family. If she did play some part in obtaining their freedom, then that freedom was not simply a gift, which is how it is presented in his *Narrative*.

Stedman's numerous efforts to obtain his slave family's freedom propels the transracial love story in his published *Narrative*. Here is how the story of their journey toward freedom unfolds. As the day for his departure draws near, the new owner of Faukenberg, Mr. Lude of Amsterdam, agrees to sell both mother and son for 2,000 florins (approximately £200), an enormous sum that Stedman realizes he does not have. Mrs. Godefrooy comes to their rescue when she offers to lend him the money for their manumission, instructing him to "go and redeem Innocence, good Sense, and Beauty, from the Jaws of Tiranny—insult, and Oppression." When Stedman conveys the news to Joanna, she exclaims—"Gado Sa Blesse da Woma"—and insists on being mortgaged to Mrs. Godefrooy until the debt is repaid (Price and Price 1988, 385). This is the only time in the entire narrative that Joanna's speech is rendered in Creole. The orality of her words gives greater authenticity to her noble sacrifice. Joanna subsequently throws herself at Mrs. Godefrooy's feet to be received as her new slave. However, the lady informs her that she is to be her companion, not her slave, and offers to build her a house in the orange garden and have her own slaves wait on her, a sure sign of Joanna's change in status. Mrs. Godefrooy tells her that, based on her "Extraction and Behaviour" (386), she can request her manumission any time she chooses. In this manner, the mulatto woman's white paternity and virtuous conduct earn her the right to be free. Stedman reports in his *Narrative* that when he initially asked Mrs. Godefrooy to post a bond for Johnny, she refused. Now that Joanna has agreed to be mortgaged to her, she agrees to post the bond. Stedman presents Joanna as having made a sacrifice for him rather than their son, whose freedom he takes full credit for obtaining.

Alluding to the sentimental story that became a paradigm for interracial love in the Americas, Stedman sees himself as "having Acted the

Counter part of Incle & Yarico" (Price and Price 1988, 599). The story
tells of Thomas Inkle, an Englishman, who is rescued by an Amerindian
woman, Yarico, from her people's raid on their landing party. They
become lovers, and he promises to take her back to England where he
will clothe her in silks. Yarico finds a ship bound for Barbados to rescue
them, but once Inkle enters English territories, "the prudent and frugal
young Man" (cited by Hulme 1992, 236) contemplates the money and
time he has lost and sells his lover and their unborn child into slavery.[23]
Although Stedman does not make slaves of his wife and child, his diary
shows that he was as "prudent and frugal" a man as Inkle.

In his diaries, Stedman records that he requested Mrs. Godefrooy to
post a bond for both his slave wife and son (and not just Johnny, as he
reports in his *Narrative*), which suggests that he had the purchase price
for both of them (Thompson 1962, 180). She refused, as he explains in
his *Narrative*. After a series of negotiations, she agreed to an arrangement that Stedman considered to be financially advantageous for him
and socially preferable for Joanna:

> This day I visit Mrs. Godefrooy with whom I strike a bargain, infinitely
> more to my advantage, and that of Joanna, as had she been the caution,
> viz: I *let* Joanna to herself so long as she lives, but then she is to have
> her liberty at Mrs. Godefrooy's entire expense, whose capital is her cau-
> tion. I profit 900 florins, and the buying of a yard and house. Joanna
> is with *a mother* not with *a mistress,* and free from all taxes and assizes,
> and sure of her liberty, with all the appendages at her lady's death, which
> were not in my power to give her. I also form a request to free Johnny.
> (Thompson 1962, 183–84)

The diary entry is telling, as it demonstrates that, although manumission appears to be instantaneous in the abstract, it was in reality a
much more drawn-out and complicated process. The manumitter not
only had to pay the purchase price and taxes but was also required by
law to post a bond to ensure that the freed slave would not be a liability
to the colony (Brana-Shute 1989, 42–43). As Stedman states, since he
was leaving Surinam, it was not in his power to grant Joanna her freedom. And, even if she had been manumitted, it might not have been
so desirable for her, as freedom would have cut her off from her slave
family. A series of amendments to the 1733 manumission law placed
greater restrictions on manumitted slaves by prohibiting them from

marrying or having children with slaves, requiring them to support their patrons if they should fall into poverty, and permitting a reversion to slavery for insolence against whites. A 1761 amendment prohibiting freed slaves from attending slave dances is an indication of the drastic measures taken to ensure against social interaction between freemen and slaves (Brana-Shute 1985). The most that Joanna could perhaps hope for was the manumission of her son, which she managed to accomplish. Stedman's diary shows that he did as much as he possibly could to ensure that she would not be mistreated and that she would eventually be free. However, the entry also makes clear that the question of his family accompanying him to Europe was never part of the arrangement.

Joanna's domestic virtues screen Stedman's duplicity toward his readers, for his *Narrative* presents his return to Europe without his Surinam wife as her desire rather than his own. According to his published account, he offered to purchase and educate her, and to make her his Christian wife in Europe, but she responded by saying that she did not want him to be shunned for marrying a slave:

> I am born a low contemptible Slave, to be your Wife under the forms of Christianity must degrade you to all your Relations and your Friends, besides the expence of my Purchase and Education, but I have a Soul I hope not inferior to the best European, and blush not to acknowledge that I have a regard for you who so much distinguishes me above the rest—nay that now independent of every other thought I shall pride myself / by in the way of my Ancestors / to be yours all and all, till fate shall part us, or my Conduct Shall give you Cause to Spurn me from your Presence. (Price and Price 1988, 100)

These words, apparently spoken by Joanna, establish her humanity through the heroic virtue of self-sacrifice. In other words, by sacrificing her own happiness for Stedman, she demonstrates that she is equal to any European. In this manner, the question of her humanity is inseparable from the noble virtues that she possesses. Joanna is a "virtuous slave" because she is proud but not prideful; heroic because she places his interests above her own. What Stedman is establishing, however, is less the noble sensibility of an honest slave than the sincerity of a guilt-ridden man who feels he has abandoned her.

Joanna's speech, described as "the genuine Speech of a Slave who had simple nature for her only education" (Price and Price 1988, 101),

is in fact Stedman's performance of a ventriloquism. Her refusal to accompany her husband to Europe is less the indication of a slave woman
speaking her mind than the author assuming her voice so that she might
speak his desires. As author, Stedman wants to leave no doubt in the
reader's mind that the decision to remain in Surinam was hers. He represents Mrs. Godefrooy as repeatedly offering to have Joanna and Johnny
accompany him to Europe, and Joanna refusing to do so over and over
again: She "Nobly as Firmly Refused" and "was unmoveable even up
to Heroism" (Price and Price 1988, 470, 507). As he prepares to leave
Surinam, Stedman tries to convince her once again to accompany him.
And once again she declined his offer,

> first from a Conciousness that with propriety she had not the disposal
> of herself—& Secondly from pride, wishing in her Present Condition
> Rather to be one of the first amongst her own Class in America, than as
> she was well Convinced to be the last in Europe at least till such time as
> fortune should enable [him] to establish her above dependance. (Price
> and Price 1988, 603)

In view of the merit to a statement that suggests Joanna was better off
in Surinam among her friends and family than in Europe, it is conceiv-
able that perhaps she did choose to stay behind. However, we should be
hesitant to be so quick to assign her this kind of agency. To recognize
Joanna's status as a slave and secondary wife, rather than a free woman
as Stedman would have his readers believe, is to see that the choice was
not hers to make.

Stedman's employment of European sentimental ideals for representing his relationship to Joanna led his readers to believe that she was
his lawful wife. But William Thomson, a professional editor hired to
improve his prose, also encouraged this belief by censoring evidence
of the plantocracy's sexual misconduct. He deleted all references to
Surinam-style marriages, which included Stedman's detailed description
of the practice as well as his references to Joanna's mother serving her
father "with the Duties of a Lawful Wife" (Price and Price 1988, 88) and
to her sister being the secondary wife of Mr. De Lamarre. Also deleted
were Stedman's declaration of his intention to make Joanna his lawful
wife in Europe and her response in which she refuses to degrade him
by becoming his Christian wife. Were these deletions made to shelter
the book's middle-class readers from the immorality of concubinage, or

do they reveal an objection to the intimacy between slave women and white men betrayed by the term *wife*? For the most part, the changes are in keeping with more pervasive editing that emphasizes the division between the races. These changes, as the Prices indicate, reflect both the editor's proslavery position and the new legitimacy of racist doctrines in the period between the time Stedman wrote his *Narrative* in 1790 and its publication in 1796 (Price and Price 1988, lx–lxv).

Yet, there are also inconsistencies in the alterations that make it difficult to argue that they simply emphasize the racial division between Stedman and his mulatto wife. The Johnson edition included the statement that "a decent wedding" attended by "respectable friends" took place and Stedman "was as happy as any bridegroom ever was" (Stedman 1806 [1796], 1:62). The Prices are puzzled by this insertion and speculate that Stedman may have added it "as a step toward righting the balance" of the editor's efforts to depersonalize his relationship with Joanna (1988, xcv, 54n). One cannot say with any certainty who was responsible for the changes, author or editor, but their sum effect was to clear the ambiguity surrounding Joanna's status as a secondary wife in favor of a domestic norm. And, I want to argue, the only kind of slave who could represent this ideal of domesticity was a light-skinned mulatto woman.

Through the figure of Joanna, Stedman's *Narrative* introduces a new stereotype for the mulatta, who was otherwise perceived to be an arrogant, vain, and superficial woman. Janet Schaw, who visited Antigua and St. Kitt's in 1774, characterized mulatto women as "a spurious and degenerate breed" who were "licentious and insolent past all bearing" (Andrews 1939, 112). Moreton describes them as "extremely proud, vain and ignorant" women who had "no idea of virtue or fidelity" because they were interested in white men only for their money (1790, 125, 159). Both he and Long accuse concubines of feigning affection for their keepers in order to appropriate their property when they die (Long 1774, 2:323; Moreton 1790, 161). It is possible to read in these descriptions the signs of a "cunning" often employed by slaves. In *Noises in the Blood*, Carolyn Cooper invokes a Jamaican proverb—"Thief from thief Massa God laugh"—for explaining the concubine's appropriation of her keeper's property (1995, 32). Stedman's *Narrative*, however, offers no possibility for seeing Joanna as a trickster figure. As a simple, modest, and self-sacrificing woman, she stands apart from her greedy and duplicitous sisters.

The Joanna of Stedman's *Narrative* is no historical woman but a mixed-race version of the Noble Slave, who was an exceptional or uncommon individual by virtue of his or her ancestry and character. The reader is informed not only that Joanna's father was a Dutch gentleman but that her "Mothers Family were Distinguished people on the Coast of Africa" as well (Price and Price 1988, 386). Her lowly birth into slavery enhances her noble ancestry, for it shows that her virtues are natural rather than acquired. Wylie Sypher identifies Aphra Behn's Oroonoko as the paradigmatic Noble Slave, whose female equivalent was Richard Steele's Yarico. Although they are both tragic figures, there existed a different desired emotive response to the male and female Noble Slave. "If Oroonoko astonishes," writes Sypher, "Yarico evokes unadulterated pity" (1942, 127). Stedman's elevation of Joanna to a Noble Slave who is too good for the cruel society in which she lives is designed to evoke feelings of pity, compassion, and sympathy for her. In *The Theory of Moral Sentiments* (1759), Adam Smith identifies sympathy as the source of the ability to feel pity and compassion and to act benevolently. Sympathy is specular in the sense that it involves "the individual's imaginary substitution of himself for the suffering Other through spectatorship" (Benedict 1994, 2). But an identification with the suffering Other also distances the spectator from the one who is suffering, for the observer alone is in a position to ameliorate their condition (Sharpe 1993, 52). Sympathy operates through an imaginary substitution through which the ability to feel for the Other is precisely not to be the Other.

The trope of sympathy paradoxically established the kinship of Europeans and Africans, while placing the former in a position of superiority over the latter. This tropological construction explains why the female version of the famous Wedgwood cameo—"Am I Not a Man and a Brother?"—which was made to denote the shared sisterhood of white and black women, shows the slave woman kneeling in a supplicant position before the European (see Figure 8).[24] While the slave woman's hands are bound together with chains, suggesting that she is not in a position to free herself, the European woman is holding out one hand to lift her out of her misery and carrying the scales of Justice in her other hand. The specular structure of sympathy is also visible in Stedman's description of his reaction to the news that the estate to which Joanna belonged was to be sold:

Figure 8. Abolitionist roundel with the emblem "Am I Not a Woman and a Sister?" Courtesy of Wilberforce House Museum, Kingston upon Hull.

I now felt all the Horrors of the Damn'd bewailing my unlucky fortune that did not enable me to become her Proprietor my self and figuring in my Mind her ensuing dreadfull Situation—Me thought I saw her, mangled, ravished, ridiculed, and bowing under the weight of her Chains calling aloud for my assistance—I was miserable—Indeed I was truly wretched labouring under such Emotions as had now nearly deprived me of all my faculties.[25]

This is the only moment in Stedman's *Narrative* that the reality of Joanna's enslaved condition is presented as holding the potential for her being physically, sexually, and verbally abused. Stedman sympathizes with her condition inasmuch as he experiences the full horror of what it means to be bought and sold as a slave. These feelings of sympathy position him as a potential owner and spectator—an impassioned one but a spectator nonetheless. As a result, the force of his emotions produces an image in which he sees her as a forlorn and pitiable slave calling for his aid. Joanna's cry for help struck a chord with British and American abolitionists. Since the desired effect of antislavery literature was to evoke in readers sympathy for the pitiable condition of slaves, which would prompt them to humanitarian action, her story could be turned into an antislavery statement.

THE TRAGIC MULATTO MAID

The period during which Stedman's book appeared was one of intense lobbying on the part of the Society for Effecting the Abolition of the Slave Trade, which Granville Sharp, Quakers, and other social reformers had formed in 1787. The former slave Ottabah Cuguano published his antislavery pamphlet in 1787, and Olaudah Equiano's slave narrative appeared two years later. Both claimed to have been Africans who had survived the Middle Passage and, along with John Newton (a slave trader turned abolitionist), testified to the horrors of the Guinea coast trade. It was during this period that Josiah Wedgwood designed the abolitionist society's seal, which showed a supplicant slave in chains with the emblem "Am I Not a Man and a Brother?" and was reproduced on chinaware, decorative boxes, jewelry, and stationery. The emblem exhibits one of the more powerful strategies of the movement, which was to show the desire for freedom and equality coming from the slave rather than simply to have abolitionists speak on his behalf.

Yet abolitionists also suffered a setback following the violence of the San Domingue rebellion in 1791, which would lead to the free black republic of Haiti in 1804. The widespread killings and destruction of property reconfirmed the belief of the plantocracy that the emancipation of slaves would unleash anarchy and savagery on their world.[26] British abolitionists concentrated their efforts on ending the slave trade in the belief that cutting off the supply from Africa would make slaves a more valuable commodity and force planters to take better care of them. The Society for Effecting the Abolition of the Slave Trade and, after the abolition of the slave trade in 1807, the Society for the Mitigation and Gradual Abolition of Slavery (known as the Anti-Slavery Society), which was formed in 1823, emphasized an amelioration of the slave's condition through reform rather than full emancipation.

Stedman himself was no abolitionist, as he defends the slave trade in his *Narrative* and opposes the introduction of a free labor system to the West Indies. He presents slaves as faithful dependents who would give their undying loyalty to masters who treat them well. His description of the slave who was fortunate to have a kind master paints a rather romantic picture of slavery. Stedman characterizes the slave's work day as no more than "Healthy Exercise" that leaves him free to hunt, fish, and cultivate his own garden (Price and Price 1988, 534–35). Since this slave happens to be his own (indicated by the initials of J. G. S. branded on his chest), his happy state belongs alongside Joanna's domestic bliss as evidence of the author's refusal to acknowledge his own participation in the oppressiveness of slavery he documented.

Stedman's graphic descriptions of the Dutch plantocracy's mistreatment of their slaves caused his *Narrative* to become caught up in debates over the abolition of the African slave trade. "We have never opened any work which is so admirably calculated to excite the most heart-felt abhorrence and detestation of that grossest insult on human nature,—domestic slavery" declared one review ("Stedman's Narrative" 1796, 53). Another predicted that the book "will stimulate vigorous and effectual exertions for the speedy termination of the execrable traffic in human flesh" (L. M. S. Sept. 1796, 226). Certainly, the horrors of slavery Stedman documented had particular appeal to abolitionists. But the book's love story also fired their imagination. Stedman's description of Joanna's sincerity, modesty, youth, and beauty already reflected the primitivism and sentimentalism of antislavery literature. Moreover, he convinced his readers, through his marriage and expressed devotion to her, that the inequalities between a white man and slave girl could be overcome. The circulation of their love story in fictional and historical form reflects a growing interest in interracial relationships in the nineteenth century.

Joanna was reborn as a literary figure in abolitionist pamphlets and romantic plays and stories.[27] *Die Sclavin in Surinam* (1804), a play written by Franz Krotter and performed in Frankfurt, ends with the Joanna character (who is renamed after her mother, Cery) accompanying Stedman back to Europe (Sollors 1998, 123). This ending reflects the desire to see the triumph of love over social taboos. Joanna's story was also excerpted from Stedman's *Narrative* and published in London in 1824 as "Joanna, or the Female Slave; A West Indian Tale." Stedman is not credited as author, although the title page does claim that it was "founded" on his *Narrative*. Still, the editor takes some liberties with the original inasmuch as he, quite paradoxically, assumes the author's voice to condemn Joanna for participating in so immoral a practice as concubinage.

The editorial changes to the 1824 excerpt from Stedman's text make Joanna into a more pitiable woman than she appears even in the Johnson edition. While Stedman, in his 1790 manuscript, describes her as collapsing bereft into a chair when he leaves Surinam, the Johnson edition has her falling into "the arms of her adopted mother" (Stedman 1806 [1796], 2:427). This editorial change emphasizes the tragic breakup of Stedman's family for which the maternal role of Mrs. Godefrooy alone can compensate. "Joanna, or the Female Slave; A West Indian Tale" makes the parting even more tragic by having Joanna die in Mrs. Godefrooy's arms: "Joanna now shut her beauteous eyes; her lips turned the pale colour of death; she bowed her head, and, motionless, sunk in the arms of her *adopted mother*. My Joanna was gone! Again and again I pressed her lifeless form to my bosom" (Stedman 1824, 174). In having Joanna die of a broken heart, the editor was perhaps punishing her for her life of sin, for he also condemns her for choosing to live out of wedlock with a white man over marriage to her own kind. The question of the displaced colored man is thus introduced but only in the interest of enforcing "virtue and a virtuous life" among black people (xi).

Joanna's story, then, is presented as an example of how slavery "reduces the female slave to a life of ignominy" (Stedman 1824, 46). However, as the editor (in the voice of the author) proceeds to explain, "ignominy" does not refer to the heroine's status as slave, for she may be a free woman. Rather, it designates her enslavement to a "vanity" responsible for her choosing an immoral lifestyle. The trope of reciprocity in Stedman's *Narrative,* which is based on the premise that Joanna is capable of exercising her free choice, permits the editor to hold her responsible for her degraded situation. She is thus introduced as a woman whose tragic life is as much a condition of her misplaced affections as it is of slavery:

> [A]s poor Joanna is, I think, for so slight a sketch, one of Nature's master-
> pieces, she will, I trust, be equally favoured, and her sorrows and her

sufferings not only plead her own cause, but likewise that of her hapless countrywomen, and shew *in her own fate* the wretched existence of even those who blindly see their pre-eminence in the mistaken favour of the *"white man"* [emphasis in the original]. (Stedman 1824, v–vi)

Elements of the tragic mulatto, whose flaw is her devotion to the white man she can never have, are visible in the editor's moral indictment of Joanna. Werner Sollors identifies Joanna as the prototype for the character of the tragic mulatto that was developed by the American abolitionist Lydia Maria Child. What interests me about this passage, however, is how Joanna's agency is raised only to make her a victim of her choice. Lacking vision over her own condition for having "blindly" placed her faith in the "mistaken favour" of a white man, she cannot enunciate her oppression. Instead, her "sorrows and her suffering" will speak on her behalf and that of her fellow slave women. As a framing device, the author's dedication shifts agency from Joanna to the antislavery pamphlet as the textual enunciation of her life.

The excerpt of Joanna's story from Stedman's *Narrative* was published once again in Boston in 1834, which is the same year the Emancipation Act went into effect. Simply called "Joanna," the tale appeared in *The Oasis,* an antislavery collection edited by L. Maria Child, who also edited *Incidents in the Life of a Slave Girl, as Written by Herself.*[28] This edition of Stedman's text was reprinted again in 1838 as a book entitled "Narrative of Joanna; an Emancipated Slave, of Surinam" (Child 1838). What is noticeable about antislavery abridgements of Stedman's *Narrative* is that Joanna has displaced the author as subject of its story. The changing status of her identity—from female slave to emancipated slave—is an indication of her being invested with the political objectives of the antislavery movement. While the London edition of Joanna's story makes her incapable of voicing her oppression, the packaging of the Boston edition turns her into a spokesperson for the abolitionist cause. The title, "Narrative of Joanna; an Emancipated Slave, of Surinam," draws attention to her eventual emancipation even though she remained a slave until her death. Child's edition emphasizes Joanna's free status because it is perhaps only as an emancipated slave that Joanna can speak on behalf of the antislavery cause.

The pictures that accompanied the text made Joanna conform more closely to a female-gendered antislavery paradigm. The slim volume includes a frontispiece engraved by G. G. Smith, who modified the

Holloway engraving of Joanna in the Johnson edition so that her naked breast was no longer exposed. The visual image of Joanna is desexualized so that she can appeal to a Victorian sensibility of womanhood. But it also emphasizes, unlike the Holloway engraving, her domestic roles as mother and wife. Four additional plates, of which only the third appeared in Stedman's *Narrative,* are dispersed throughout the volume: "Joanna at the slave market," "Joanna visiting Capt. Stedman at 'The Hope,'" "Capt. Stedman's residence, 'The Hope,'" and "Capt. Stedman taking a final leave of Joanna." The first and last plates, which depict a weeping Joanna standing before the auctioneer and several weeping children around her as she kisses Stedman goodbye, draw on popular antislavery images. Appended to the story are two poems: "A Negro Mother's Appeal" in which a black woman tells white women of how the pleasures of motherhood are denied her, and "The Slave-Dealer" (from Pringle's "African Sketches"), which tells of a mother who hardly recognizes the son driven mad by the memory of his cruel deeds as a slave-trader. Joanna is less the sexual object of desire that she is in Stedman's *Narrative* than a wife and mother like these other women, black and white, slave and free.

By bringing Joanna into a universal model of womanhood, the packaging of the Boston edition expresses the gender politics of women abolitionists like Child. The antislavery discourse of women abolitionists established the humanity of female slaves through the domestic virtues they shared with white middle-class women. The argument was designed to create in white women an empathy with the slave women who were sexually violated and whose children were removed from them. By defining slave women's lives as simply the negation of the domestic happiness that white women enjoyed, however, this discourse fails to contend with the kind of domesticity white men established with their concubines in the colonies.

Child believed Joanna to have been Stedman's lawful wife, even though she must have known that slaves could not marry. What allows the fiction of marriage to be maintained is Joanna's cultural whiteness as expressed by her civilized and virtuous conduct, which is the reason Mrs. Godefrooy gives for receiving her as a daughter rather than a slave. Unlike the editor of the 1824 edition, Child admires the romantic attachment Stedman has for Joanna. At the same time, she is careful to assert that she does not encourage interracial marriages. As she reassures her readers, "the Abolitionists have no wish to induce any one to marry a mulatto, even should their lives be saved by such an one ten times" (Child 1838). But, even as she praises Stedman for having married a mulatto slave, she notices several inconsistencies in his story:

> Such is Capt. Stedman's own account of the beautiful and excellent Joanna. In reading it, we cannot but feel that he might have paid Mrs. Godefroy, and sent for his wife to England, long before 1783. His marriage was unquestionably a sincere tribute of respect to the delicacy and natural refinement of Joanna's character. Yet we find him often apologizing for feelings and conduct, which are more truly creditable to him than any of his exploits in Surinam; and he never calls her his *wife*. Perhaps Joanna, with the quick discernment of strong affection, perceived that he would be ashamed of her in Europe, and therefore heroically sacrificed her own happiness. (Child 1838, 56–57)

Child wonders why Stedman did not pay Mrs. Godefrooy what he owed her and have Joanna join him in England after he left Surinam. She is also puzzled as to why he never calls her his wife. Yet, the heroic virtue of self-sacrifice that Stedman attributes to Joanna is such a noble quality that she recasts it as a domestic virtue to endorse his version of events. Endowed with the feminine virtue of "strong affection" that gives her a womanly insight into her husband's true feelings, Joanna has become in Child's text the domestic woman that guided Stedman's narrative reconstruction of their life together in Surinam. Child raises the slave woman's agency only to put to rest any suspicions that the crossracial relationship might not quite have been the one of reciprocity that he describes. By the mid-nineteenth century, there was no Joanna outside of the pages of Stedman's travel book or the abolitionist recovery of her life. With each new narrativization, the historical woman receded even further behind the image of the mulatto wife she had come to represent.

3.

"Our History Was Truly Broken"
Writing Back to a Slave Past

Although Joanna never made that fateful journey to Europe except in the imagination of abolitionists like Lydia Child, her story can be read as an allegory for the postwar migration from the West Indies to England. This migration is generally dated from 1948, the year that the *Empire Windrush* docked at London with 492 Jamaicans anticipating a better life. What awaited them instead was a confinement to low-paying unskilled jobs and the racial prejudices of English people who considered them inferior. Like the first generation of immigrants who in hindsight wished that they had never left the Caribbean, Joanna expressed a preference for staying in Surinam, claiming "Rather to be one of the first amongst her own Class in America, than as she was well Convinced to be the last in Europe" (Price and Price 1988, 603). After her death her son, Johnny, joined his father in England but later died off the coast of Jamaica. The watery grave of Stedman and Joanna's biracial son represents, within this allegory, the death of what George Lamming calls "the tragic innocence" of Afro-Caribbeans who thought that in journeying to England they were going home (1991, xxxvii). I have presented an allegorical reading of Joanna's life story that is less concerned with a historical faithfulness to the era in which she lived than it is in describing the conditions under which her memory is revived. My purpose in doing so is to stage the play between past and present at work in black British historical fiction.

Much of the literary effort to engage the memory of slavery comes from British-Caribbean writers, for whom England's implication in slavery constitutes a point of departure for explaining their own presence in a nation that has traditionally been white-identified. Black Britain, a political and cultural movement that emerged in the 1980s in response to the homespun racism of Enoch Powell and the state racism of the Thatcher government, does not present itself simply in terms of the postwar migration of people from the colonies to the imperial center. Rather, the label is intended to signal England's long history of transracial relations that was the outcome of its ever-expanding Empire. During the late eighteenth century, when Stedman was writing his book, the population of people of African descent in England was estimated at anywhere from ten to twenty thousand (Fryer 1984, 68). Jingoists like Powell could identify the 1950s as the beginning of the nation's "race problem" only because the history of black Britons had been successfully erased. Alternatively, black British writers engage the historical documents on slavery in order to make visible the transatlantic crossings that took place long before the *Empire Windrush* made its legendary journey. Their diasporic vision thus serves as a corrective to a national imaginary that has historically excluded black people. A literary retracing of a black Atlantic history can be read, then, as a response to Paul Gilroy's lament (in his book of the same name) that "there ain't no black in the Union Jack!"

Beryl Gilroy's *Stedman and Joanna—A Love in Bondage: Dedicated Love in the Eighteenth Century* (1991) and Caryl Phillips's *Cambridge* (1991) are two British-Caribbean novels that rewrite colonial accounts of slavery in order to give black people greater visibility in Britain's national past. Gilroy's work is a historical fiction—what she calls a "faction of colonial gender encounters" (1998, 53)—loosely based on Stedman's travel narrative and written memoirs, the language of which she updates for a contemporary audience.[1] *Cambridge* is a postmodern historical novel written in the anachronistic prose of late eighteenth- and early nineteenth-century travel diaries and slave narratives such as *Lady Nugent's Journal* (Cundall 1907) and *The Interesting Narrative of the Life of Olaudah Equiano* (1987 [1789]). Although both novels were published the same year, they make very different interventions into antislavery discourse. While *Stedman and Joanna* acknowledges the contribution of black people (both in England and the Caribbean) to the idea of a universal humanity that led to the emancipation of slaves, *Cambridge* returns to a slaveholding past to implicate Victorian England in the West Indian plantation system from which it disassociated itself. While Gilroy gives the character based on Joanna an agency that exceeds Stedman's narrative control, Phillips unsettles the reader's desire for an authenticating voice of black resistance. While Gilroy's novel reconfirms a humanist faith in the possibility for mutual compassion across the master-slave divide, Phillips's novel shows how even the most benign and sympathetic position does not transcend the unequal relations of power under slavery.

The differences between the narrative perspective of each novel might be explained by the generational differences of each of their authors. Born in British Guiana (now Guyana), which is adjacent to Surinam, Gilroy belongs to the first generation of West Indian immigrants who came to Britain in the fifties.[2] Since Phillips was three months old when he emigrated from St. Kitt's in 1958, he is closer to the second generation of British-born Caribbean writers. While Gilroy came of age during the civil rights struggle for a color-blind society through racial integration, Phillips belongs to a generation that witnessed the collapse of Martin Luther King's dream through the persistence of racism in a multicultural, integrated society. Since antislavery writings continue to govern our readings of slave agency, it is useful to see how each novel engages the efficacy of antislavery as a grand narrative of liberation. The different perspective on abolitionist discourse that each work has to offer will move us closer to articulating a female-gendered slave subjectivity.

THE VOICE OF ANTISLAVERY

In *Stedman and Joanna,* Gilroy makes those aspects of Stedman's writing that are unique to his travel diary—his insights into the cruel treatment of slaves and acknowledgment of a universal humanity—into the product of several transracial encounters. Shortly prior to leaving for Surinam, the fictional Stedman visits London, where he hears a sermon by the abolitionist Granville Sharp and the testimonies of the former slaves Patrasso and Gronniosaw.[3] Their stories cause him to consider the humanity of other races for the first time, and he begins to see people of color in a different light. Gilroy's depiction of Stedman's London visit is a literary invention, as there is no reason to believe that he was familiar with its free black population of around 1,200 people, most of whom lived on the margins of society. Yet, as Trinh T. Minh-ha explains about the narrative force of the story over history, "if we rely on history to tell us what happened at a specific time and place, we can rely on the story to tell us not only what might have happened, but also what is happening at an unspecified time and place" (1989, 120). Gilroy entertains the possibility of what might have happened if Stedman had met the black authors whose work he records in his memoir and travel book. The author of *Narrative of a Five Years' Expedition* indicates his knowledge of "The history of Patrasso, a negro" (Thompson 1962, 110), and praises the "Poetical Genious" of the American slave Phillis Wheatley, who visited London in 1773, and the "Sublime Letters and Sound Philosophy" of Ignatius Sancho, an African who was born on a slave ship, taught himself to read and write, and whose *Letters* were published posthumously in 1782 (Price and Price 1988, 516–17). He also shows his familiarity with antislavery writings like Thomas Clarkson's essays on the abolition of the African slave trade. In transforming these literary references into actual meetings, the novel draws attention to the political climate and social environment in which Stedman wrote.

The London of Gilroy's novel is a thriving seaport peopled by black servants, gypsies, and enterprising Chinese men, and a city abuzz with the early stirrings of the antislavery movement. Stedman hears about Judge Mansfield's ruling in the Somerset case, which set a precedent for preventing slaves from being forcibly removed from England. On his last night in London, he attends a christening party for a black man whom abolitionists had assisted in obtaining freedom. Stedman's trip to London marks the beginning of his journey toward recognizing the evils of slavery. Instrumental in this recognition is his life with Joanna. The three-part structure of the novel—"Before Joanna," "Joanna," and "The Sea Change"—makes her central to the sentiments of the entire travelogue rather than a digression for which the author is forced to apologize. While in Surinam, the character based on the historical man learns from Joanna how to feel compassion for slaves, while her family allows him to see that, despite their denigrated status, they have maintained their humanity. He also meets two exceptional black people at a free mulatto ball: Graman Quacy, a reputed obeah man who was freed for discovering a bark that cured tropical fevers, and Elizabeth Sampson, the first black woman to legally marry a white man in Surinam.[4]

These famous free black Surinamese appear in the original text, where Stedman calls Graman Quacy "one of the most Extraordinary Black men in Surinam or Perhaps in the World" but also "an indolent dicipating Blockhead" (Price and Price 1988, 581–82). He also reports with relish the interracial marriage that created such a stir in Surinam: "A great Hubbub was made here on account of a free Negro Woman call'd Eliz. Sampson going to be married to an European, she was worth above a hundred thousand pound Sterling inherited from her Master whose Slave she had formerly been and having addressed herself to their High and Mightinesses her Request was Granted, and accordingly being Christened she entered in the Lawful Bond of Matrimony with one Mr. Zubli" (79). By highlighting the appearance of black people like Graman Quacy and Mrs. Sampson in Stedman's *Narrative,* and adding additional encounters of her own, Gilroy claims a European travel narrative for a black Atlantic history. Crucial to this history is a culture that slaves could call their own.

Gilroy combines her intimate knowledge of Afro-Creole culture with ethnographic evidence of slave life to present a series of portraits of how slaves maintained their humanity through their traditions and religious practices. One of the more detailed descriptions of slave rituals in the novel is a ceremony commemorating Joanna's marriage to Stedman. The only record of a marriage ceremony in Stedman's *Narrative* is the brief statement that a "decent wedding" took place. As noted in the previous chapter, all references to Surinam-style marriages were deleted from Stedman's manuscript and the statement about a decent wedding was added to make the interracial relationship more palatable to the book's white, middle-class readers. Yet this explanation does not address what Surinam-style marriages meant for the women. Gilroy presents the demand for a "decent wedding" as coming from Joanna's mother and, in doing so, shifts the narrative perspective from European visitor to slave inhabitant. In Gilroy's novel, Cery informs Stedman that Joanna may be a slave "but slaves have family" (49) and insists that the wedding take place at the Fauconberg plantation where they live. The marriage involves an elaborate Creole ceremony beginning with Joanna's grandfather blessing the couple and ending with Cery counseling them. While visiting Fauconberg for the wedding, Stedman learns from Cery that, since so many slave children have lost their families, "black slaves mother all children who slavery robs of parents" (50). In this instance, a slave woman makes the same argument about the separation of black families as did women abolitionists. Cery's antislavery statement, however, is spoken from within an Afro-Caribbean culture. Whereas Euro-American abolitionists emphasized the destruction of the nuclear family under slavery,

Cery identifies an extended family structure that acts in its place. She characterizes black women as having, much like the warrior woman of Goodison's poem about Nanny, maternal feelings for slave children that are not their own. By depicting the secret lives of slaves that Stedman's *Narrative* fails to represent despite its detailed ethnographic observations, Gilroy shows how slaves maintained their humanity through a culture they could call their own.

Through scenes of Joanna's extended slave family, Gilroy invites the reader to imagine mulatto culture as a creolized form of European and African cultures rather than a lesser version of white culture that European eyewitnesses perceived it to be. She notices in the novel's afterword that Stedman never referred to Joanna as his wife in his published narrative but only as "my mulatto!" (181), an omission that signals to her (in a way that it did not for Child) the information being suppressed. When Stedman calls Joanna his mulatto, he is doing more than simply eliding her domestic role as wife; he is also establishing a racial identity that (following Bhabha's writing on colonial mimicry) I call "not quite/not white." The racial identity of the "mulatto" as a domesticated Other who mimics white culture negates Joanna's Afro-Creole heritage. Yet travelers to Surinam in the early nineteenth century, when concubines were more likely to be free mulatto women, noted a greater heterogeneity to their racial makeup than is suggested by Stedman's literary reconstruction of his slave wife (see Figure 9). There exists in Stedman's portrait of Joanna the occasional touches of exoticism, such as her beaver hat and ankle bracelets, but the reader knows nothing about her language, religion, beliefs, or even what made her "an incomparable nurse." In view of how culturally white he makes her, we are likely to forget that her mother, Cery, was an African slave. If Joanna had been identified as Negroid in any way, she would not have been worthy of the narrative attention Stedman gave her.

The appeal that a mulatto woman like Joanna had for eighteenth-century readers who wanted to believe in the universal humanity of humankind is that her existence proved that Africans and Europeans were not two different species, which is what those who opposed racial-mixing claimed.[5] Yet, to offer a mixed-race heritage as evidence of a shared humanity inevitably involved privileging the slave's white blood over black. This privileging is present in Stedman's introduction of Joanna in his *Narrative* as "a Gentlemans Daughter Reduced to the Situation of a humble Slave" (Price and Price 1988, 8). In *Stedman and Joanna,*

Figure 9. These ethnographic sketches by Jean-Baptiste Madou for P. J. Benoit's
Voyage à Surinam (1839) show the heterogeneity of "missies" (as the concubines
were known) that is missing from Stedman's *Narrative*. The top sketch depicts
a mixed-race woman (probably belonging to the free colored class) taking her
child to be baptized, accompanied by slaves. Benoit indicates that she is wearing a lady's attire and a large skirt to conceal her bare feet, which suggests that
she was attempting to pass, since Surinam had a racially defined dress code.
The bottom sketch is of a young slave, carrying a bouquet for a festival, flanked
by two "missies"—one is in the prime of her youth and the other in old age.
These images display the same ethnographic impulse as Holloway's engraving of
Joanna, but the women are not as Europeanized and their clothing is not used to
voyeuristic effect. Rather, the black naked body of the slave woman that Benoit
identifies as a "negress" represents (through her proximity) the sexuality of the
youthful concubine. While Stedman's picture of Joanna freezes her as an image
of eternal youth, the presence of an elderly "missie" in Benoit's travel book re-
introduces the temporality of aging into a white male fantasy of the mulattress.

by contrast, the lasting bonds of Joanna's slave family (rather than her possession of white blood) are presented as the basis for black people's humanity. After living in Surinam and spending time with her people, Stedman realizes that he shares with them a common humanity, a recognition that sets him apart from the rest of his race. He condemns his own race for their uncharitable treatment of the black people he has come to call his own: "I had learned to love the black people. I had come to know their kindness, their loyalty, and their humanity and could not understand why they were treated in such an unchristian way by those who claimed an enlightened life as their heritage" (130). Humanist statements of this kind are out of character for a late eighteenth-century European man, even one as sympathetic to the predicament of slaves as was Stedman.

Undoubtedly, the author of *A Narrative of a Five Years' Expedition Against the Revolted Negroes of Surinam* protests the sadistic treatment of slaves and presents Joanna as possessing a soul equal to that of the best European. He is attentive to black culture in the information he provides about the slave's Coromantyn language, Afro-Creole vocal and instrumental music, personal hygiene, and manner of dress. But Stedman also characterizes their religious practices as "strange Peculiarities" resembling a less enlightened era of Europe's own past (Price and Price 1988, 523). And he reproduces the racial stereotyping of Africans as savages, complete with images of their "human meatshops" that was popularized in European travel literature.

Stedman's book reflects the contradictions of an era informed not only by the abstract principle of a universal humanity but also by the particularities of racist doctrines. He calls the antislavery effort "ill-placed humanitarianism" and, indicating how transport to the colonies saves slaves from the "horrors and devestations" of life in Africa, concludes that "it is a perfect truth, that from a private evil, is derived a general good" (Price and Price 1988, 170–71). Although his documentation of the cruel treatment of slaves made it possible for abolitionists to use his *Narrative* to further their cause, he did not write his book with the intention of it serving as an antislavery tract, which is how the narrator of *Stedman and Joanna* presents the inception of his book. In contradistinction to his historical counterpart, the fictional Stedman, deeply affected by Joanna's death, feels "compelled to stand up for the injustice she had experienced" (165) and vows to expose the horrors of slavery he witnessed.

In choosing to tell the story of Stedman's growing recognition of the humanity of slaves, Gilroy projects onto an eighteenth-century male-authored travel narrative a perspective on slavery that was developed by nineteenth-century women abolitionists. Her novel reflects the antislavery position that emerged after 1824, when the British abolitionist and Quaker Elizabeth Heyrick called for an immediate end to slavery. The shift in focus from amelioration to full emancipation placed the question of black people's rights at the forefront of the antislavery argument. Heyrick's radical antislavery position was further developed in the United States by the Boston abolitionist Lydia Maria Child. In *An Appeal in Favor of That Class of Americans Called Africans* (1996 [1833]), Child condemns white America for its racial prejudices and argues in favor of black people as a class to be assimilated into the American nation rather than as a biologically distinct race to be repatriated in Africa (see Figure 10).

Child's pamphlet is a transracial document in the sense that the extensive research she conducted before writing it included the correspondence and antislavery writings of African Americans (1996, xxiv). Unlike so many other white abolitionists, whose pamphlets refused to endorse slave revolts, she makes a case for their rebelliousness as acts of self-defense and celebrates the achievements of the Jamaican maroon leaders, Juan de Bolas and Cudjoe, as well as Toussaint L'Ouverture, leader of the ill-famed San Domingue rebellion. In her defense of the intelligence and moral character of the Negro race, she gives examples of not only the literary talents of educated black men and women, as does Stedman, but also the monumental achievements of the ancient civilizations of Africa. Instead of presenting Africa as an uncivilized place, she holds Europe responsible for turning it into the dark continent:

> While commerce has carried books and maps to other portions of the globe, she has sent kidnappers, with guns and cutlasses into Africa. We have not preached the Gospel of peace to her princes; we have incited them to make war upon each other, to fill our markets with slaves. While knowledge, like a mighty pillar of fire, has guided the European nations still onward, and onward, a dark cloud has settled more and more gloomily over benighted Africa. (161)[6]

Inasmuch as she traces the violence in Africa to the slave trade, Child does not reverse the trope of enlightened Europe and barbaric Africa.

Figure 10. This version of the popular image of the supplicant slave was used as the frontispiece for Lydia Maria Child's *Appeal in Favor of That Class of Americans Called Africans* (1833). Through the slave woman's jewelry and clothing, an African identity is emphasized over a slave one. Rather than appealing to white women to save her, she is making her plea to God.

Rather, she explains how Europe placed its superior weaponry and world-class navies in the service of the slave trade in order to undermine any chance Africa had to develop. The historical antecedents to the well-known argument of Guyanese scholar and activist Walter Rodney about how Europe underdeveloped Africa are to be detected in Child's text. It is not surprising, then, that elements of Euro-American antislavery writings should appear in a black British novel like *Stedman and Joanna;* their arguments form one of the multiple strands belonging to the creolized and hybrid language of postcoloniality.

In her postcolonial rewriting of Stedman's *Narrative,* Gilroy makes the narrator's point of view conform more closely to the radical position of abolitionists like Child, who integrated a black perspective and introduced gender issues into the antislavery argument. *Stedman and Joanna* exposes the sexual violation of slave women even in those instances in which its narrator willingly participates. In the original text, Stedman writes of how, during a visit to the home of a wealthy Surinam planter, "a Masculine young Negro-woman, as black as a Coal" forced herself upon him (Price and Price 1988, 42–43).[7] He withholds the details of the sexual encounter, claiming to draw "a Sable Curtain over it" because it offers "little instruction or entertainment to the reader" other than serving as a warning to visitors of "the general Character of the negro Girls" (43). Thus does the stereotyping of black women's sexual licentiousness cover over a white man's misconduct. Just as Child says that in publishing Linda Brent's story she is showing "this peculiar phase of Slavery . . . with the veil withdrawn" (Jacobs 1987 [1861], 337–38), *Stedman and Joanna* draws aside the "sable curtain" to expose the violence behind a sexual encounter of the kind reported in Stedman's *Narrative.* In the novel, the slave woman proceeds to tell Stedman that her master commanded her to have sex with him under the threat of being flogged. In order to prevent her whipping, Stedman reports back to the planter that she was "willing and obliging" (41). The novel follows abolitionist literature in presenting the slave's "will," expressed through her apparent willingness to perform sexual services, as not her own but externally controlled by the master's whip.

The next time Stedman accepts the "gift" of a young quadroon girl from a planter, however, the incident is filtered through a postcolonial lens that emphasizes the slave's resistance. The girl, whose name is Cecily, remains silent when Stedman chooses her, but her body language conveys to him "her distaste for her position and her contempt for the service she was expected to render" (74). When Stedman visits the plantation again, he learns that she was to be sold for having attacked the overseer with a knife. Cecily's open resistance to her sexual abuse leaves her fate undetermined, although Stedman makes an offer for the free black woman, Mrs. Sampson, to buy her. He thinks he is helping Cecily out of sympathy with her pitiable condition, but he acts only after Joanna forces him to acknowledge his own contribution to the girl's misery. His slave wife articulates to him the conditions of slavery that he, as a white man, is unable to see.

Gilroy brings a female-gendered antislavery discourse into Stedman's *Narrative* by having Joanna reveal to Stedman how slavery withholds from her the domestic happiness that he wants her to experience. In other words, the fictional Joanna delivers a metacritique of the marriage plot that governs her appearance in Stedman's *Narrative*. The fictional Stedman follows his historical counterpart in representing himself as different from other European men in the high regard he has for Joanna, declaring his intentions to marry her, and resenting it when his friends treat her as a slave. But Joanna, unlike her historical predecessor, informs him that she can only be his concubine, whom he must hire from the owners of Fauconberg, thereby frustrating his desires for a marriage that can transcend the inequalities between them. The novel reveals Stedman's inability to comprehend his slave wife while endowing her with a voice of her own.

Gilroy reconstructs Joanna's subjectivity around the speech that so resonated with abolitionists—that she was "a low, contemptible slave" whose soul was equal to a European's—in order to give her the competence of a free woman who is forced to behave as a slave. As the daughter of a Dutch gentleman and an African slave woman, Joanna has two identities that cannot be reconciled. In the novel, Stedman learns that, since she was educated by her father, she is literate in Dutch and German and can speak English. Yet, she rarely speaks any language other than Surinam Creole or reveals that she is educated for fear of being accused of overstepping her station. When he declares his intentions to make her his wife and not his slave, she informs him that, so long as she remains a slave, their marriage can only be a lie:

I must live wearing yet another coat of deception—educated but un-
educated, your wife but yet a slave girl who must be hired from the
owners of Fauconberg, who wears the given dress of a woman of mixed
race sometimes and a lady's dress when we are alone. I must never forget
that I am a slave. And will you mind when your drunken friends accost
and command me? (46)

Joanna identifies, through the mimicry of secondary wives, how men like
Stedman and Thistlewood created an illusion of domestic life within the
privacy of their own homes. And, her words allude to how fragile this
illusion was, as is evident in Stedman's diaries but not in his published
narrative. Yet, the idea of slavery as a "coat of deception" suggests that
Joanna's true identity is that of the educated daughter of a Dutch gentleman, which contradicts the Afro-Creole lineage the novel creates for her.

An abolitionist privileging of the enlightened and educated slave exists
in tension with a postcolonial privileging of Afro-Caribbean culture in
Gilroy's novel. While Joanna's formal education allows her to articulate
her oppression, her informal training in herbal knowledge permits her
to defend herself against sexual abuse. Although she asks Stedman what
he would do if one of his friends should accost her, he does not become
her protector. In response to his inquiry as to how she received a bruise
on her face, she tells him that a soldier demanded to go home with her
but had to leave after developing stomach pains from a drink she offered
him. Stedman fails to understand the implication of her words even
though on a prior occasion, when he asked her what she would do if she
were ordered to service visitors to Fauconberg, she responded by opening one of the medals she wore around her neck and showing him the
herb it contained. "Parents cannot control our ends," she tells him, "but
we are all taught how to take care of ourselves—only we must never
be found out" (57). This encounter alludes to how planters lived under
the constant fear of being poisoned, especially by their domestic slaves
who had an easy access to their food coupled with a knowledge of herbs
that could produce effects that were indistinguishable from tropical illnesses. However, it is difficult to know whether the slaves accused of
poisoning their owners actually did so or were held responsible for the
deadly effects of improperly stored food or diseases that were unknown
to the European settlers. What the planter's paranoia does indicate is
that household slaves were not loyal and trustworthy servants. Rather,

they instilled fear and suspicion in their owners (Bush 1990, 75). Gilroy represents Joanna as a woman who is capable of producing illness in white men in order to exercise some control over her choice of a sexual partner. This image simultaneously disrupts the comforting stereotype of the nurturing native, while suggesting that the mulatto slave chose domestic partnership with a European man.

Stedman and Joanna clears up the ambiguities in the original text—particularly in the Johnson edition where references to Surinam-style marriages were deleted—in favor of representing Joanna as Stedman's wife rather than his concubine. Noting in the afterword that Stedman's Surinamese family does not show up on his genealogical chart, Gilroy remarks that "it was as if this true story never occurred" (181). The exclusion of Joanna and Johnny from Stedman's family tree is structured by a national amnesia about the racial mixing that was part of Britain's history, which would explain why Gilroy would want to show that Stedman regarded Joanna as his lawful wife even if legally he was prevented from marrying her. Yet, in doing so, she also makes slavery external to their relationship rather than constitutive of it.

Although the novel reveals, in a way the historical text does not, that theirs was "a love in bondage," it simultaneously endorses Stedman's claim that love (or, to use the novel's title, "dedicated love") between a white man and a slave girl could exist. Stedman's relationship to Joanna appears in the novel, as it does in the original text, as separate and distinct from the ones he has with other female slaves. He falls in love with Joanna the first time he sees her and expresses his desire to marry her, to educate her, and to take her back to Europe. In the novel he recalls the first night they spent together as being "gentle," "tender," and "loving" (113), which is far removed from the dalliances with multiple partners that appear in the diaries. When Joanna confronts him about his sexual appropriation of other slave women, she accuses him of behaving like other white men when he is with them—a statement that suggests that he does not act like a white man with her. She tells him: "Being European is not your color. It is what you do" (80). This formulation, which belongs to an antislavery humanism that distinguishes slavery as a corrupting influence from the people who participate in it, is the novel's premise for the possibility of Joanna returning Stedman's love. If she does not love him at first, it is not because he is a white man who is purchasing her services, but because slavery has killed all desire in her. The fear of being sold prevents her from expressing her feelings, which she is able to do once Mrs. Godefrooy purchases her freedom.

There is no qualification of Joanna's manumission in the novel as there is in Stedman's *Narrative*. Instead of offering to earn the money to pay back Mrs. Godefrooy, Joanna is christened and accompanies her husband to a free mulatto ball. Stedman notices that, once his slave wife is free, slavery ceased to drive a wedge between them. "For the first time," he records, "I was able to lie beside her in love without the ghosts of slavery beclouding our hearts. It was only then that I realized the barrier to our feelings that slavery had been" (121). The ghosts of slavery mentioned here are the shadows slavery casts on their relationship rather than the ways that sexual relations between white men and slave women continue to haunt the present. When Stedman returns to Holland and is asked how he could have loved a slave, he replies, "There were no barriers to love. In my arms my Joanna was just a lovely woman" (156). The depth of their love is confirmed not only by the narrator (as in the original) but by Joanna as well. Stedman receives a letter from Mrs. Godefrooy reporting that Joanna has refused to remarry out of her devotion to him. He also learns from their son, Johnny, when he joins him in England after his mother's death that she had kept their "great love" alive "in song, dance, story, and ritual" (171). In the end, the novel's reader learns that true love and affection were possible between a white man and a female slave. "What remains the crowning achievement of the novel," remarks one reviewer, "is the depiction of the love between Joanna and Stedman. It is a love that transcends color and class" (Newson 1993). Pratt's observation about Stedman's *Narrative*—that "romantic love mystifies exploitation out of the picture" (1992, 97)—can be extended to Gilroy's fictional reenactment of Stedman and Joanna's story. Her presentation of a crossracial marriage as an act of mutual choice and affection extends rather than interrupts the trope of reciprocity belonging to Stedman's narrative of the anticonquest.

An understanding of concubinage as romantic love, rather than as the woman's seduction of white men or the master's rape of slave women, is the one that resonates with today's multicultural societies. Witness, for instance, the CBS miniseries *Sally Hemings: An American Scandal*, which recounts Thomas Jefferson's relationship with one of his slave girls as the story of star-crossed lovers.[8] As a historical romance, *Stedman and Joanna* does not simply resurrect the idea of interracial love present in

Stedman's *Narrative*. Rather, by having Joanna articulate how slavery placed restraints on their love, it creates a new "mystique of reciprocity" (to use Pratt's term) for a postcolonial, multicultural era like our own.

Gilroy has described her literary project as one that engages "such concepts as subjectivity, choice, free will and individuality, thus counter-balancing the belief that society, its structure and its laws should bear responsibility for the outcomes of individual lives" (1998, 31). Her novel reflects this perspective inasmuch as it stages the conflict between Stedman and Joanna's love for each other and the laws of a slaveholding society that prevented them from consummating their desire. Yet, there could be no consensual relations between white men and slave women when the women were not in a position to choose their partners or to refuse the sexual advances of their masters and overseers. As Hortense Spillers explains, "under these arrangements, the customary lexis of sexuality, including 'reproduction,' 'motherhood,' 'pleasure,' and 'desire' are thrown into unrelieved crisis" (1987, 76). *Stedman and Joanna* manages this crisis through its representation of Joanna as a slave woman who, due to her husband's efforts, successfully gains her freedom. In this regard, Gilroy follows Child's plotting of Joanna's life as a journey toward emancipation.

Is Gilroy's literary restoration of Joanna to her "proper" place of wife any different from Child's perception of her as domestic woman rather than concubine? Although Gilroy does not go so far as to suggest that Joanna was Stedman's lawful wife, she does make their Surinam-style marriage equal to a Christian one rather than the exchange of sexual and domestic services for payment, which is what the term *concubinage* implies. To speak of Joanna's marriage to Stedman as merely an economic exchange would be to reduce the slave woman to the sexual capacity in which she performed. To acknowledge her sexual preference for a white man, on the other hand, eliminates the inequalities governing her "choice." I have been arguing that only by considering concubinage as a form of domesticity that cuts across the division between slavery and freedom, exploitation and marriage, a black and white world, can we address agency in terms other than the white man's absolute power over his slave wife or the slave woman's exercise of her free will.

Because Gilroy wants to suggest that Stedman's marriage to Joanna was equal to a Christian one, her novel does not entertain the possibility that he did not offer his mulatto wife the choice of accompanying him to Europe. As does her historical counterpart, at least as reported by Stedman, the fictional Joanna says that she would rather remain among her own kind than be treated as a "rescued slave girl" by his friends and family in Europe (105). When framed by scenes of her family life that are not present in the original, Joanna's refusal does not appear in the spirit of heroic self-sacrifice as it does in Stedman's *Narrative* or even domestic self-sacrifice as in Child's commentary on his text. Moreover, Joanna informs Stedman that she has spoken to Elizabeth Sampson, who, having just returned from England, warns her, "You must belong to the abolitionists, or you are ill regarded" (143). Mrs. Sampson's words make evident that freedom and racial equality were no more guaranteed in England than they were in Surinam. At the same, the novel presents Joanna as being offered a choice that, as stated in the previous chapter, was not hers to make.

The elimination of exploitation from the marriage allows for structural similarities to be established between Joanna's situation and that of Elizabeth Sampson. Mrs. Sampson was a wealthy manumitted slave whose income was derived from the several estates her owner had left her (Van Lier 1971, 67). In 1764, at the age of fifty, she petitioned for marriage to a thirty-year-old white man. Since there was no law prohibiting interracial marriages, she hired a solicitor in Amsterdam and took her case directly to the board of directors. When she presented a second European candidate named Zubly (or Zobre) for a husband a few years later, her request was granted.

Elizabeth Sampson appears as a memorable and colorful character in *Stedman and Joanna,* where she is described as "a woman of commanding stature" (104) who was known to make a fan of the credit notes from Dutch planters who had borrowed money from her. Stedman appears to know her well as he instructs Joanna to befriend her, saying she is "a mulatto also married to a white man" (59). He dances with Mrs. Sampson at a mulatto ball, where she reports to him, having just returned from England, the news of the antislavery movement. She confides in Stedman the gossip that Zobre married her for her money, to which he replies, "Where there is love, it matters not" (104). This imaginary exchange between Stedman and Mrs. Sampson romanticizes the problematical status of interracial relations in eighteenth-century Surinam. The history of black and colored women's sexual availability through concubinage makes the desire of an independently wealthy black woman to marry a white man more than simply the expression of love. Her action is overdetermined by the racial hierarchy and class structure existing in Surinam at the time.

The novel presents the two interracial marriages as equally transgressing the conventions of Surinam society, despite the fact that historically Stedman's Surinam-style marriage produced none of the scandal created by Zobre's legal one. The public opinion of the latter marriage is summed up by the official response to Mrs. Sampson's first petition to marry a white man. "Such a marriage," wrote the Hof van Politie to the directors of the society in the Netherlands, "is repugnant and revolting, it being a most serious disgrace for a white man to enter into a marriage of this kind, whether he be motivated by perverse sensuality or by a desire for gain, as it has always been held in contempt here" (cited by Van Lier 1971, 68). The Dutch found Mrs. Sampson's marriage to be particularly distasteful because it reversed the power relations of concubinage. A black woman (far worse for the Dutch than a mulatto) was purchasing a white husband rather than the other way around. But even if Mrs. Sampson were mulatto, the marriage would have been condemned. As Bryan Edwards observes, "no White man of decent appearance . . . will condescend to give his hand in marriage to a Mulatto! The very idea is shocking" (1807, 2:26). The historical Stedman would not have married Joanna, however strong his feelings for her might have been, and in this regard he remained a man of his place and time.

Gilroy's intervention into a late eighteenth-century document like Stedman's *Narrative* is to turn it into the kind of antislavery statement that nineteenth-century abolitionists would have liked it to have been. In *Stedman and Joanna* there is no metanarrative critique of the travel narrative's reworking of the raw materials in the diaries, or of the diaries as a textual mediation of the incidents and events recorded therein. As a fictional rewriting of an actual travel book, the novel gives greater reality—a reality already confirmed by abolitionists like Child—to the author's assertion of his devotion to a slave girl and, through the voice of Joanna, authenticates his romantic reconstruction of their relationship. Inasmuch as the abolitionist desire for a happy ending to Stedman and Joanna's story expresses the wish for a new egalitarian society in which the color of one's skin was no barrier to love, Gilroy revives this utopian dream. Yet this vision, being based on the triumph of individual will over social laws, does not contend with the racial hierarchies that prevented such a union from taking place. As a literary revision of a European

travel narrative, *Stedman and Joanna* speaks more to the integrationist
sentiments of the civil rights era than it does to the segregated society of
eighteenth-century Surinam. It is a utopian vision of what could have
been rather than a literary intervention into what was. Since Gilroy is
rewriting an existing document on slavery, however, she is accountable
to its past even if she is not obligated to remain faithful to it.

A DEAD MAN'S JUMBY SPEAKS

Phillips also introduces a Victorian perspective to a late eighteenth-
century document, but his is a metacritical act designed to expose
the racial hierarchies that persisted long after the evils of slavery were
widely recognized. *Cambridge,* which is set just a few years before the
emancipation of slaves in 1834, consists of a brief prologue and epilogue
that frame an English woman's travel journal, an African slave's confession, and an official report on the murder of an overseer. The novel's
presentation of multiple overlapping perspectives draws attention to the
uncertainty in determining the truth of the events that transpired and
exposes the opacity or "thickness" of language that prevents the document from being a transparent window on the past. The English woman's travel diary reveals the racial prejudices in even the most benevolent
of European attitudes. The diary is followed by a slave testimony that
shows the traveler's presumed knowledge to be derived from a racial
superiority that sanctions an ignorance about black culture and the lives
of slaves.[9] But even the slave who addresses his audience as a narrating
"I" does not speak from outside the racial hierarchies that his testimony
exposes. As a freeman who was baptized, he believes in the superiority of
English culture and that Christianity is the one true religion.

The fictional documents are a pastiche of late eighteenth- and
early nineteenth-century narratives with no indication of their source.
Phillips's disregard of their historicity, however, does not translate into a
disregard for history. In response to critics like Fredric Jameson and Hal
Foster, who consider the pastiche of postmodern fiction to be profound-
ly ahistorical, Linda Hutcheon characterizes it as a form of parody that
ironically reworks historical material. "Postmodern parody," she writes,
"does not disregard the context of the past representations it cites, but
uses irony to acknowledge the fact that we are inevitably separated from
that past today—by time and by the subsequent history of those representations. There is continuum, but there is also ironic difference, difference induced by that very history" (1989, 94). Phillips establishes an

ironic distance from the historical texts he imitates through the anachro-
nism of his language, the racial prejudices of the English woman's journal, and the colonized mind of the African slave. Yet, his postmodern
parody of preexisting documents also positions the reader as a traveler
into the past by allowing us to see slavery through the eyes of a Victorian
woman and African-born slave. Phillips's citations are so close to the
originals that there appears to be no parody at all. However, through
subtle changes, he dramatizes the race, class, and gender hierarchies un-
derpinning the historical document as a record of the past. "The larger
historical question regarding memory," he explains about his novels on
slavery, "has to do with our own collective memory of history as a community, as a society. So my way of subverting received history is to use
historical documents, use first-person voices, digest what they're saying,
and somehow rework them" (Sharpe 1995b, 157). By creating fictional
documents that approximate real ones, Phillips exposes the fiction on
which history is founded—namely, that real events tell their own story.

The partial and subjective nature of the document is made all the
more apparent if one considers that the third part of the novel is no
literary invention but an excerpt from an actual travel diary, Mrs. Flannigan's *Antigua and the Antiguans* (1844), a source that he does not
identify. By placing an actual historical document at the end of his
novel, Phillips frames its version of the past with his own storytelling.
By not alerting the reader to its historicity, he blurs the distinction between fact and fiction. A reviewer for the *New York Times,* believing the
third part of the novel to be yet another literary invention, evaluates it
as an official report that misreads the events that have already transpired
(Garrett 1992). The reviewer is right in his evaluation, except that the
"events" the historical document apparently misrepresents are fictional
recreations. As a postmodern representation, fiction serves as a refer-
ent for factual evidence rather than the other way around. The reader
thus recognizes in Mrs. Flannigan's diary the mindset Phillips creates
for his character, Emily Cartwright, who pens a journal much like her
historical predecessor. As an English woman who visited Antigua on the
cusp of emancipation, Mrs. Flannigan judges slavery to be "a foul and
hideous monster, which ought to be exterminated from every corner of
the world" (162–63). Yet, she also betrays her distaste for the Negro race
as much as the most fervent defender of slavery.

Mrs. Flannigan's racial prejudice is evident, despite her efforts to assume the objective voice of the annals, in the tale she tells of a murderous and vengeful slave, Cambridge, who bludgeoned his overseer to death. She recounts how the murderer was tracked down to his hut, where he was caught in the act of washing his bloodstained hands. There is no doubt in her mind that the man committed the crime of which he was accused. His guilt is reconfirmed by his sentencing, which is death by hanging on the same spot where the murder was committed as an example to other slaves. True to the form of the travel literature to which her book belongs, she embellishes her narrative with drama and local lore: "Long did his whitened bones glisten in the moonbeams; and as the wind shook the chains which held the body, many a little negro who had strayed that way in search of guavas, fled from the spot, for fear of the 'dead man's jumby'" (92). Thus ends the story of the man known only as Cambridge. From this fragment of a life, which exists in Mrs. Flannigan's travel book for no other reason than to entertain, Phillips begins to tell a different tale.

Cambridge resuscitates the dead man whose jumby is doomed to wander by wrenching "factual evidence" about him out of Mrs. Flannigan's narrative and adding two additional perspectives on the incidents being described. Emily Cartwright's journal entries are a pastiche of late eighteenth- and early nineteenth-century travel diaries by women like Lady Nugent, Janet Schaw, and Mrs. Carmichael, as well as J. B. Moreton's *Manners and Customs of the West Indies* (1790) and M. G. ("Monk") Lewis's *Journal of a West Indian Proprietor* (1834). The characterization of Monk Lewis, a successful writer who inherited two Jamaican estates that he visited in 1815–16 and 1817, as "a cultured English gentleman who has a sincere if somewhat misguided interest in the welfare of negroes who have suddenly become his property" (Ragatz 1970, 228) is an apt description of Emily, who is commissioned to visit the West Indian estate that belongs to her father, its absentee owner. Yet she is unable to assume the position of benevolent master as did a cultured gentleman like Lewis. As an unmarried woman with no income of her own, Emily has limited options in life. On her return to England, she is to marry a fifty-year-old widower and to assume the responsibility of raising his three children. She wants to protest the future that her father has planned for her but finds herself forced to keep her thoughts to herself.

The novel opens by establishing certain resemblances between Emily and the slave women whom she later meets, resemblances that are absent

from the historical travel diaries. Victorian womanhood is characterized in the prologue as a form of bondage, one in which Emily's desires
are made to conform to the "lonely regime which fastened her into
backboards, corsets and stays to improve her posture" (4). As a woman
forced into a marriage of convenience, she shares with slaves the state of
subjugation to patriarchal authority. Like the slave women who appear
to agree with her in their powerlessness to speak, "her voice unspooled
in silence" (4) before her father. When she arrives on her father's plantation, she discovers that she does not have any real power over the men
who are running it. Rather, they consider her to be somewhat of an
inconvenience. Allowing herself to be seduced by the white overseer,
Emily finds herself competing with his concubine for his attention.
Since the overseer is a cruel and uncouth man whom she loathes at
their initial meeting, it soon becomes clear that her romantic fantasies
about him are fueled by her rejection of the oppressive life that awaits
her back home. She is able to keep her sexual relationship with him hidden until it becomes known that she is pregnant with his child. Evelyn
O'Callaghan explains that Emily's journal shows "the indeterminacy of
the title 'mistress,'" one in which the powerlessness of the mistress of
the Great House overlaps with the illegitimacy of the mistress of the
overseer (41). Emily's powerlessness and illegitimacy suggest that she dif-
fers little from the black or mulatto concubine. Indeed, by the end of
the novel, the plantation lady is a "fallen woman" who is unable to save
her honor through marriage because the overseer has died, murdered by
the slave Cambridge. However, unlike her slave counterpart, the English
woman is able to participate in a discourse of power that maintains her
in a position of superiority over slaves.

Emily begins keeping a journal, which constitutes the first of the two
fictional documents in the novel, under fairly innocuous circumstances
as a woman's diary of private reflections. She records the thoughts she is
unable to share with her Spanish female servant, who dies on the journey over. Her journal very quickly changes into a more public record intended to "encourage Father to accept the increasingly common, though
abstract, English belief in the iniquity of slavery" (8). Once she arrives
in the West Indies (the specific island is not identified), she is swayed by
the proslavery argument, and her report starts to reflect the perspective
of the men who run the plantation. It is a sign of her own powerlessness
and marginalization that she defers to the authority of these men. At the

same time, she assumes a position of authority when she decides to take their message back to England. Although she sees slavery as an ineffi-cient labor system that is coming to an end, she also thinks that it is not the abomination abolitionists have made it out to be. She believes that, as one who has witnessed plantation life firsthand, her opinion will carry some weight back home. Emily's journal soon becomes the instrument for her own emancipation once she realizes that she can earn a living giving lecture tours in England. Her character makes evident that the shared oppression of white women and black slaves does not create the conditions for a common sisterhood.

Phillips exposes, through Emily's journal, that the power to imagine oneself as a slave is derived from the ontological fact that one is not a slave. The ethnographic impulse to descriptions of slave life in travel diaries like Stedman's is guided by a separation of the subject who knows from the object being described and classified. Emily records the slave's work schedule, eating habits, domestic life, and customs with the accu-racy of an anthropologist. Her detailed description of slave villages are among the many passages Phillips copies from Monk Lewis's *Journal.* Here are two passage for comparison, the first from Emily's journal and the second from Lewis's:

> I have never witnessed so picturesque a scene as a negro village. Each house is surrounded by a small garden, and the whole village criss-crossed by miniature lanes bordered with sweet-scented flowering plants. The gardens of the negroes are not like the kitchen-gardens of England, planted with functional, plain vegetables, and the odd shrub of goose-berry or patch of strawberry. No, the negro grows his provisions in his mountain-grounds and harvests them once a fortnight, as I have described. These village gardens are decorative groves of ornament and luxury, and filled with a profusion of fruits which boast all the colours of the rainbow from the deepest purple to the brightest red. If I were to be asked if I should enter life anew as an English labourer or a West Indian slave I should have no hesitation in opting for the latter. (Phillips 1991, 42)

> I never witnessed on the stage a scene so picturesque as a negro village. I walked through my own to-day, and visited the houses of the drivers, and other principal persons; and if I were to decide according to my own taste, I should infinitely have preferred their habitations to my own. Each house is surrounded by a separate garden, and the whole village

is intersected by lanes, bordered with all kinds of sweet-smelling and flowering plants; but not such gardens as those belonging to our English cottages, where a few cabbages and carrots just peep up and grovel upon the earth between hedges, in square narrow beds, and where the tallest tree is a gooseberry bush: the vegetables of the negroes are all cultivated in their provision-grounds; these form their *kitchen*-gardens, and these are all for ornament or luxury, and are filled with a profusion of oranges, shaddocks, cocoa-nuts, and peppers of all descriptions. (Lewis 1929, 95)

Both real and invented narrators authenticate their possession of an intimate knowledge of slave culture through the details of their accounts. The absentee owner in each instance is no outsider to plantation life but one who mingles with his or her slaves. The exchange between Self and Other is far more dramatic in Lewis's declaration of a preference for living in a slave hut over the Great House. What makes the negro village more desirable is the lure of the traveler's desire for the exotic, as indicated in the contrasts made between an English and West Indian provision garden.

The contemporary reader who has little or no knowledge about the everyday lives of slaves is likely to find oneself seduced by the ethnographic detail of Emily's report. It is difficult to find descriptions indicating the care with which slaves tended to their provision gardens (often planted on the worst land) in their own testimonies. The slave narrative is sparse on information about how slaves maintained their social beings against a system that dehumanized them. For strategic purposes, it emphasized the breakup of black families rather than the extended networks of kin on which runaways relied, the cruel treatment of slaves rather than their strategies of survival. As such, it lacks the ethnographic record of slave culture found in the travel literature. The narrative force of Emily's documenting of slave culture lies in the totalizing effect of the details of everyday life. At the same time, her obsessive fascination with the color of the slave's skin and her reliance on racist systems of meaning continuously interrupts the reader's desire to see the slave village "as it is." Because there is no authorial voice to instruct or distance one from her narration, the tension between being pulled by the ethnographic lure of her descriptions and repulsed by her racist observations makes for uncomfortable reading. But that is precisely the point of Phillips's novel. Rather than confronting slavery from a time and place removed from the past, the reader is forced to consider that past as a condition of existence for his or her privileged place of reading.

The power of the ethnographic voice lies in the native informant's reconfirmation of what the European observer already knows. Lewis reports how often his slaves told him that they were happy he was their master and expressed their desire to remain slaves. Yet, as his description of their celebration of his arrival indicates, such expressions of joy and happiness were excessive to the degree of being disturbing: "Whether the pleasure of the negroes was sincere may be doubted; but certainly it was the loudest that I ever witnessed: they all talked together, sang, danced, shouted, and, in the violence of their gesticulations, tumbled over each other, and rolled about upon the ground" (60). In *Cambridge,* slaves also repeat back to Emily what they think she, as their owner, wants to hear—that they are satisfied with their lives on the plantation and do not want to be free. Since a superficial familiarity with slaves forms the grounds for "preliminary truths," she paints a rather benign picture of slavery (38). As Cambridge later testifies, Emily's "not altogether un-surprising posture of social superiority" prevented her from valuing his opinion (164). In fact, she is an unreliable narrator who misreads practically everything she sees. This includes her understanding of the slave she calls Hercules, which is the name she gives Cambridge because of his large size and brute strength.

Cambridge appears in Emily's journal the same way his namesake does in Mrs. Flannigan's—as a troublemaker and a thief. However, it is also clear in Phillips's fictional rendition of the travel diary that we do not have the whole story. The first time Emily sees Cambridge, he is being whipped by the overseer, Mr. Brown, who explains to her the reason for his action: "The old fool you call Hercules is the chief trouble-maker of the estate. He steals, lies and provokes the others to acts of minor rebellion which must be quashed at once" (59). Emily is taken by surprise when this same malcontented slave quizzes her "in highly fanci-ful English" as to her views on slavery (92). She later learns that his name is Cambridge and he is educated and can read the Bible. Like Joanna in *Stedman and Joanna,* Cambridge is forced to conceal his education and knowledge of English. By making the brutal slave in Mrs. Flannigan's journal into an educated Christian, Phillips is signifying on the West Indian practice of naming slaves after university towns in mockery of their presumed ignorance. Cambridge's revelation of his intellect to

Emily undermines her effort to give him a name that reduces him to his body. She soon learns that Mr. Brown offered him the position of head driver as a way of thwarting any respect field slaves might have had for him, but he refused to cooperate. This refusal provoked the overseer into disciplining him for the slightest infraction. Emily's journal ends with the news that Brown has been murdered by "same *intelligent* negro with whom he waged a constant war" and that "now the negro is hanged from a tree, no longer able to explain or defend his treacherous act" (128). But the reader does get to hear his defense, if only posthumously, in the form of a confession taken prior to his execution.

A shadowy figure in Emily's journal, Cambridge emerges as the subject of his own story once he is granted "the powers of self-expression in the English language" (133). He tells of how he was born in Africa and was kidnapped and transported on a slave ship across the Atlantic, a journey that severs him from his home. His observation to the person recording his words—"Our history was truly broken" (137)—is also a metanarrative statement on the incomplete nature of the existing records on slavery. However, unlike Gilroy, Phillips does not fill in the holes with the information of slave life that is missing. Rather, he unravels the colonial documents whose gaps and contradictions his fiction inhabits.

Cambridge's confession is structured along the lines of the well-known slave narrative *The Interesting Narrative of the Life of Olaudah Equiano* (1789) and incorporates elements of Ukawsaw Gronniosaw's *Narrative* (1774) into it as well. Phillips confounds the racial stereotyping of black men by introducing the possibility that Mrs. Flannigan's brutal and vengeful slave could be an educated Christian like Equiano and Gronniosaw. The reader who hopes to find an authenticating text of resistance in Cambridge's testimony, however, will be disappointed. The confessional mode and Christian ethos that structure his words prevent any direct statement of rebelliousness. Cambridge appears to be a good Christian who believes in the superiority of Western civilization; his rebelliousness lies less in his insubordination than it does in his moral outrage, Christian piety, and highmindedness. He expresses remorse for having committed the crime of which he is accused, saying that he is "truly frightened of [his] actions and the fearful consequences of [his] heathen behaviour" (167). But is Cambridge saying what he thinks or does he want to gain the sympathy of his judge and executors?

As a criminal confession, Cambridge's testimony conceals evidence as much as it reveals the truth about his identity. In this regard, it resembles a document like *The Confessions of Nat Turner* (1831), which is now acknowledged to be more the product of Thomas R. Gray, the lawyer who recorded the testimony. As Michel Foucault reminds us about the confession, "the agency of domination does not reside in the one who speaks (for it is he who is constrained), but in the one who listens and says nothing; not in the one who knows and answers, but in the one who questions and is not supposed to know" (1980, 62). Turner, who led an uprising of sixty or seventy slaves in Virginia on the night of August 21, 1831, appears in his confession as a bloodthirsty megalomaniac who went on a killing spree after butchering his owner (whom he calls "a kind master") and his family with a hatchet (Gray 1975 [1881], 12–13). In making the respectable slave narratives of Equiano and Gronniosaw into a suspect document like the criminal confession, Phillips draws attention to the kind of black subjectivity the slave testimony can produce.

Like his historical predecessors who remade themselves in the image of a Christian Englishman, Cambridge is an African-born slave who becomes a "virtual Englishman" and "black Christian" (156, 161).[10] Olumide, which is Cambridge's African name, tells of how he was sold into slavery and transported to England, where he converted to Christianity and married an English woman who was employed as a servant by his master. When his owner died, he and his wife toured England to promote the Christian missions in Africa. He decided to go to Africa to join the missionaries after his wife's death but was robbed by an unscrupulous captain and sold as a slave. This is how he ended up on the Cartwright plantation in the West Indies. Both Equiano's and Cambridge's testimonies follow the ocean voyages of their protagonists from African freedom, to European enslavement, and on to Christian redemption. But Equiano's worst fears as a free man—of being resold into slavery—are made into a reality for his fictional counterpart.

Although Equiano purchased his manumission while in the West Indies and assumed the post of captain on a ship, he finds himself treated like a slave each time he docks on land in the Americas. He is almost kidnapped and resold into slavery in Georgia, while in Montserrat he is obliged to advertise himself like a slave each time he leaves the island. He longs to return to England, which he describes as a place where his heart lies. Written for English readers in the service of the abolitionist cause, Equiano's narrative contrasts the freedom he enjoys as a black Englishman with the "mockery of freedom" experienced by freeman in the West Indies (1988, 89). However, slaves could be bought, sold, and bequeathed in wills in England, and runaway slaves continued to be hunted down and returned to their owners long after the Somerset case in 1772. This is indeed what happened to Equiano's friend John Annis, whose owner forcibly removed him from their ship while it was docked on the Thames in 1774. Despite Equiano's efforts to obtain a habeas corpus to prevent his friend from being carried abroad, Annis was returned to St. Kitt's, where he was flogged and placed in irons. This is the one place in Equiano's autobiography where he is so disillusioned that he says he wants to leave England and never return. His spiritual conversion en route to Turkey, however, sutures over this narrative rupture, thereby preserving the progress of his journey toward Christianity and freedom. Cambridge's life story, by contrast, undermines the trope of Christian conversion that is so central to Equiano's spiritual autobiography, as his conversion does not lead to freedom but to reenslavement and death by hanging.

Cambridge's testimony reveals that for a black man (or woman, as we will see in the case of Mary Prince) to live in England is precisely not to be free. Although abolitionists interpreted Judge Mansfield's decision in the Somerset case in terms of Blackstone's declaration in his *Commentaries* that no slavery could exist on the free soil of England, both Blackstone and Mansfield maintained a distinction between waged workers and slaves, who were not entitled to payment for their labor (Shyllon 1977, 24–27). Slavery continued to exist in the form of indentured servitude in Britain and was not officially abolished until it was ended in its colonies in 1834 (Fryer 1984, 125–26, 203–4). When Cambridge first arrives in London, his master instructs him (as did Gronniosaw's in Amsterdam) that he is not a slave but a servant; however, the difference is semantic rather than legal. As the servant-slave explains, although his master spoke against the slave trade that had ended, he was among the many slave-owners "happily accommodated in the bosom of English society" (141). Cambridge is witness to a city in which "darling blacks" are fashionable appendages, African children are sold as exotic animals, and free blacks live on the margins of society as prostitutes, street entertainers, and beggars. This small but vital black community is not visible in Equiano's narrative, yet it is present in the detail with which he describes the customs and social practices of Africa. Although presented as his own memories of the land he left behind, the account is potentially the collective memory of displaced Africans living in London. This is all the more likely if, as Vincent Carretta claims, Equiano may have been born into slavery and invented a free African identity for rhetorical purposes (1999).

Like Gilroy, Phillips finds a place for Black Britain in a historical document that is not centered on life in England. He uses the slave testimony to sow the seeds for a black Atlantic identity that does not originate in the postwar migration to which he himself belongs. Transforming the nineteenth-century idea of a black Englishman as one whose color prevents him from being a true Englishman, Cambridge claims an English identity that is both black and free:

> Truly I was now an Englishman, albeit a little smudgy of complexion! Africa spoke to me only of a history I had cast aside. . . . We who are kidnapped from the coast of Africa, and bartered on the shores of America, occupy a superior and free status in England, although an unsatisfactory reluctance to invoke the just English law permits the outward appearance of slavery to be enacted by some persons. This creates in the minds of many true Englishmen a confusion as to the proper standing of the black people in their presence. (147)

Cambridge's words are addressed to the novel's readers to remind them of the slave-trading history that brought him to England, even as he acknowledges that he is not considered a "true Englishman" because of a national identity formed through a collective amnesia about the history of black Britain. By resurrecting the voice of a dead slave in order to make him part of Victorian England, the novel shows how an English national culture is haunted by its slave past.

In modeling his narrator after Equiano and Gronniosaw, Phillips follows the political objective of the slave testimony, which was to overturn the perception of black people as an ignorant and superstitious race who were deserving of their enslavement. As Charles T. Davis and Henry Louis Gates Jr. explain in their introduction to *The Slave's Narrative,*

> the recording of an authentic black voice, a voice of deliverance from the deafening discursive silence which an "enlightened" Europe cited as proof of the absence of the African's humanity, was the millennial instrument of transformation through which the African would become

the European, the slave become the ex-slave, the brute animal become the human being. (1985, xxvi–xxvii)

The narrative effect of demonstrating the slave's humanity, however, was to produce an "authentic black voice" that was both European and Christian. Cambridge's testimony may have been recorded in the West Indies, but the identity of the narrating "I" is a black Briton. Cambridge, being an outsider to West Indian slavery as was Equiano, does not have much to report about the everyday lives of slaves.

Emily's journal, more so than Cambridge's testimony, gestures toward the black subjectivities hovering at the edges of an eyewitness report. Just as Lewis finds the exuberance of his slaves disturbing, Emily expresses the discomfort she feels over a free man's deference and suspects (although she can never really know for sure) him of mocking her. She is convinced that slaves are superstitious but also complains that they "make something of a convenience of their *jumbys*" (70). In such instances, Phillips foregrounds the trickster figure that colonial observers unknowingly recorded. He similarly unpacks the stereotype of the black mammy in the character of Stella, whom Emily describes as a woman with a "smiling ebon face and broadly grinning lips" (78). Stella is the most trustworthy of the slaves, who attends to her mistress's every need. When Emily attempts to get her presumably loyal housekeeper to "share her knowledge" of concubinage with her, however, Stella remains silent (76). As Emily chatters on about how black women do their utmost to attach themselves to white men, whom they consider superior beings, and that they know how to abort their babies if a pregnancy should inconvenience them, she notices that Stella "manifested her rage not by overt onslaught, but by covert smouldering" (76). The slave woman's voice unspools in silence before her mistress just as Emily's did before her father. However, the reader is aware of how wounding these words are for Stella, even if Emily is not, because she has already recorded that Stella was "a fine breeder" whose children had been sold to other plantations. The housekeeper's excessive show of maternal concern toward her charge is a form of noncooperation, as she tries to prevent her mistress from making her inquiries to the overseer by insisting that she protect herself from the hot midday sun. Although the novel suggests that Stella's agency lies more in her silence and refusal to cooperate than insubordination and rebelliousness, her story remains untold, as does that of other slave women. In a postmodern novel like Phillips's, there is nothing outside the documents it mimics, not even an omniscient narrative or authorial voice from which to assume a critical perspective. As a result, the slave woman as subject is conspicuously absent.

A particularly enigmatic character is Christiana, who like Cambridge is a literary embellishment of a slave mentioned in *Antigua and the Antiguans.* Mrs. Flannigan introduces Christiana as the overseer's "amour," whom Cambridge wished to murder out of revenge for having informed on the slaves. Phillips recodes the colonial signification of the concubine's loyalty by making Christiana into an obeah woman and wife of the intractable slave who stands accused of murder. Emily describes Christiana as a "coal-black *ape-woman*" (73) and "arrogant black wench" (89) who attempts to seat herself next to Mr. Brown at the dinner table in the Great House. When Emily orders to have her escorted away, Christiana begins "howling and hurling abuse like some sooty witch from *Macbeth*" (74). Emily later learns that the slaves are afraid of her because she is obeah, and this fear is confirmed when she sees her scratching lines in the dirt outside her bedroom. Her inquiries into the nature of obeah elicit such predictable responses as it being "the devil's work" and a "primitive belief in witchcraft" (96, 98). Although we know that this description reflects the racial prejudices of her European informers, we are also not supplied with the information of what the practice meant to slaves or how a range of African-based religious practices were included under the label of "obeah." The only hint of Christiana's practicing something other than witchcraft lies in Cambridge's description of her as "an exceedingly strange, yet spiritually powerful young girl" (158) who brought him food and water when he first arrived at the Cartwright plantation. Yet, this brief reference to her spiritual power is easy to overlook because she is not identified by name.

Emily's perspective on Christiana as an arrogant and self-deluded slave is contradicted by Cambridge, who tells a more tragic story of her life. He describes her strange behavior as the result of a series of unhappy incidents beginning with her being coupled at age ten with a much older slave in order to breed and culminating with the overseer's raping her. Cambridge befriends Christiana and moves her into his home as his wife. He claims that the violence of the rape had unhinged her mind and she imagined that she was the mistress of the Great House, a fantasy the overseer encouraged. She started to eat dirt and practice "other abominations" until Emily's arrival drove her into "her final and irrevocable madness"

(163). Cambridge confirms Christiana's bad behavior toward the real mistress of the Great House but only because "she now considered herself little more than a common animal, and she was acting accordingly" (165). We hear no more of Christiana after this, other than that she has run away. One might say that Phillips employs the literary device of eliminating her as a character because he cannot tell her story. It is a difficult story to tell, for to do so would be to suggest that not all white men's concubines were vain and arrogant women, as reported in European travel literature, and not all sexual relations between overseers and slave women were rape, as reported in male-authored slave narratives.

Christiana appears as an evil witch in the English woman's journal and a helpless victim in the confession of an Anglicized Christian slave. Between the white woman's diary and black man's testimony, the black woman as subject disappears. Gilroy, on the other hand, uses dialogue to introduce slave women's subjectivities into a male-authored text. Through the contradictions established between Stedman's perception of his wife as a woman who is incapable of acting on her own and Joanna's own explanations of her actions, the reader catches a glimpse of the slave woman that the European male narrator is unable to see. But *Stedman and Joanna* also displays the pitfalls of humanism through its faith in an empirically determined reality, belief in the possibility for mutual empathy and compassion across the master-slave divide, and privileging of a self-determining individual. Inasmuch as my own study is suspicious of teleological narratives and a unified coherent subject, I favor a postmodern approach. Yet I also recognize the value of the literary effort to right a historical wrong by representing a black female subjectivity that has been disarticulated in the records. Is it possible, then, to work between these two positions?

The struggle to trace a line from the myths and stereotypes surrounding slave women to the women themselves forces the question of whether a black female subjectivity is more likely to be found in the slave woman's testimony in which she appears as a narrating "I." This is a question that the next chapter addresses in its reading of *The History of Mary Prince*. Yet, as I turn now to the third woman of my study, I find the need to disengage her subjectivity from the slave narrative with which it has become identified. As in so many slave narratives, the plotting of the narrator's life in *The History of Mary Prince* anticipates the Christianized fugitive slave in the consciousness of the slave. Although this anticipation served the political objectives of the antislavery movement, which was to demonstrate the slave woman's competence as a moral individual, it also made her capable of an agency that would have been impossible under slavery.

The double objective of the slave narrative—to establish the humanity of the slave while showing the dehumanizing effects of slavery—presented a paradox for abolitionists that could be resolved only through a splitting of the slave narrator away from slave life he or she left behind. This splitting meant that the narrated "I" (that is, the slave) spoke only inasmuch as he or she was on the path toward Christianity, enlightenment, and freedom. In the next chapter, I make a case for separating an academic agenda from the political one of the antislavery movement. An agency that is more appropriate to the constraints placed on slave women can be made available by placing the slave testimony in articulation with other documents, including such disreputable ones as proslavery propaganda. Curiously enough, Mary Prince exists in these intersecting narratives as Cambridge and Christiana rolled up in one, appearing as a morally upright Christian in her own testimony and a foul-mouthed heathen in the writings of the proslavery lobby that denounced her. By locating a black female subjectivity between these contradictory representations, we see that even highly suspect documents like proslavery propaganda need to be incorporated into our understanding of slave women's lives. And, the slave testimony is but a beginning rather than the end of the story to be told.

4.

"A Very Troublesome Woman"
Who Speaks for the Morality of Slave Women?

The slave narrative was a means by which an unlettered black woman such as Mary Prince could express herself in writing. But it also exhibits the triangular relationship between slaves, their readers, and evangelical sponsors. Although the testimony was written at Prince's request, it was sponsored by the secretary of the Anti-Slavery Society in London, Thomas Pringle, who decided to publish it in response to her owner's efforts to discredit her. In keeping with the genre of antislavery pamphlets to which it belongs, Prince's narrative was intended to create sympathy for the Negro race by showing slavery from the perspective of its victims. Pringle fulfills this political objective by presenting Prince as *both* the abused victim of cruel masters *and* a socioethical being who is active in obtaining her freedom. Her actions converge so as to reconfirm the political mission of the antislavery campaign. As the retrospective reconstruction of Prince's life from a historical present that envisions the end of slavery, *The History of Mary Prince* moves from ignorance to enlightenment and from slavery to freedom.

The antislavery requirement to anticipate the free and enlightened ex-slave in the consciousness of the slave imposed restrictions on what could be considered appropriate or acceptable forms of agency. Prince is shown chastising her owners for their cruelty, expressing a desire to be free, and working hard toward her manumission. The slave woman acts, then, only inasmuch as she exhibits the *moral* agency of an enlightened individual. The slave narrative makes no mention of Prince attempting to gain freedom through extramarital relationships with white men, including a Captain Abbot who was employed by her owner, John Wood. In a document intended to overturn Wood's claim that his runaway slave was a dishonest and sexually depraved woman, even the slightest hint of sexual impropriety could have destroyed Prince's credibility. But her testimony is also silent about her rape at the hands of her master.

That sexual abuse of Prince would cast doubt on *her* character shows that she was expected to adhere to standards of morality that were impossible under slavery (see Figure 11). Harriet Jacobs is critical of such universal moral standards in her *Incidents in the Life of a Slave Girl* when Linda Brent begs her readers to forgive her for having become Sands's concubine: "The condition of a slave confuses all principles of morality, and, in fact, renders the practice of them impossible. . . . I feel that the slave woman ought not to be judged by the same standard as others" (385–86). Jacobs is able to offer this critique only because she combines the slave testimony with the sentimental novel in order to clear the space for a narrative form adequate to slave women's stories (Smith 1990). Publishing under the pseudonym of Linda Brent and the sponsorship of a radical abolitionist like Child also gave Jacobs a literary license that is missing from an as-told-to testimony like Prince's. The latter offers no criticism, either direct or indirect, of the model of womanhood against which slave women's actions were measured. Since Prince did not write her life story herself but told it to abolitionists who then wrote it down, she exercised minimal narrative control.

The paradoxical position of the slave woman as one who existed outside the structures of domesticity but had to uphold its ideals points to an inherent contradiction in the speaking subject of *The History of Mary Prince*. While having no self-autonomy as a slave, she was expected to exercise a sexual autonomy over her body. This contradiction is the product of the narrative requirement to present Prince as an authoritative witness to the dehumanizing effects of slavery. Inasmuch as the truth of her testimony depended on demonstrating that she was a decent Christian woman, her narrative authority was linked to her sexuality. The intimate connection between her authority and sexuality might explain why the advocates of slavery attacked her credibility through examples of her sexual misconduct. These examples provide a way into reading a different kind of gendered slave subjectivity than the one produced by the requirements of the antislavery movement.

Like Jacobs, Prince appears to have established sexual relations with

Figure 11. "The Abolition of the Slave Trade, Or the Inhumanity of Dealers in human flesh exemplified in Captain Kimbers treatment of a Young Negro Girl of 15 for her Virgin Modesty." This abolitionist cartoon published in 1792 depicts a captain punishing a slave girl for resisting his sexual advances. The words of the sailor stringing her up ("My Eyes Jack our Girls in Wapping are never flogged for their modesty") allude to the hypocrisy of the proslavery advocates who maintained double standards for black and white women. Courtesy of Wilberforce House Museum, Kingston upon Hull.

men as a means of challenging her master's authority. Unlike Jacobs, the conditions of her sexual relations were closer to prostitution, which made her actions all the more damning in the eyes of British abolitionists. This is why her testimony is silent about this aspect of her life as a slave. Commenting on the silences that structure the slave narrative, Toni Morrison reminds us that it is equally a record of what must be forgotten about slavery as it is of what must be remembered: "In shaping the experience to make it palatable to those who were in a position to alleviate it, they [slaves] were silent about many things, and they 'forgot' many other things" (110). She places the word "forgot" in quotation marks to emphasize how it was an active forgetting or self-imposed silence.

How can we read the slave narrative as a record of what the slave could not speak into being or was obliged to forget? Here a Freudian understanding of memory as a screen-discourse can be useful. Freud describes the mnemic trace as the product of two opposing forces, whereby the effort to record an experience comes up against a resistance (1963). The product of the double force of remembering and forgetting, repetition and erasure, legibility and illegibility, a screen memory is not a record of what happened but of the way it was remembered to have happened. This two-handed operation moves us away from considering the singularity of agency in any record of the past. Following a Freudian understanding of memory, we see that it is not enough simply to confirm slave agency; we also need to be aware of the models of understanding on which our readings are based. In failing to consider what is forgotten, erased, or illegible in the slave narrative, we are often forced to rely on the evidence abolitionists considered noteworthy. Such a reliance involves showing a preference for the Christianized slave, one who resembles the Cambridge of Caryl Phillips's fictional testimony discussed in the last chapter.

The British antislavery movement did not condone practices that went against the Protestant ideals of obedience, self-discipline, hard work, and moderation. Moreover, abolitionists believed that, although slaves had natural rights, they had no access to these rights except through Christian conversion and Western civilization. Understanding African culture to be the negation of a European civilization that served as the norm, they located the moral deficiency of black slaves in both the negative influence of slavery and their "Africanness" (Sharpe 1993, 41).

The slave that had to be freed, then, was not only an enslaved body over which the master had absolute control but also an African body bound to "heathenism" and savagery. The antislavery position, like its proslavery counterpart, articulated a racial hierarchy but one that was culturally rather than biologically determined. By acceding to the abolitionist preference for the enlightened individual, we risk equating slave agency with a movement toward Christian emancipation.

THE MAGICAL POWER OF THE ROOT

An understanding of literacy as empowerment is due, in part, to its prior narrativization by black abolitionists like Olaudah Equiano and Frederick Douglass (Gates 1987, 98–124; 1988, 127–69). In his 1845 *Narrative of the Life of Frederick Douglass, An American Slave, Written by Himself,* Douglass explains how his master, Hugh Auld, unwittingly revealed to him the power of the book. When Auld discovered that his wife had been teaching the young Douglass to read, he informed her that she had broken the law. Slave literacy was considered dangerous because it allowed runaways to forge passes from their masters. But for Douglass, the written word has a deeper ontological significance. When Auld declared that reading "spoils" a slave by making him dissatisfied and unmanageable, he disclosed the secret of white men's power. Douglass describes the effect this disclosure had upon him:

> It was a new and special revelation, explaining dark and mysterious things, with which my youthful understanding had struggled, but struggled in vain. I now understood what had been to me a most perplexing difficulty—to wit, the white man's power to enslave the black man. It was a grand achievement, and I prized it highly. From that moment, I understood the pathway from slavery to freedom. (1987 [1845], 275)

Douglass embarks upon the path to freedom by surreptitiously teaching himself to read. The books he reads provide him with a language with which to express his previously inarticulate desires to be free: "The reading of these documents enabled me to utter my thoughts, and to meet the arguments brought forward to sustain slavery" (279). But they also make the state of subjugation even more unbearable. The adult Douglass, looking back on that moment, describes how the knowledge he gained from books distanced him from other slaves: "In moments of agony, I envied my fellow-slaves for their stupidity. I have often wished

myself a beast" (279). By equating illiteracy with the slave's ignorance
and lack of humanity, Douglass positions himself as an outsider to the
orality of slave culture even though he was still a slave. As Valerie Smith
remarks about this passage, "to link reading and writing inextricably
with social development is to display an inherent bias toward Anglo-
American uses of language" (1987, 4). It is also to denigrate the residual
knowledge of Africa, which appears in an episode describing the magical
power of a root.

   The episode centers on Douglass's defeat of Mr. Covey, a cruel overseer who had the reputation of being a slavebreaker. After suffering
repeated physical abuse from Covey, Douglass ran away and hid in the
woods. While in hiding, he met up with a slave called Sandy Jenkins,
who gave him a root that he claimed had the power to protect him from
white men's violence. Jenkins instructed Douglass to keep the root in his
right pocket at all times. Douglass says he took the root only to please
Jenkins and was skeptical of its powers until "the virtue of the *root* was
fully tested" (297). The next time Covey attempted to whip him, he was
seized by a new resolution to fight and ended up beating the overseer
bloody. This is how Douglass records what happened:

> but at this moment—from whence came the spirit I don't know—
> I resolved to fight; and, suiting my action to the resolution, I seized
> Covey hard by the throat; and as I did so, I rose. He held on to me, and
> I to him. My resistance was so entirely unexpected, that Covey seemed
> taken all aback. He trembled like a leaf. . . . I felt as I never felt before.
> It was a glorious resurrection, from the tomb of slavery, to the heaven
> of freedom. My long-crushed spirit rose, cowardice departed, bold defi-
> ance took its place; and I now resolved that, however long I might re-
> main a slave in form, the day had passed forever when I could be a slave
> in fact. (298–99)

Critics explain Douglass's ability to thrash Covey and escape punishment for his deed as a moment that is equally constitutive of his identity
as the earlier episode in which he understands the power of literacy. In
fact, Douglass explicitly states that after having beaten the man responsible for breaking him "in body, soul, and spirit" (293), he was lifted
toward "the heaven of freedom."

   However, this episode is also structured by a silence. Unlike the
mystery of the book, which is revealed to both Douglass and the reader,

the source of his resolution to fight remains an enigma. In a footnote, Douglass lays to rest any suspicion that he might have believed in the power of the root by condemning the practice as a "superstition [that] is very common among the more ignorant slaves" (303). This disavowal might explain why most critics tend to downplay the importance of the root (see, for example, Baker 1984, 46–47).[1] Douglass cannot legitimate residual forms of knowledge, for the authority of his eyewitness account rests on his ability to demonstrate that he is an enlightened man. In his narrative there is no way to determine whether he believed in the power of the root, although one suspects that he did not.[2] The episode is none-theless present as the marker of an opposition to slavery that did not originate in the antislavery movement.

Douglass's statement that he was a slave in form but no longer in fact offers a counterintuitive understanding of factual evidence in which the fact is constituted not by what is spoken or seen but what remains unspoken and unseen. A consideration of what is unspoken or unseen presents the reader with the contradictory status of one who is and yet is not a slave. Douglass's sense of freedom is derived from an experience of self-empowerment rather than liberation as such.[3] The contradictory status of existing between freedom and bondage is of interest to this study and is to be placed alongside Linda Brent's assertion of having "something akin to freedom" as Sands's concubine. It offers an alterna-tive path to the narrative plotting of Prince's life story in *The History of Mary Prince,* where she appears as both a victim to be saved and an enlightened individual.

In order to address the life experiences that Prince could not speak or had to "forget," we must break down the opposition between the slave woman as speaking subject of the slave narrative and as "spoken for" object in the pro- and antislavery debates. The signs of her subjectivity appear across several documents, including the proslavery propaganda and courtroom cross-examination that were intended to discredit her. Prince's *History* demonstrates how an articulation of moral agency in the slave narrative screens those aspects of black women's culture that were in response (but not reducible) to the conditions of slavery. In drawing attention to the political demands of the antislavery movement that shaped Prince's narrative, I do not mean to suggest that she was merely an instrument of the abolitionists or that fugitive slaves were unable to disrupt the conventions of the genre. Nor do I negate her use of the testimony as a powerful tool for gaining a voice in a society in which black people were marginalized. Rather, I focus on the narrative restraints placed upon the slave woman who told her story in order to disclose the limits of an abolitionist discourse on freedom and thus to complicate an academic recovery of a black female voice.

THE MORAL IMPERATIVE OF SPEECH

The History of Mary Prince is the product of a unique set of circumstances having to do with the role British abolitionists played in transmitting the stories of black slaves. Prince belonged to a privileged group of household slaves who had the opportunity to travel to England, where in theory (if not always in practice) they were free. In 1828 she accompanied her owners, Mr. and Mrs. Wood, on a trip from Antigua to England to serve as a nursemaid for their child. She reports in her narrative that, after several disputes involving her refusal to do heavy laundry, Mr. Wood threatened to send her back to Antigua, have her incarcerated, or turn her out of the house. Prince told him that her own desire was to return to Antigua, but only if she could be free. Wood responded by forcing her out of the house, saying that she could now see what it was like to experience freedom.

That liberty could be used as a threat against slaves who traveled to England is evident in the testimony of another domestic slave, known only as Polly, who accompanied her owner from Trinidad in 1827. A Quaker woman who interviewed her reports that "she knew she was thought free in England, but she thought she was more a slave than in the West Indies, as she had none of her acquaintance to speak to" (quoted in Midgley 1992, 91). This statement shows the importance of community in maintaining some semblance of freedom within slavery. Prince expresses a similar sentiment when she says, "I knew that I was free in England, but I did not know where to go, or how to get my living; and therefore, I did not like to leave the house" (210). The predicament of runaways shows that the line between slavery and freedom was not clearly defined. There was no question of a slave woman simply choosing freedom if she had no means of supporting herself. Nor could she turn for help to London's free black community, which, consisting primarily of servants, street entertainers, and beggars, was small and relatively powerless. When Prince decided to leave her owners, Wood ruined any chances she might have of securing another domestic position. He stated in her reference papers that he was letting her go because "she [did] not evince a disposition to make herself useful." He was also careful to note that she requested to accompany him to England and was "at liberty to . . . go where she pleases" (Prince 1987, 217). Having nowhere to go, Prince claims she appealed to Mash, a shoeblack in the Wood household, whose wife secured her a position as a charwoman. She was eventually able to obtain references from a Mrs. Forsyth who, having visited the West Indies, "was accustomed to Blacks" (213).

In the meantime, Prince was in contact with the Anti-Slavery Society, whose secretary, Thomas Pringle, petitioned Parliament for her right to return to Antigua a free woman (reprinted in Ferguson 1987, 116–17). Pringle decided to use her case to challenge the ruling made the previous year in the Grace Jones case. Jones was a domestic slave who traveled with her owners to England in 1822 and was returned to Antigua the following year, possibly against her will. In response to complaints by abolitionists, custom officials seized her on her arrival at Antigua, declaring her reenslavement to be illegal. However, the Vice-Admiralty Court of Antigua ruled that Jones was still a slave, and Lord Stowell upheld its verdict in the High Court of Admiralty in England. Stowell decreed that the slave who walks free in England "goes back to a place where slavery awaits him, and where experience has taught him that slavery is not to be avoided" (cited by Goveia 1980, 155). The ruling dealt a particularly severe blow to the antislavery cause. What did it mean to say that slaves had the right to freedom in England so long as it did not conflict with their masters' right of ownership in the West Indies? Abolitionists hoped to resolve this contradiction by submitting a series of parliamentary petitions on behalf of runaway slaves. Mary Prince's was one of the more publicized cases. When its petition on her behalf failed, the Anti-Slavery Society offered her owner, John Wood, money for her manumission. He refused to sell her, claiming that she was too immoral a woman to be allowed to go free. The Woods left for Antigua without Prince in December 1829, at which time Pringle began employing her as a domestic servant. She was legally a slave until slavery was ended in Britain's overseas colonies in 1834.

Moira Ferguson, who is responsible for the republication of *The History of Mary Prince* and has done an excellent job of documenting its narrator's life, was unable to discover what happened to Prince after the publication of her narrative. The postscript to the second edition indicates that her health was failing, and she was going blind (Ferguson 1987, 118). Prince vanishes from the official records after February 27, 1831, when she appeared as a witness in a libel suit Wood filed against Pringle. Her sudden disappearance from the archives is a reminder of the highly mediated nature of her story.

As Pringle explains in his preface, the twenty-three-page story was recorded "from Mary's own lips" by a friend of his, Susan Strickland, and later "pruned" of redundancies and grammatical errors "so as to render it clearly intelligible" (Prince 1987, 185). Like the author's dedication to *Joanna, or the Female Slave; A West Indian Tale,* his statement deauthorizes the speaker in the very act of authorizing the written record of her words. Prince probably spoke patois, the creolized speech of slaves that combined English, Spanish, French, and West African languages. The need to render her story into standard English is a comment on the perceived inferiority and unintelligibility of her speech.[4] The shift in authority from slave woman to text is also enacted through the extensive footnotes in which Pringle elaborates upon what she says and a supplement in which he defends her character. The documentation that generally accompanied slave narratives—photographs to establish the existence of narrators, letters to reconfirm the truth of what was being said, prefaces to assure readers that the accounts were unembellished—shows that the authority of the fugitive slave was not presumed but had to be proved. Prince's authority was even more precarious not only because, as a woman, she was considered an unreliable witness but also because, as a black woman, she had to overcome the sexual stereotyping deployed by her owner. An indication of the precariousness of her authority can be seen in the attitude of the Birmingham Ladies' Society for Relief of Negro Slaves, which agreed to raise money for her defense fund only after verifying the whip marks on her back (Midgley 1992, 91).

Framed by the political demands of the emancipation campaign and the evangelical views of abolitionists, Prince's testimony exhibits many of the literary conventions designed to establish the authenticity of the account and to elicit pity and sympathy from its readers. It opens with Prince explaining that she was born into slavery in Bermuda. Her master died while she was still an infant, and she was purchased, along with her mother, as a gift for a little girl, Miss Betsey Williams. She says that she was ignorant of her enslaved condition at the time because of the kindness of Miss Betsey's mother. This opening convention, which follows the biblical plotting of an Edenic existence before the Fall, establishes black slaves as God's children created in a state of innocence. Equally important is a need to depict benevolent slaveholders, usually a mistress, in order to demonstrate that they are not inherently cruel; rather, it is the system of slavery that corrupts them. The existence of a kind mistress also reassures readers that slaves are loyal and obedient workers so long as they are treated well. As Prince states: "My obedience to her [Mrs. Williams's] commands was cheerfully given: it sprung solely from the affection I felt for her, and not from fear of the power which the white people's law had given her over me" (188). Being contingent upon the owner's good will, any happiness within slavery is precarious. With the death of Mrs. Williams, Prince and her sister are sold to different masters, thus being separated from each other and the rest of their family. Her sale marks the beginning of her descent into "the horrors of slavery" (200). Prince's description of the dissolution of her family follows yet another convention designed to create sympathy in middle-class English women for the female slave.

As a black woman, Prince was less likely to be employed in the household, since domestic positions were usually held by racially mixed slaves. However, on small plantations like the one owned by her third master, Captain I——, there was no division of labor between field and domestic slaves. In addition to her domestic duties of cooking, cleaning, and caring for the children, Prince had to tend to the animals and pick cotton. Very early in the narrative Captain I—— flogs a pregnant slave Hetty to death because a cow got loose from the stake to which she had tied it. This episode exhibits yet another convention of the slave narrative. An initial description of a slave (usually a woman) being brutally beaten establishes the narrator as a reliable eyewitness and prepares the reader for the narrator's own abuse (see Figure 12). After Hetty's death, Prince assumes her duties and ill-treatment. Like her predecessor, she is punished for wrongdoings for which she is not responsible, such as "breaking" a jar that is already cracked and "letting" a cow get loose from its stake. The captain's wife is a "savage mistress" who makes her slave "know the exact difference between the smart of the rope, the cart-whip, and the cow-skin" (194). The knowledge Prince possesses at this stage of her life is the pain of suffering and the violent death that awaits her.

After five years of working for Captain I——, Prince is sold to an even more vicious master, Mr. D—— of Turks Islands in the Bahamas.

Figure 12. *Flagellation of a Female Samboe Slave* from Stedman's *Narrative of a Five Years' Expedition against the Revolted Negroes of Surinam* (1796). In defiance of the West Indian perception of Sambos as a racial downgrading, Stedman characterizes the subject of this engraving as "a truly beautiful Samboe girl." The similarity between this image and the abolitionist cartoon of Figure 11 suggests an underlying convention for depicting the cruel treatment of slave women. Courtesy of Special Collections and Archives, University of California at Irvine Libraries.

He sets her to work in his salt ponds—a job that involved standing in shallow lagoons of seawater and raking the evaporating crystals to the shore. The sun reflecting off the salt was blinding to the eye and blistering to the exposed skin. Prince describes how her feet and legs were covered in boils from standing in the salt water all day. The ten years she spent working in the salt ponds may well have been the source of the rheumatism that would cripple her later in life. Prince says she was relieved from the crippling work only after Mr. D—— retired to Bermuda and took her with him to care for his daughters. His real motivation for moving her from the salt ponds and into his home was probably sexual in nature. However, his sexual appropriation of her is possible to discern only through her expression of the disgust and shame she felt at having to wash his naked body (Ferguson 1987, 9–10).

There are other silences in this part of Prince's story. Her narrative gives no indication of the higher incidence of slaves running away from the salt-producing Turks and Caicos Islands.[5] Evidence of slaves escaping the harsh conditions on the island would unravel the thread of a story that ties their sorrowful lives to the English. The intimate knowledge Prince has about slavery is conveyed to her readers so as to rouse them into action: "I have been a slave—I have felt what a slave feels, and I know what a slave knows; and I would have all the good people in England to know it too, that they may break our chains, and set us free" (Prince 1987 [1831], 200). Her statement conforms to a logic that locates the agency for social change in England. The conventions of the slave testimony considered thus far position Prince as a victim to be saved.

However, a parallel narrative of emancipation, beginning with her religious conversion and ending with her appeal to English people, runs throughout her life story. Prince claims to have had no knowledge of God until after the age of twenty-five, when she was purchased by her fifth and final owner, Mr. John Wood of Antigua. While working in his country home during Christmas, she attended a Methodist prayer meeting that, she says, left a lasting impression on her. Prince's religious conversion is a turning point in her life as it gives her access to a free black community. It is through the Moravian Society that she meets her future husband, Daniel James, described as "an honest, hard-working, decent black man" who earned the purchase price of his freedom and encourages her to do the same (207). It is also after her conversion to Christianity that she is first able to articulate her desire for freedom, when she expresses to Mrs. Wood that "to be free is very sweet" (208). Moravian missionaries did provide slaves with a language for expressing the desire for emancipation as a human right; however, the liberation they offered was a contradictory one. Missionaries did not condone the violence of rebellion, emphasizing instead obedience, diligence, loyalty, submission, and the belief that God will provide (Goveia 1980, 272–85).[6] Prince demonstrates these virtues throughout her narrative, while also indicating that she does not have complete faith in the Christian maxim that God will provide. She reports that, despite her minister's advice for her to open her heart to God, she "find[s] it a hard and heavy task to do so" (Prince 1987 [1831], 214).[7]

Narrative ruptures of this sort allow critics to identify a black female subjectivity that is distinct and separate from the abolitionist presentation of Prince's life. Helen M. Cooper reads the testimony for the effect it had on its English audience, arguing that Prince reverses their ethnocentric gaze, claiming for herself the moral decency belonging to the English through observations of her master's bestiality (1996, 200–202). Sandra Pouchet Paquet gives evidence of a black vernacular that Pringle's "pruning" failed to efface. Arguing that Prince maintained authorial control over her narrative, she concludes that "through her distinct voice, the slave narrative as evidence of victimization and document of legal history, is transformed into a triumphant narrative of emergent West Indian subjectivity in the gendered space of a black woman and a slave" (Paquet 1992, 131). The subjectivity Paquet identifies is that of a political activist, a black woman who spoke on behalf of not simply herself but also a community of slaves. She charts this activism throughout Prince's life, beginning with an incident in which the domestic slave attempts to stop her master from beating his daughter. The man in question is Prince's fourth owner, Mr. D—— of Turks Islands, and the incident occurs after they move to Bermuda. When he starts to whip her instead, she reminds him that he cannot treat her so cruelly as they are no longer on Turks Island. Prince reprimands Mr. D—— yet again when he gives her a particularly severe beating for breaking some plates. This is how the episode appears in *The History of Mary Prince:* "He struck me so severely for this, that at last I defended myself, for I thought it was high time to do so. I then told him I would not live longer with him, for he was a very indecent man—very spiteful, and too indecent; with no shame for his servants, no shame for his own flesh" (202–3). Alluding to this passage, Paquet identifies the position from which Prince speaks as "the high moral ground" (139) of one who opposes the base values of slaveholders. Prince's testimony shows the slave woman speaking out against the cruelty of her owners on at least two more occasions: when she tells Captain I—— that she ran away to her mother because she was unable to stand the floggings, and when she accuses Mrs. Wood of not caring whether she lived or died. Each time she speaks up she is not beaten. And when she tells Mr. D—— she can no longer work for so indecent a man, he hires her out to another household.

But let us examine such instances of voice-agency more closely. As much as Prince's scolding of Mr. D—— shows a slave woman standing up to her master, one has to wonder whether morally upright speech could prevent a lashing from so ruthless a man. The episode has the narrative effect, however, of proving that a moral high ground can control the slaveholder's abuse of power. In doing so, it renders less morally upright forms of self-defense, such as verbal abuse or acts of insubordination, inappropriate as responses to slavery. The antislavery requirement to demonstrate that Prince was a decent and hardworking Christian woman cannot accommodate less ennobling forms of protest or escape. Because she treats the as-told-to story of Mary Prince as the expression of a black female consciousness, Paquet accepts at face value its emphasis on honesty, industry, decency, and propriety. However, these virtues are more a projection of the kind of slave women Prince's antislavery readers wanted to see.

In *Subject to Others,* a study of the civilizing discourse in British women's antislavery literature, Ferguson is more aware of the restraints suffered by the slave woman who told her story to abolitionists (1992, 281–98). She argues that "weighty silences" alone speak the sexual practices Prince was not allowed to name. However, she also indicates that Prince surreptitiously admits evidence of her sexual abuse at the hands of Mr. D—— and her relationship with Captain Abbot through veiled references that invite one to read between the lines. Calling *The History of Mary Prince* a "double-voiced discourse," Ferguson shows how its narrator negotiates Pringle's effort to shape the meaning of her words. On the basis of such negotiations, she asserts that "Mary Prince claims herself as a speaking, acting, thinking subject with an identity separate from Anglo-Africanist constructions of her past and present reality" (282). Like Paquet, Ferguson locates an autonomous black female subjec-

tivity in the control Prince exercises over the telling of her story. By
equating agency with the autobiographical act, however, this position
interprets the life experiences of the slave woman from the perspective
of the fugitive slave. In this manner, it follows the logic of an abolitionist discourse that anticipates the free and enlightened ex-slave in the
consciousness of the slave. Hence, Prince is shown "acting" in the West
Indies only inasmuch as her action prefigures her escape to freedom. For
example, Ferguson explains Prince's religious conversion as a strategy
that guaranteed the aid of Moravians on the trip over to England and
gave her the courage to contact the Anti-Slavery Society in London (1992,
285, 291). Yet, as we have already seen in Douglass's *Narrative,* there were
discourses of self-empowerment and freedom that did not originate in
Christianity.

In her poem "mary prince bermuda. turks island. antigua. 1787"
(1992), Gale Jackson presents a slave narrator whose thoughts of freedom
do not arise from Christian doctrines but rather, the stories of rebellion
that circulated among slaves.[8] Like the slave narrative on which it is
based, the poem begins by enumerating the sorrowful events in Prince's
life. In *The History of Mary Prince,* a community of slaves is established
through their shared suffering. "In telling my own sorrows," declares
Prince, "I cannot pass by those of my fellow-slaves—for when I think of
my own griefs, I remember theirs" (201). In Jackson's imaginative retelling, this community is established through the stories of rebellion and
escape that slaves whisper to each:

> from haiti we heard past the mask of silence
> in haiti they built black armies burned the slave
> fields killed the masters black revolt
> [. . .]
> . . . i heard
> lula burned at the stake for making poison
> "oh mary"
> burned nat turner alive gabriel they hung
> then fired his remains but slaves swear
> they got away
> slaves swear they got away (Jackson 1992, 7)

Word of the free black republic of Haiti, about which abolitionists
and missionaries are silent, reaches Prince, as does news of less successful

rebellions and individual acts of resistance. Since Nat Turner's rebellion occurred after Prince left the West Indies, the poem does not offer a faithful chronology of events in the past so much as remind contemporary readers of oral stories that exist outside the frame of reference of *The History of Mary Prince.* The stories Jackson imagines Prince to have heard belong to the memories of black slaves over whose prostrate bodies, to invoke Walter Benjamin, the triumphal march of history takes place. Although the rebels are burned to ashes, in the eyes of the slaves the absence of a body is evidence of their escape to freedom. Jackson's poem draws on the merging of fact (in its naming of historical persons and events) and fiction (in the power of the story to engender subsequent revolts) that exists in oral histories. By foregrounding the transmission of stories—what was heard and not simply what was spoken—the poem reminds us of the community of slaves to which Prince belonged in the West Indies and without which she was lost in England. This community was crucial to her ability to maintain some autonomy over her life even though she was a slave.

The vast majority of West Indian slave women do not appear as speaking subjects in the archives because their action did not lead them to the Anti-Slavery Society in London. Unlike the United States, where there existed an Underground Railroad and (until the Fugitive Slave Acts) the possibility for escape to the North, there was little or no way to escape from the islands. Nor could slaves escape to the free maroon communities once these self-governing townships had settled with the colonial government. Although some fugitive slaves attempted to pass for free coloreds, most ran away to force their masters into improving work conditions or selling them to owners of their choice (in many instances to be closer to family members) (Heuman 1986, 99–108). Prince herself ran away to her mother to escape being abused by Captain I——, knowing full well that she would be returned to him. The act of running away in the West Indies needs to be read as not only a quest for freedom but also a struggle for greater autonomy within slavery.

The narrative force accorded to moral speech in *The History of Mary Prince* encourages critics to overlook the more protracted and circuitous means by which Prince negotiated greater autonomy from her owners. The episode in which she chastises Mrs. Wood for not caring whether she lived or died does not end there. Mrs. Wood proceeds to complain to her husband, who does not whip Prince but instead gives her a note of sale and tells her to go look for another owner. Prince reports in her narrative that she did not mean to sell her but wanted to frighten her and to please his wife. Instead of being scared into submission, she returns with an offer from Adam White, a free black cooper or barrelmaker. Wood informs him that she is not for sale and flogs Prince the next day. This response, within the formal restraints of the slave narrative, can be understood only as yet another instance of the cruelty and ir-rationality of slaveholders. The incident is immediately followed by a similar sequence of events that occurred five years later. Prince tells Mrs. Wood she is too sick to work; Mrs. Wood complains to her husband, who in turn instructs Prince to look for another owner. This time a white cooper, Mr. Burchell, offers to buy her. Prince had given Burchell one hundred dollars to which he added his own money to make up the total purchase price. In exchange, she agreed to work for him for a limited time (Prince 1987, 208). Given the high price of manumission, limited-term contracts of this sort were the more likely path to freedom. Wood's response, however, was the same as before.

In addition to Adam White and Burchell, a second white man, Cap-tain Abbot, approached Wood about buying Prince. His relationship to her is not explained in the narrative, but it is presumed to be the same as Burchell's. Both monetary transactions are subsumed within a larger frame of the Protestant work ethic as the guiding light to free-dom. The following lines, in which Prince explains how she earned money through hard work and good market sense, follow quickly on the episodes describing the failure of White and Burchell to negotiate her manumission. Her higglering, that is, the buying and selling of goods at local slave markets, is cast in the more favorable light of honest work and good economic sense:

> I did not sit still idling during the absence of my owners; for I wanted, by all honest means, to earn money to buy my freedom. Sometimes I bought a hog cheap on board ship, and sold it for double the money on shore; and I also earned a good deal by selling coffee. By this means I by degrees acquired a little cash. A gentleman also lent me some to help to buy my freedom—but when I could not get free he got it back again. His name was Captain Abbot. (205)

What this account elides is that it was next to impossible for slave women to earn enough money to purchase their freedom, especially since they were not trained in the artisanal skills that allowed male slaves to hire themselves out. Higglering was one of the few occupations that gave slave women the mobility of male slaves who hired out their labor (Simmonds 1987, 32–33); the other was concubinage or prostitution (Bush 1990, 33–50; Handler 1974, 32–37).[9] Prince's purchase price was $300 (equivalent to £67.10s sterling), a sum not easy for her to raise. It is likely that she made an arrangement with Abbot to serve as his concubine in exchange for her purchase price. By suggesting that the money was a loan, the slave narrative excludes such negotiations as a legitimate means to manumission. As we will later see, much of the information Prince gave Strickland regarding her sexual connections with men was expunged from the published version of her *History.*

Inasmuch as Pringle imposes such silences on Prince's text, he effaces an unsavory aspect of slave culture that black women turned to their advantage. Yet he also assumes a position of authority by speaking on her behalf. In his supplement, Pringle alludes to the relationship with Captain Abbot about which Prince herself is forced to remain silent. In doing so, he offers the reader an explanation that acts in the place of her own. The explanation is provided by Joseph Phillips, an abolitionist living in Antigua, who wrote to Pringle as a character witness for Prince. Phillips confirmed that she was Abbot's concubine and that such relationships are commonplace in the West Indies:

> Of the immoral conduct ascribed to Molly [Mary Prince's slave name] by Mr. Wood, I can say nothing further than this—that I have heard she had at a former period (previous to her marriage) a connexion with a white person, a Capt.——, which I have no doubt was broken off when she became seriously impressed with religion. But, at any rate, such connexions are so common, I might almost say universal, in our slave colonies, that except by the missionaries and a few serious persons, they are considered, if faults at all, so very venial as scarcely to deserve the name of immorality. (Prince 1987, 227)

Despite Phillips's admission that Prince might not be as morally upright a woman as Pringle claims, the conversion narrative in Prince's *History* remains intact. According to the logic of his statement, she did not know she had sinned because her actions were condoned in the colonies; however, once she recognized herself as a sinner, she revoked her past life. Prince reinforces this explanation in her testimony when she confesses: "I never knew rightly that I had much sin till I went there [the missionary church]. When I found out that I was a great sinner, I was very sorely grieved, and very much frightened" (207). The evangelical demand that she see herself as "a great sinner" explains the sexual availability of slave women as their moral weakness. The abolitionist leader Thomas Cooper makes this clear in his response to the well-known "fact" that black women willingly entered into sexual relationships with white men because they perceived them as superior beings:

> I have been assured, on the best authority, that the White men are not more ready to connect themselves with Black or Brown women, than the latter are to receive their unlawful amours. Indeed, they are said to think it an honour to be thus employed. They regard the Whites as a superior species, and are, therefore, flattered by any attentions from them. Hence, in the estimation of their own community, that is to them an honour which, in a moral respect, ought to be viewed with abhorrence. But here, again, it may be fairly asked, whether they are not, in a great degree, objects of pity? Their ignorance must be taken into the account, and also, that it is quite out of their power to enter into the married state. Slavery sinks them beneath the condition of women, and to slavery a great part of their immoralities must be imputed. (Cooper 1824, 40)

Cooper wanted to shift the responsibility for black women's sexual misconduct to their enslaved condition. But he could do so only by turning them into objects of pity—namely, ignorant women who are the victims of slavery. In arguing that they "chose" concubinage with white men as a substitute for the marriage with black men that was denied them, he failed to question the motives given for the women's apparent willingness. Although Phillips's allusion to Prince as a sinner whose sins are pardonable is perhaps more generous than Cooper's statement, both statements presume the women's moral weakness, thereby reproducing the stereotyping of black women's sexual promiscuity.

By excising from Prince's testimony evidence of Mr. D——'s rape of his domestic slave and her relationship with Captain Abbot, Pringle placed two kinds of sexual practices under the single sign of an immorality that cannot be named. In this manner, he eliminated important differences between the white man's abuse of slave women and the slave woman's use of white men. Prince attached herself to free men as a way

of loosening the knot of control her owners had over her. I would include among these relations her marriage to the free black man, Daniel
James, whom she met seven years after ending her relationship with
Abbot. She kept her marriage a secret from the Woods for three or four
months, and they found out only because Burchell told them. In her
History, Prince reports that Mrs. Wood, on hearing Prince had married
a free man, had her whipped, saying that "she would not have nigger
men about the yards and premises, or allow a nigger man's clothes to
be washed in the same tub where hers were washed" (Prince 1987, 208).
Underlying the overt racism of Mrs. Wood's protest is the fear of a loss
of control over her domestic slave that her marriage to a free man represents. And there were other free men in Prince's life. Only one of them,
Captain Abbot, is mentioned in her narrative, and then simply as one
who lent her money that she returned when Wood refused to sell her. A
consideration of the tactics by which slaves negotiated greater autonomy
within a labor system that denied them self-autonomy allows us to
distinguish between the sexual appropriation of slave women and the
women's reappropriation of their presumed availability. Yet such tactics
are particularly difficult to detect in the slave narrative because they are
overwritten by, to use William L. Andrews's phrase, "the rhetoric of antislavery moral absolutism" (1993, 476).

THE SLAVE WOMAN'S SCANDALOUS TONGUE

In her *History*, Prince's voice-agency is linked to her sexuality inasmuch
as the truth of her testimony hinges on her abstinence from extramarital relations, forced or otherwise. This might explain why the proslavery lobby attempted to destroy her credibility through examples of
both her scandalous behavior and her abusive speech. An article in the
Bermuda Royal Gazette simply accuses her of prostitution ("The Anti-
Slavery Society" 1831), while James Macqueen, writing in *Blackwood's
Magazine* (1831), presents the picture of a foul-mouthed, contentious,
and dissolute slave who was deserving of the punishment awarded her.
Much of Macqueen's evidence against Prince relies on the testimony
of Martha Wilcox, a free mulatto woman whom the Woods hired as a
nursemaid. Prince characterizes her as "a saucy woman" who took pleasure in asserting her authority over slaves (204). According to Wilcox,
Prince's dissatisfaction stemmed from Wood's locking the yard at night
to prevent her from letting in strange men. This did not stop Prince,

she continues, for she would send a boy to steal the key from the master's bedroom. Wilcox concludes with the following indictment: "She took in washing and made money by it. She also made money *many, many* other ways by her badness; I mean, by allowing men to visit her, and by selling . . . to worthless men" (emphasis and ellipses in the original) (cited by Macqueen 1831, 749).

Macqueen produces another witness, a "respectable female," who claims that Prince was used to dressing "more like the mistress than the servant" and that "Molly's violence and scandalous language" drove her from the Woods' household, particularly since "she threatened to kill [the witness] more than once or twice" (749). In her *History,* Prince gives no indication of the superior attitude or violent language suggested by this report. Due to the feminine modesty demanded of her, she says that she could not even repeat the "ill-language" used by Mrs. Wood. One could dismiss Macqueen's evidence of Prince's insubordination as proslavery propaganda, except that West Indian slave women were notorious for "that powerful instrument of attack and defence, their tongue," which is the phrase used by a government official for justifying the flogging of female slaves (quoted in Mathurin 1975, 13). Harryette Mullen reminds us that verbal modesty offered little defense to women whose bodies were exposed on the auction block and made available for physical and sexual abuse. She argues that the sharp tongue of slave women returns the violence enacted against them (1992, 245).

A reading of Prince's voice-agency needs to consider the forms of speech capable of contending with the violence of slavery. Such a reading cannot be derived from *The History of Mary Prince* because of the antislavery requirement to prove that its narrator was a decent and docile slave. The picture of Mary Prince that emerges from a symptomatic reading of proslavery propaganda is an outspoken and resourceful woman who considered herself as something more than simply a slave. Wood's contention that she was a disreputable and dishonest woman represents his attempt to ensure that she knew her proper place. Prince's refusal to be subservient is evident in the name "Mary, the Princess of Wales," given to her in mockery of her superior attitude. Pringle restores Mary's paternal name to the published version of her testimony as a means of countering "the habitual contempt with which they [colonialists] regard the negro race" (Prince 1987, 207). Yet his attempt to endow Prince with dignity is a contradictory one, for it replaces the sign of self-pride with that of patriarchal authority.[10] Moreover, he appears to be in agreement with the proslavery assessment of her violent nature and superior airs, as he admits that her "defects" are a "somewhat violent and hasty temper, and a considerable share of natural pride and self-importance" (230).

Capitalizing on the contradictions between the eyewitness reports and what he calls "Mary's washing-tub tales," Macqueen blames Pringle for using the runaway slave to destroy the Woods' good name. Pringle subsequently sued the publisher of *Blackwood's Magazine* for libel and won. Wood followed with a countersuit against Pringle, who lost by default because he could not produce any witnesses from Antigua. Prince did appear in court as a witness for the defense; however, the judge must have agreed with Wood's solicitor that her testimony was "exaggerated" ("Wood v. Pringle" 1833). The evidence given by a female slave was thus treated as insignificant in what amounted to a legal battle between white men. Prince's court testimony does reveal something about the teleology of freedom in *The History of Mary Prince*.

When compared to the same report that appears in her *History*, Prince's court statement shows that she was a member of the Moravian Society *before* she started seeing Abbot and stopped attending their meetings once she started living with him. This chronology disrupts the narrative of religious conversion, which demands that she revoke the immorality of her past life:

> She knew a free man of the name of Oyskman, who made a fool of her by telling her he would make her free. She lived with him for some time, but afterwards discharged him. That was when she first went to Antigua, and Oyskman was the first man who came to court her. She parted from Captain Abbot on his killing a man on board one of the plaintiff's [Wood's] vessels. She had been a member of the Moravian Society, and discharged herself in consequence of her connexion with Captain Abbot. She was kept out of the class for seven weeks. She told all this to Miss Strickland when that lady took down her narrative. These statements were not in the narrative published by the defendant. ("Wood v. Pringle" 1833)

Since this information is elicited under cross-examination, one cannot take it at face value. But, then, is not *The History of Mary Prince* also the product of a cross-examination? Prince's court testimony cannot be considered any more true a statement than her *History*; rather, it can be used to disrupt the abolitionist discourse on slave women's extramarital relations.

Contrary to the assumption of abolitionists and planters alike—that black women are flattered by the attention of white men—here was a black woman who "discharged" one as soon as he fell into disfavor with her owner. This is not to suggest that Prince exercised a sexual autonomy over her body by ending her relationship with Abbot. Rather, we must question the use of a model of a self-determining agent for explaining power relations under slavery. To speak of the slave woman's sexual avail-ability in terms of her consent or coercion positions her as either the consort of white men or a body to be appropriated. Advocates of slavery concealed slave women's negotiations for power behind the stereotype of their sexual licentiousness. For abolitionists, the transformation of abused slaves into decent Christian women was contingent upon view-ing concubines as ignorant victims to be pitied. The pro- and antislavery arguments were governed by the same assumption that a good slave was one who was loyal rather than untrustworthy, humble as opposed to defiant, a hard worker and not one who shunned his or her duties. The two positions thus complement each other even though one was intend-ed to show Prince's sexual depravity and the other her decency.

The antislavery requirement to show that Prince was a morally up-right woman fails to contend with her status as a commodity that could be bought and sold. The assertion of her moral agency in her *History* is intended to negate her object-status as a slave. But, in doing so, this position extends to her the subjectivity of the free individual, thus creat-ing conditions that were impossible for her to fulfill. To consider slave women's immorality is to see that, by offering their bodies in exchange for money, they were reappropriating the place of their economic and sexual exploitation. This argument is not to be found in *The History of Mary Prince* or any of its supporting documents. It is available, however, in a slave song that J. B. Moreton recorded in his *Manners and Customs in the West India Islands* (1790).

The song, entitled "What Care I for Mam or Dad," opens with the singer establishing her identity as a black, not yellow (that is, racially mixed), slave woman, who like Prince (at least according to Macqueen's report) "willingly" engaged in prostitution (154–55). Through the asser-tion of this identity, the singer distinguishes black women, who were more likely to engage in sexual activity with simultaneous partners, from mulatto women, who were more desirable as secondary wives or serial partners. She also alludes to the possibility of her black paternity, thereby inserting the absent black man into a scene of interracial relations:

> Altho' a slave me is born and bred,
> My skin is black, not yellow:
> I often sold my maidenhead
> To many a handsome fellow. (154)

The singer's response to her status as a commodity is one in which she proves herself to be an astute seller who fetches the highest price for herself (rather than for her master) by making each man think he is the first. As Carolyn Cooper explains, "she may be a legal 'slave' but she is free nevertheless to exploit her status as commodity in the sexual marketplace" (1995, 29). This assessment points to the paradoxical subjectivity of a slave woman who gains control over her exploitation through self-exploitation rather than self-determination.

The song proceeds to describe the slave woman's life as one in which her secretive sexual practices are revealed through the color of her children's skin. The singer admits to having been kept by her master, who dressed her up in fineries to win her "sweet embraces." However, when her baby is born black, the master whips her, strips her of her fancy clothes, and sends her to work in the fields. She then becomes the sexual property of the overseer, who also gives her "gown and busses." This time her baby is born white, "almost as white as missess." When the mistress sees the light-skinned baby, she whips the slave woman because she thinks it belongs to her husband. He in turn calls his wife a "'lyin bitch!'/And tell her, 'buss my rassa!'" which is patois for "kiss my arse."

"What Care I for Mam or Dad" is a verbal attack on the master and mistress, a slave woman's way of getting back at them for having whipped her. When made to issue from the mouth of the white master, the denigrated language of slaves brings him down to their level. The singer also signifies on white women, for whom the color of their offspring was often the only evidence of their own sexual transgressions. Hence, the song not only alludes to how slave women had clandestine relations with black men while pretending to be faithful to their white keepers; it also disengages miscegenation from white men's relations with black women by introducing the interracial sexual relation that could not be named—that of white women with black men.[11]

This slave song confirmed for the unsympathetic Victorian that female slaves were not decent Christian women but crude and oversexed. Michael Scott's fictional travelogue, *Tom Cringle's Log,* alludes to an early nineteenth-century version of the song as a "vulgar Port Royal ditty" (179). For abolitionists, on the other hand, the song was evidence of the master's tyrannical power over slave women. Moreton remarks that "it is pity that there is not some law to protect them [slave women] from abuses so tyrannic, cruel and abominable" (155). The terms of the slavery debates thus establish an either/or opposition that prevents an exploration of other narrative possibilities.

There is yet another understanding of the song, one that is likely to have been recognizable to the slave women who sang it and, as such, is a form of subaltern knowledge.[12] The singer reveals that, by virtue of her sexual availability, a slave woman is placed at greater risk of violence and subjected to the jealousy of both the master and his wife. She knows that she cannot escape punishment but in the song neither do her owners. Having stepped outside the bounds of decency by having her master abuse his wife, she ends by declaring her innocence from sin and, by extension, any part in disrespecting her owners:

> Me fum'd when me no condescend;
> Me fum'd too if me do it;
> Me no have no one for 'tand my friend,
> So me am for'cd to do it.

> Me know no law, me know no sin,
> Me is just what ebba them make me;
> This is the way dem bring me in;
> So God nor devil take me! (154–55)

Whereas Prince's testimony is underpinned by the fiction that the slave woman was indeed a subject under the law and hence accountable for her sins, this woman assumes a position outside of the law in order to proclaim her innocence.[13]

Being outside the law did not free slave women from the restrictions slavery placed on them. After all, for them to exist outside the law also meant that they were not protected by it, as is evident in the countless failed efforts of those who sought justice through a racially biased court system (Mathurin 1975, 17–18). But the song does assert a subjectivity in the act of negating one. The singer claims no agency—"So me am for'cd to do it"—and no identity—"Me is just what ebba them make me"—in order to gain "mastery" over her sexual exploitation and physical abuse. As Jean "Binta" Breeze declares about the idea of being a victim of the system: "My hand might be tied but my mouth free" (1994). By calling attention to how white people "make" the black woman into whatever they will, the singer declares a knowledge of how her identity is made to conform to a racial stereotype of which she is not the author. By virtue of her ability to identify the impossibility of self-representation, she asserts an identity that exceeds the one that has been made for her. A black female subjectivity exists through its differential relationship to a dominant discourse on black women, in terms of what the slave woman cannot declare herself to be rather than what she says she is. Yet, as a speech act, "What Care I for Mam or Dad" brings that which is not supposed to exist into being. As a means of disengaging Prince's subjectivity from her testimony, I want to introduce this vulgar, duplicitous, and immoral voice into a reading of *The History of Mary Prince*.

THE SEXED BODY OF THE SLAVE NARRATIVE

This chapter began with a description of the slave narrative as a screen memory in order to foreground the incidents in Prince's life that were forgotten or erased. A Freudian model of reading suggests that, by treating silences as productive of meaning, we can make manifest what is unspoken or unsaid. My explication of limited choice under slavery is derived from a symptomatic reading of Jacobs's *Incidents in the Life of a Slave Girl* and Douglass's *Narrative,* whose authors had greater narrative control over their writings. Due to the highly mediated nature of an astold-to story like *The History of Mary Prince,* even a symptomatic reading cannot deliver an alternative to the abolitionist plotting of freedom. For this, it is necessary to understand events in Prince's *History* as intersecting with (rather than opposing) evidence that appears in proslavery propaganda and her court testimony.

A model of reading the slave woman's subjectivity across different documents is available through the narrative structure of Caryl Phillips's *Cambridge.* His novel offers a unique opportunity to view the same event—the murder of an overseer—from a number of different perspectives, something that the archives rarely provide. A comparison of the same event across several documents allows a critic to identify what each one does or does not say. Their intersecting narratives offer a wider perspective on "what happened" even if, as fragments, they do not add up to a totality. As a means of creating similar conditions of overlapping narratives, I want to place *The History of Mary Prince* alongside her court testimony and the proslavery literature—but not in the interest of demonstrating the limited perspective of each document, as Phillips does in his novel. Rather, a more useful approach to the texts is available from writers whose critique of teleological narratives is rooted in an oral storytelling tradition.

Whereas Phillips suggests that there is nothing outside the written record, Olive Senior derives from oral storytelling a viable alternative to his postmodern perspective on the past. She integrates the great loops, digressions, and repetitions of oral storytelling into the short stories collected in *Arrival of the Snake-Woman* (1989), several of which address the problem of racial stereotyping and the restricted gender roles available to Caribbean women.[14] In doing so, she makes the life histories of marginal female characters emerge from the interstices of overlapping narratives that center on other, more prominent figures. Unlike an autobiographical model that privileges the narrating "I" or a Freudian model that focuses on textual silences, the one suggested by Senior's stories allows us to see how Prince's subjectivity cuts across seemingly incompatible documents in which she appears, not as a first-person narrator, but as "the woman Molly" and "she (witness)."

It is possible to map the intersecting narratives of a single event across three documents: *The History of Mary Prince,* Macqueen's article in *Blackwood's Magazine,* and Prince's court testimony. The incident was initially publicized by John Wood in a letter requesting the governor to refuse Prince's petition to return to Antigua a free woman. The letter alludes to his domestic slave's sexual connections with men as proof that her "moral character is very bad, as the police records will shew." Wood adds that "she would be a very troublesome character should she come here [to Antigua] without any restraint" (Prince 1987, 220). The implication of his use of the word *troublesome* is that Prince was a disreputable and dishonest woman and, as such, was socially unfit to be free. When asked whether slave women would work if flogging was prohibited, a planter also uses the word *troublesome* to describe them, saying, "I think it is likely they would become excessively troublesome; they are, generally speaking, much worse to manage than the men" (Parliamentary Papers 1831–32, 337). This statement places a different emphasis on the meaning of the word in Wood's claim; Prince is not a sexually depraved woman so much as an unmanageable slave.

Reprinting Wood's letter in his supplement to Prince's narrative, Pringle deletes the incident, declaring it to be "too indecent to appear in a publication likely to be perused by females" (Prince 1987, 220n). Macqueen, however, does not hesitate to publicize the incident, as reported to him by the mulatta nursemaid:

> A woman, named *Phibba,* came to lodge a complaint to Mrs Wood, that Molly had taken away, not her *"pig,"* but "her *husband,"* and she, Molly, in the presence of Mrs. Wood, and myself, fought the woman until she tore her down on the steps. The woman then took Molly before a magistrate *(Mr Dyett,)* where she was punished. (Macqueen 1831, 749)

Wilcox is alluding to an episode in *The History of Mary Prince* in which Prince describes how Mrs. Wood ordered her to be placed overnight in a barred cell for holding intractable slaves and flogged the next morning, all for quarreling with another slave woman over a pig. According to Wood and his proslavery allies, Prince was justifiably punished for stealing another woman's husband and behaving in an unruly manner. *The History of Mary Prince,* by contrast, represents her as being wrongly punished for claiming a pig that was rightly hers:

> I was also sent by Mrs. Wood to be put in the Cage one night, and was next morning flogged, by the magistrate's order, at her desire; and this all for a quarrel I had about a pig with another slave woman. I was flogged on my naked back on this occasion; although I was in no fault after all; for old Justice Dyett, when we came before him, said that I was in the right, and ordered the pig to be given to me. (Prince 1987, 204)

The emphasis here is on the innocence of the slave woman and the cruelty of her owners.

Prince's court testimony reveals that Macqueen's account conflates two separate incidents in which Prince appeared before the magistrate. She was brought before Justic Dyett by a woman she had "licked" after having discovered her in bed with Captain Abbot in the hut he shared with her.[15] The magistrate dismissed the other woman's complaint and told her that he would place her in the stocks if she ever told such stories again. The reference to a "husband" in Macqueen's report alludes to the woman's effort to replace Prince as Abbot's concubine rather than Prince's stealing another woman's spouse. Prince *was* flogged after appearing before Dyett, but on a different occasion involving a complaint over a pig.

A comparison of the two published versions with the one in the court testimony shows that in order to demonstrate Prince's innocence the antislavery pamphlet also renders her powerless:

> Witness [Mary Prince] had a pig given to her for some money which was owing to her by a woman. She complained of this mode of payment to Mrs. Wood. Mr. Wood was sent for, and he hit witness two knocks, and told the woman to take the witness before a magistrate. On going before the magistrate the woman stated that Mr. Wood would not let her rest until she had made a complaint. Mr. Wood's nephew, Mr. Judkins, attended for Mr. Wood before the magistrate, who dismissed the complaint, and witness was afterwards flogged with a cat-o'-nine-tails. She bled very much. The next morning she saw Mr. Wood, and begged him to sell her. She was afterwards taken before another magistrate, who decided in her favour. ("Wood v. Pringle" 1833)

In this version, the quarrel is not over a pig but money that was owed Prince. The punishment, which is ordered by Mr. Wood and not his wife, makes better sense in terms of what the transaction represents—namely, Prince's efforts to raise money for her purchase price. Wood makes the other slave woman register a formal complaint to ensure that Prince learns her rightful place. Despite Dyett's orders to have her whipped, Prince nonetheless seeks justice through the court system that ruled against her by making her owner bring the case before a different magistrate.

Why should Prince seek justice through a court system that did not recognize the legal rights of slaves? As Lucille Mathurin points out, slave women "established their nuisance value" (1975, 18) by bringing charges against their owners, particularly in response to their disregard of the amelioration laws. During the 1820s, appeal courts or councils of protection were instituted throughout the British West Indies for enforcing laws that banned the use of branding, restricted the amount of flogging (particularly of women), and established a minimum requirement for food, clothing, and holidays. Slaveholders generally ignored these laws, and the courts only loosely enforced them. Magistrates, who were slaveholders themselves or friends of the plantocracy, rarely made judgments in favor of those slaves who registered complaints. Mathurin reports that "in twenty-one cases of complaints in Port Royal in the 1820's which were lodged by women slaves against their owners, eighteen cases were thrown out as being 'trifling,' 'groundless,' 'false,' or 'malicious,' and the complainants were in a few instances discharged, the majority were punished" (1975, 17–18). The threat of punishment did not deter these slave women from appealing to the courts for justice, and their appeals might have empowered them in a more subtle way. When asked about the frequency of the rape of slave women on plantations, one witness reported in 1832 that "the overseer had stated that in former times such a thing was practicable; but that for the last 20 years it was impossible, and that no overseer dare to make such an attempt" (Parliamentary Papers 1831–32, 381). Although this statement overestimates slave women's ability to prevent their rape, it nonetheless indicates their use of the amelioration laws for challenging the overseer's authority.

Prince's case is unusual inasmuch as she did obtain justice through the court system—but only after she begged to be sold. Whenever Wood threatened to sell her, he was reminding her that, as his property, she could easily be sold if she should displease him. However, each time she returned with someone to purchase her, she transformed his will into hers through the statement that she wanted to be sold. She reversed his statement that she was a bad slave into one that commented on his cruelty as a master. For Wood to sell her then would confirm her version of events rather than his own. Prince's move is a tactic that draws on the power of the slaveholders to sell their slaves at will. We already saw her use this tactic when she brought Adam White, Mr. Burchell, and Captain Abbot forward to purchase her—except this time she, rather than her owner, initiated the sale.

A simple and linear plotting of the slave's quest for emancipation is inadequate for explaining negotiations through which Prince undermined her master's right of ownership by asserting her status as property. If we are to read *The History of Mary Prince* in the interest of the slave rather than the fugitive slave, then we must acknowledge the limitations of a subjectivity based on notions of self-autonomy and/or free will. It is not simply a question of presenting all of Prince's actions as evidence of her desire to be free. It may well be that she was meeting Wood's threats with one of her own. This would especially be the case if she did not have enough money for her purchase price. But the antislavery model of freedom cannot accommodate negotiations for power within slavery, which might explain why Prince may have withheld from her *History* evidence that Wood did on at least one occasion agree to sell her. As she confessed under cross-examination during the libel suit against Pringle: "Some years afterwards, when the plaintiff [Mr. Wood] was about to sell her, she went on her knees and entreated Mrs. Wood to persuade him not to sell her. She did not mention that fact to Miss Strickland" ("Wood v. Pringle" 1833).

Did Prince not want to be sold because it was not to a master of her own choosing? Or did she realize that she was better off with Wood than somebody else? The records do not yield an answer. What they do tell us is that she knew that the Anti-Slavery Society would not take her case if she had indicated to Miss Strickland that she "chose" to stay with her master. Having no choice at all, except that which belonged to the fiction of the free individual abolitionists extended to her, Prince was in a relatively powerless position. Elizabeth Sampson's admonition to Joanna in *Stedman and Joanna*—that she must belong to the abolitionists in England—can be extended to Prince as well. For this reason, *The History of Mary Prince* needs to be read as a testimony of the power relations between master and slave in the West Indies, on the one hand, and the West Indian slave woman and abolitionists in England on the other. Prince's censored story is not merely the result of Pringle's pruning; its silences are also self-imposed. Yet, to read such self-imposed silences simply as the sign of her narrative control halts an inquiry into relations of power under a coercive labor system like slavery and manifests a failure to see how its inequalities extended all the way across the Atlantic to England.

Afterword

In a city like Los Angeles, which is dominated by the Hollywood film industry, it is difficult to ignore the euphoria over the Oscars for best actor and best actress in leading roles both being awarded to African Americans for the first time in the history of the Academy of Motion Picture Arts and Science. Halle Berry's recognition for playing Leticia in *Monster's Ball* (2001) is undoubtedly an achievement of a sort, just as Hattie McDaniel's was for the supporting role of Mammy in *Gone with the Wind* (1939). Yet the stereotyping of black women in both roles—despite the actresses' efforts to inject some dignity into their characters—is still another indication of how the more things change, the more they remain the same.

Monster's Ball does not lament the fall of the Old South, as did *Gone with the Wind,* but rather it confronts the entrenchment of Southern racism long after the end of segregation. Who cannot help but cringe when Buck Grotowski, a corrections officer and family patriarch so excellently played by Peter Boyle, unleashes one of his racist diatribes against a couple of black children who dare to venture on his property to visit his grandson, Sonny? The film positions the viewer to see racial hatred in all its ugliness. Hence, we sympathize with Sonny when he kills himself in protest of the sustained physical and verbal abuse he suffers at the hands of his father, Hank. And we applaud Hank (who provokes Sonny into shooting himself) for eventually rejecting the misogyny and bigotry on which he was bred.

What makes *Monster's Ball*'s critical stance on racial and patriarchal violence difficult to endorse is that its story of a white man's spiritual redemption is enacted through the body of a black woman. A pivotal moment in the film's plot is when Leticia graphically gives herself to Hank by pulling down her tank top and offering him her exposed breast. The relationship that is born of their mutual desire and compassion forces him to overcome his racism and contempt for women. Salman Rushdie's observation that "every story one chooses to tell is a kind of censorship, it prevents the telling of other tales" (1984, 72–73) prompts the question: What other kinds of stories about black women does this one censor?

The audience is introduced to Leticia as the wife of a black man who is on death row in rural Georgia. After witnessing his brutal execution, we see her life reach a crisis point as she proceeds to have a string of bad luck. She is served with an eviction notice, her car breaks down, and she is fired from her job as a waitress for coming late to work. Although she practically reaches the end of her rope when her son is run over by a car and killed, she manages to find relief from her misery and despair in a relationship with Hank, who assists her at the scene of the hit-and-run accident. Little does she know that, like his father before him, he works as a corrections officer on death row. Nor is she aware that the white man with whom she initiates a sexual relationship was involved in executing her husband. The scene of their first sexual encounter is explicitly staged to reverse a prior scene in which Hank engages in impersonal sex with a white prostitute whom he can approach only from behind. When he looks up at Leticia's face while she straddles him, it is clear that she occupies the dominant position. Yet the scene is also voyeuristically shot—from a hidden camera positioned as "peeping tom"—to establish the racially marked female body as a sexual object of desire.

The white male fantasy of the mixed-race woman as an object of desire is not an image resurrected from the past but one that is very much alive today. Angela Bassett all but stated this when she told *Newsweek* that she had turned down the role of Leticia because "it's such a stereotype about black women and sexuality" (cited in Samuels 2002). Despite its acknowledgment that Bassett was criticizing the movie industry rather than Berry, the press chose to present her comment within the scenario of one black woman attacking another. The unwillingness of the popular press to reflect on the criticism being made denotes its inability to recognize the rootedness of the film's sexual fantasy in slavery. As one columnist confesses about Bassett's remark, "I just don't see what there was about this heartrending role that makes it a 'demeaning stereotype'" (Smith 2002).

Behind the image of Leticia offering herself to Hank flits the ghostly presence of Joanna. A little over two hundred years ago, Stedman cleansed himself of the guilt he felt over abandoning his slave wife by writing about an interracial relationship capable of overcoming the violence of slavery. *Monster's Ball* performs a similar purification ritual for the burden white America bears over its inability to rid itself of the racism that is the legacy of its slaveholding past. When Leticia learns that Hank was her husband's executioner, her discovery does not appear to affect their relationship. As the Swiss-born, American-trained director Marc Forster explains, "Confronting him (Billy Bob) that she knows he was the executioner of her husband will not change anything. The only way to move on and overcome is to forgive" (Schiller 2001). But where does the movie's ending leave black America? As a number of African American commentators have observed, Leticia is a distressed black woman who does not turn to her extended family, church, or community for comfort and assistance, but rather finds sexual and emotional relief in the arms of a racist stranger. And, instead of leaving Hank when she discovers the part he played in her husband's execution, she resigns herself to staying with him. In the movie's message of forgiveness, the burden of overcoming racism is hers alone. *Monster's Ball* may have exorcised some of the nation's demons, but the ghosts of slavery are with us still.

Notes

INTRODUCTION

1. Much of the effort to rewrite the historical records on slavery has come from writers living in what George Lamming calls the "external frontier" of the Caribbean: Britain, Canada, and the United States. Writers from within the English-speaking Caribbean address the problem of history in the legacy of slavery during the post-Emancipation period.

2. Ulla Haselstein, for example, is too quick to articulate Brent's agency in terms of a model of self-autonomy or "self-possession," which is the term she uses. This critical move leads her to the conclusion that "the model of relationship suggested here [Brent giving herself to Sands] is not the relation of master and slave but of two independent subjects engaged in a free exchange of gifts" (1998, 133).

3. Although de Certeau is addressing the popular consumption of culture in his study, I find his theoretical model helpful for explaining how slaves made use of a world that was not of their own making. For an earlier formulation of the argument I make here, see Sharpe (1995a, 46, 54n).

4. Although the pacified maroons were self-governing societies, they were still subject to the colonial government that ruled.

1. "THE REBELS OLD OBEAH WOMAN"

1. The first use of the word *maroon* is ascribed to *Sir Francis Drake Revived* (1628), where "Symerons" are described as "black people which about eighty years past fled from the Spanish their masters" (Beckwith 1929, 189). According to Edward Long in his *History of Jamaica* (1774), the word is derived from the Spanish for a young pig, *marráno,* to designate the skill of the fugitive slaves as hog-hunters. Bryan Edwards includes in his history an entry from a French

encyclopedia that attributes the term to *Simaran,* the Spanish for monkey, "par-cequ'ils se retiroient comme ces animaux aux fonds des bois et n'en sortoient que pour cueillir des fruits qui se trouvoient dans les lieux les plas voisins de leur retrait" [because they retreated like these animals to the depths of the jungles and lived off the fruit that they found there] (1807, 1:523n). The multiple sources of the naming of the maroons demonstrate the impreciseness of etymology as a science. It also shows how language is racially coded, as, perhaps with the exception of "hog-hunters," the origins of their name establishes an affinity between maroons and beasts.

2. *Journals of the Assembly of Jamaica,* 3:226, Jamaica, February 21, 1734, Public Records Office, London.

3. The military title of Colonel, which is a holdover from the early militant years, denotes Rowe's position as leader of the Accompong Town maroons.

4. Colonel Harris was leader of Moore Town until Nehemiah Sterling disputed his claim to leadership in 1973 ("Maroon Factions Clash" 1975).

5. Since they trace the beginnings of their community to a land patent awarding Nanny and her people 500 acres of land, the Moore Town maroons consider themselves her direct descendants.

6. Colonel Henry Rowe told the American folklorist Martha Warren Beckwith and Jesuit anthropologist Joseph J. Williams that Nanny turned her back to the soldiers and, stooping slightly, caught the bullets between her legs with her hands (Beckwith 1929, 192; Williams 1938, 398). He called the gesture "*Nantucompong,* Nanny takes her back to catch the balls" (cited in Williams 1938, 398). Jamaican historian Richard Hart claims that Rowe was "less inhibited" in describing the action to him (1985, 80).

7. The echoes of this gesture are evident in a version of the story that Colonel Harris told at a 1983 ceremony honoring Nanny: "This great Nanny, who after the signing of the Treaty caught the bullets. Of course so many people know the method that she used (makes gesture of lifting skirts) and she caught the bullets that were (interrupted by laughter). And she caught them, she caught them and returned them, whence they came" (1984, 20).

8. Tacky, an obeah man and leader of a major Jamaican slave revolt in 1760, was also known to be a bullet catcher. Long records that slaves claimed Tacky "caught all the bullets fired at him in his hand, and hurled them back with destruction to his foes" (1774, 2:451).

9. In *The Maroon Story,* which is published by a maroon press, Beverly Carey draws on her personal knowledge of maroon oral history (passed down by family historians) and extensive interviews with maroons to give a unique perspective on the colonial archives. I have found her book to be an invaluable source.

10. A notable exception is Richard Hart's "Cudjoe and the First Maroon War in Jamaica," which used the oral tradition to establish Nanny's importance

as "a leader of great bravery and ability" a full twelve years before Jamaica's independence (1950, 54).

11. Even Naipaul admires the rebellious spirit of the maroons, acknowledging that the maroon "remembered his African skills of carving, song and dance; he remembered his African religion" (1962, 185).

12. The title of "Grandee," which is derived from the Jamaican patois for "grandmother," is used as a term of endearment and respect and for establishing familial ties to Nanny.

13. At the groundbreaking ceremony for a memorial at Nanny's Moore Town grave, known as Bump Grave, Beverley Manley, wife of Michael Manley, called on Jamaican women "to take their inspiration from the Maroon Queen, Nanny, and to remain in the forefront of the struggles against domination and oppression and to seek social and economic justice for all Jamaican people" ("A Maroon Celebration" 1976).

14. Agnes Akosua Aidoo (1981) notes that the "fighting queen mothers" were postmenopausal and thus able to circumvent the ritual disqualification of women from military activity. In addition, the political role of the *ohemaa* was expanded during times when the male leadership was in crisis.

15. See Cooper 1994 for a reading of Reid as griot.

16. Carey suggests that the original maroon societies contained influences from a wide range of African and even Amerindian traditions that may have been supplanted by an Asante tradition after 1740, when the settlements were stabilized (1997, 61–63, 213–32). Maroons have long claimed that they were of Amerindian descent, a claim that was discredited because it was believed that the Spaniards had exterminated the indigenous people long before African slaves were brought to Jamaica. Yet a 1993 excavation of Nanny Town revealed it to have been built on top of an Amerindian settlement that predates it. The archaeological find suggests to E. Kofi Agorsah that a few Arawak communities may have survived, hidden and unknown to the British, and provided shelter for the African slaves who escaped to the mountains (1994).

17. Richard Price notices that at the beginning of the eighteenth century maroon leaders only very rarely claimed princely descent from Africa, tending instead to style themselves captains, governors, or colonels rather than kings (1973, 20).

18. *Journals of the Assembly of Jamaica,* 3:121, Jamaica, March 29, 1733, Public Records Office, London.

19. Ayscough to Board of Trade, with enclosures. C.O. 137/21, folio 207. Public Records Office, London. Brathwaite indicates that Nanny is further marginalized in the printed edition of the Colonial Office Papers, where the transcriber replaced "put to death by Nanny" with "put to death by hanging" (1994, 124–25).

20. "The further Examination of Sarra alias Ned taken by order of His

Excellency," October 1, 1733, C.O. 137/21, folio 42, Public Records Office, London.

21. The American anthropologist Barbara Kopytoff, for example, explains that colonial officials had a history of showing a preference for autocratic leaders and, in the absence of one existing among the windward maroons, probably chose the person who most suited their purposes (1976, 76–78). This may have been the case, as Quao is not mentioned as a leader prior to the signing of the treaty. Thicknesse, thankful that Quao was a former plantation slave who was used to dealing with the British, describes him as a "reasonable man" who spoke "tolerable good English" (1790, 75).

22. According to Major Aarons, "certain archives of the British say Nanny was transported herself from Africa with her slaves" (cited by Gottlieb 1994, 84). Some oral histories claim that all of the leaders in the first maroon war did not come over as slaves but were royalty who were banished to Jamaica. It is even suggested that they were sent from Africa to lead the revolt (Carey 1997, 155).

23. Planters did not take obeah seriously until they discovered that the slaves who had participated in Tacky's rebellion had taken religious oaths (Turner 1982, 57). As a result, laws prohibiting the practice of obeah were passed.

24. It is of some significance to the perspective of their work that both of these writers have an ambivalent relationship to the Jamaican nation. As a light-skinned, mixed-race woman who grew up socially white and came of age during the early period of national independence, Ford-Smith identifies herself as Jamaican, but one who is perceived as being "not the popular color" (Ford-Smith 1997, 215). Condé, who is from Guadeloupe and whose work belongs to the Francophone tradition, decided to write about Nanny after spending some time in Jamaica, where she visited maroon country. "I bent over the grave of Nanny of the Maroons and walked down small, almost impassable paths that had been closely guarded by the maroons," she explains. "History is still present there" (Pfaff 1996, 56).

25. Breeze explained that she performs the poem "Nanny" to a mento rhythm and uses Kumina drumming for its refrain (a conversation with the poet in November 2001). Mento, which emerged in the 1930s and 1940s, is one of the earliest styles to develop from Jamaican folk music, while Kumina is a religious music of spirit possession.

26. I am grateful to the play's artistic director, Jean Small, for providing me with its script.

27. For the oral histories on which Equiano's account of the battle was potentially based, see Acholonu 1989, 31–32. Although Equiano's contemporaries criticized his description of life in Igboland for its inaccuracies, Paul Edwards observes that, since he left Africa when he was a child, his memory would be faulty and he probably integrated information he got from discussions with other Africans (1988, ix). Equiano also references two well-known travel books

by British abolitionists to corroborate his description of life in Africa, which demonstrates the greater authority of the European traveler as eyewitness over the African inhabitant. These books could have also have served as the sources for Equiano's description of customs in Igboland. Vincent Carretta, noting that the existence of a baptism record identifying a Gustavus Vassa (which is the name Equiano used throughout his life) who was born in Carolina, introduces the possibility that his African identity was a rhetorical invention (1999).

28. Riland was born in 1778, well before the end of the slave trade in 1807, which would explain why Mahali would be African-born.

29. Clare's family name, Savage, is an ironic reversal of colonial representations of maroon savagery. The name belongs to her white ancestor, Judge Savage, who set fire to his slave quarters on the eve of emancipation because he did not want to see his slaves freed.

30. The term *amazon* comes from the Greek, meaning "without a breast." It was believed that the right breast was removed in order to divert blood to the right arm to strengthen it and to make it easier for the women to handle weapons (Alpern 1993, 4). The association of the Amazons with the all-female colony on Lesbos might explain why the Victorian traveler Richard Burton suspected that the all-female army of the king of Dahomey engaged in same-sex relations (Law 1993, 256).

31. The ritual is based on a Jamaican prenuptial ceremony described by Zora Neale Hurston in *Tell My Horse,* a work that is mentioned in *Abeng* and cited as a source (Cliff 1984, 86).

32. For discussions of homophobia in Jamaica, see Chin 1997 and Glave 1999.

33. *Viva Zapata!* (1952) is an American film (with a screenplay by John Steinbeck) about the Mexican revolutionary hero Emiliano Zapata, while *Burn!* (1969) is a Franco-Italian film about a slave rebellion on the fictitious Antillean island of Quemada in the 1830s. Both films star Marlon Brando.

34. The name is probably an ironic reference to the American painter George Fuller, know for his painting *The Quadroon.*

2. "AN INCOMPARABLE NURSE"

1. During the 1760s, the Dutch government negotiated peace treaties with the Ndjuka, the Saramaka, and the Matawai tribes, which came to be known as the pacified Bush Negroes. However, it was unable to prevent new groups of maroons from being formed. Since Surinam was not an island, it was possible for runaways to retreat deeper into bush country to avoid pursuit. Although the bands of rebellious slaves were small, their wars came at a time when the plantations were suffering the effects of overextended mortgages and high absenteeism. The maroon wars threatened to touch off a full-scale insurrection of Surinam's 50,000 slaves, who greatly outnumbered its 4,000 European inhabitants (Hoogbergen 1990).

2. The Johnson edition of Stedman's *Narrative* served as the definitive version until 1988, when Richard Price and Sally Price published a new edition based on the 1790 manuscript. As the Prices explain, the Johnson edition made significant changes to Stedman's manuscript, in many instances altering its intent and purpose. All further references to Stedman's *Narrative* are to the Price and Price edition unless otherwise noted.

3. Brathwaite attributes the poem to Reverend Isaac Teale, although he does not cite his source (1971, 179).

4. For a history of the mulatto woman as an object of desire, see Mohammed 2000.

5. Mary Seacole, who identifies herself as a "yellow doctress" in her travel book, *Wonderful Adventures of Mrs. Seacole in Many Lands* (1857), was perhaps the first woman to confer middle-class respectability on the folk healing traditionally performed by concubines. It is likely that she inherited this tradition from her mother, as she claims that her father was Scottish and her mother ran a boarding house. It is well documented that free colored women had a relative monopoly on boarding houses which their white lovers established for them (Kerr 1995, 198). Sandra Gunning argues that the respectability of Seacole's doctoring was contingent on her leaving the West Indies, where it would be more strongly associated with concubinage.

6. Price and Price 1988, 87–88. The editor of the Johnson edition of Stedman's *Narrative* deleted the comparison of Joanna with a "goddess" and replaced "olive complexion" with "the darkness of her complexion" (Stedman 1806, 1:52).

7. A similar tropological construction of a racialized Other who is explicitly not Negroid can be detected in the description of the Amerindian Friday that appears in Daniel Defoe's *Robinson Crusoe* (1719): "He [Friday] was a comely handsome Fellow, perfectly well made; with straight strong Limbs, not too large; tall and well shap'd, and as I reckon, about twenty six Years of Age. He had a very good Countenance, not a fierce and surly Aspect; but seem'd to have something very manly in his Face, and yet he had all the Sweetness and Softness of an *European* in his Countenance too, especially when he smil'd. His Hair was long and black, not curl'd like Wool; his Forehead very high, and large, and a great Vivacity and sparkling Sharpness in his Eyes. The Colour of his Skin was not quite black, but very tawny. . . . His Face was round, and plump; his Nose small, not flat like the Negroes, a very good Mouth, thin Lips, and his fine Teeth well set, and white as Ivory" (Defoe 1975, 160).

8. My reading of Holloway's engraving of Joanna is greatly indebted to a conversation with Dian Kriz.

9. I am grateful to Carolyn Cooper for bringing this song to my attention.

10. Although the practice varied from one island to another, a secondary wife could usually dine at the table when she was alone with her husband but not when he was entertaining company (Stewart 1823, 328).

11. Concubinage was practiced less in Barbados, where a larger number of white women resided and slaves were encouraged to establish lasting conjugal relations (Ward 1988, 76).

12. The overestimation of the number of concubines and their children that were granted manumission contributes to the mystique of the power mulatto women were believed to have had over white men.

13. Orlando Patterson attributes the higher manumission rate for slave women to a culture in which the women maintained a position of dependency on white men and thus were less threatening than freed men (1967, 263–64).

14. A sambo is classified as being between a mulatto and negro, which suggests that Jolycoeur's father was African. Long draws up two charts of interracial mixing: one a line of ascent by which Negro blood could eventually be bred out, and the other a line of descent, where he places sambos (Figure N.1). Notice how it takes only two generations, as opposed to five on the other side, for a mulatta to regress back to a negro. Note also how the whites in his chart are identified as male, thereby negating the possibility for a mixed-raced child to be the offspring of a white woman (Long 1774, 2:260–61).

15. For the maroon oral histories documenting the existence of spies and even counterspies during this period, see Price (1983, 153–59).

16. The term *Creole* referred to the West-Indian or island-born people, both black and white. Since all slaves were Creole after the abolition of the British slave trade in 1807, the term was used primarily for white West Indians until after Emancipation, when it was adopted by the free colored population to distinguish themselves from emancipated slaves.

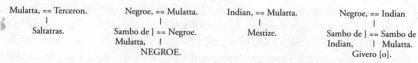

DIRECT lineal Ascent from the Negroe Venter.
White Man, == Negroe Woman.
White Man, == Mulatta.
White Man, == Terceron.
White Man, == Quateron.
White Man, == Quinteron.
WHITE.

RETROGRADE.

Mulatta, == Terceron.   Negroe, == Mulatta.   Indian, == Mulatta.   Negroe, == Indian
Saltatras.   Sambo de } == Negroe.   Mestize.   Sambo de } == Sambo de
Mulatta,   Indian,   Mulatta.
NEGROE.   Givero [o].

Figure N.1. Charts of interracial mixing drawn by Edward Long in his *History of Jamaica* (London: T. Lownudes, 1774).

17. I call Edwards's statement the reverse image of Brent's because it is underpinned by the racial assumption that the women freely gave themselves to the men.

18. The diaries are among the Monson Papers at the Lincolnshire Archives Office. Their 10,000 or so pages have been extracted and published by Douglas Hall (1989), which is the source I used in this study.

19. For Thistlewood's sexual practices, also see Beckles 1999 (38–58) and Morgan 1999 (69–74).

20. Morgan believes the transactions to be more widespread when Thistlewood was overseer of Vineyard Pen, which, as a result of having fewer slaves, was more intimate than a sugar estate (1995, 68n).

21. Thistlewood often borrowed money—up to twenty-seven pounds—from Phibbah (Hall 1989, 117, 219). The ability to lend him money, the master signifier of exchange, would certainly have raised her status above that of a slave.

22. Stedman's notebook, along with additional diaries, notebooks, and loose sheets of entries, are now housed in the John Bell Library at the University of Minnesota. His diaries have also been published by Stanbury Thompson, an English antiquarian who bought them from a junk dealer in 1940 (Thompson 1962). Thompson not only mistranscribed portions of the journals, he also took great liberties in editing them. For a more detailed account of the history of Stedman's notebooks and the changes Thompson made, see Price and Price (1988, xxvi–xxxvi). My references are to the manuscript unless otherwise indicated.

23. Peter Hulme calls the Inkle and Yarico story "the product of no single authorial consciousness but rather a story that English (and European) society chose persistently, over a period of seventy years, to tell itself" (1992, 228). He identifies Richard Steele's account that appeared in *The Spectator* in 1711 to be the most influential version of the story. For British women writers' adaptations of the Inkle and Yarico story, see Ferguson 1992 (79–90). For an explication of Stedman's employment of the story, see Sollors 1998.

24. For a history of the female abolitionist emblem, "Am I Not a Woman and a Sister?," see Yellin 1989 (3–25).

25. Price and Price 1988, 176. The Johnson edition deleted the reference to Joanna being "ravished" (Stedman 1806, 1:115).

26. The following observation by a medical doctor who visited Surinam in 1796 shows how the San Domingue rebellion entered European history as an act of unbridled savagery: "Restraint being removed, jealousy, suspicion, revenge, and all the worst passions of uncivilized man were left to rage in lawless sway. The most horrible cruelties which savage nature could invent were practised upon the whites—men, women, and children—the aged and the tender infant, all were slaughtered with one undistinguishing barbarity; and a scene of human woe was introduced such as no former age had witnessed" (Pinckard 1816, 502–3).

27. See Price and Price (1988, lxxxiii) for a complete list of literary works based on Stedman's *Narrative*.

28. Until Jean Fagan Yellin (1985) established Harriet Jacobs as author of *Incidents in the Life of a Slave Girl, as Written by Herself*, it was believed to have been the work of L. Maria Child.

3. "OUR HISTORY WAS TRULY BROKEN"

1. The sources for Gilroy's novel are the Johnson edition of Stedman's *Narrative* and Stanbury Thompson's edition of Stedman's unpublished memoirs and diaries in *The Journal of John Gabriel Stedman*.

2. Beryl Gilroy was one of the first black schoolteachers who went on to become the first black headmistress in England. She has expressed how "Caribbean writers in Britain have to deal when writing about the Caribbean with a retrospective and increasingly unrepresentative view of reality of the places they call home" (1998, 56).

3. Ukawsaw Gronniosaw, an African slave who was granted his freedom after serving in the British army, was author of *Narrative of the Most Remarkable Particulars in the Life of . . . an African Prince* (c. 1770). Gilroy includes a summary of his narrative in her novel.

4. The other black woman known to have married a white man was Elizabeth Sampson's niece (Van Lier 1971, 69). For more complete accounts of Graman Quacy and Elizabeth Sampson, see Price 1983 (153–59) and Van Lier 1971 (67–69).

5. The term *mulatto* is derived from *mule,* which is the offspring of a donkey and a horse. Defenders of slavery like Edward Long perpetrated the myth that mulatto women were barren like mules (1774, 2: 335–36).

6. The influential Quaker abolitionist Anthony Benezet makes a similar argument about Africa in *A Caution and Warning to Great Britain and Her Colonies* (1766).

7. Stedman's diary relating to this passage simply records: "I f-k one of his negro maids" (February 9 1773).

8. Sally Hemings's family history suggests a system of concubinage existed on the mainland as well. Her grandmother was an African woman impregnated by an Englishman, Captain Hemings, from whom the family took its name. Her owner, John Wayles (who was Thomas Jefferson's father-in-law), made her mother his concubine after his wife died (Hemings 1999, 255). It is a sign of the incestuous nature of slaveholding families that Sally was the half-sister of Jefferson's wife.

9. For a discussion of knowledge as "sanctioned ignorance," see Spivak 1999 (164).

10. Equiano characterizes himself as "almost an Englishman" and one who was known as "the black Christian" (51, 64).

4. "A VERY TROUBLESOME WOMAN"

1. David van Leer (1990), who explains the power of the root as an expression of Douglass's ambivalence toward Christianity and a synecdoche for his African "roots," gives a reading that is closer to my own. Also see Paul Gilroy (1993, 60–63).

2. In retelling the incident in *Life and Times,* Douglass assumes an ironic distance from his (if only momentary) belief in the purported power of the root (1962 [1892], 137–44).

3. Valerie Smith identifies a similar state of freedom within slavery in *Incidents in the Life of a Slave Girl,* when Jacobs dates her emancipation from the time she concealed herself in a crawlspace in her grandmother's house, a full seven years before she escaped to freedom (1990, 213).

4. One English traveler to St. Vincent reports that she "could comprehend little or nothing of what they [slaves] said; for though it was English, it was so uncouth a jargon, that to one unaccustomed to hear it, it was almost as unintelligible as if they had spoken in any of their native African tongues" (Carmichael 1969 [1833], 5).

5. Of the 142 runaway slaves listed in the Bahamas between 1822 and 1825, 128 of them were from Turks Islands (Saunders 1985, 82).

6. Missionaries, however, had little control over how slaves interpreted their teachings. In *Slaves and Missionaries* (1982), Mary Turner discusses the importance of religious meetings in providing a forum for black Baptists to mobilize slaves for rebellion. She argues that, at least in Jamaica, rebel slaves forced missionaries to see that their Christian values could not be reconciled with the brutality of a coercive labor system. The missionaries eventually had to acknowledge that viewing slaves as humans meant granting them freedom in this world rather than the afterworld.

7. Pringle admits in his supplement to Prince's narrative that her knowledge of Christianity was "indistinct" (Prince 1987, 231).

8. Gale Jackson describes herself as an African American activist-poet, librarian, and storyteller. She is of Jamaican descent on her mother's side and claims to have grown up in an extended family household with relatives from the West Indies passing through all the time (Jackson, Hahn, and Sherman 1992, 10).

9. Huckstering or higgling was both an integral part of the plantation economy and a constant irritant to the planters, as slaves were just as likely to sell goods stolen from their owners. As a means of controlling slave hucksters, the Antiguan government instituted a series of laws prohibiting the sale of certain goods (Goveia 1980, 161–63). As Jamaican sociologist and fiction writer Olive Senior points out, the everyday practices of slave women such as higglering, "Anancyism" or "working brain" (cunning), prostitution, and "knowing

people" has survived today in the skill of "making do," which is a term used for Afro-Caribbean women's ability to make something out of nothing (1991, 129–42).

10. Prince's father returned her to Captain I—— when she ran away to her mother, who hid her (Prince 1987, 197).

11. Brathwaite reports his discovery of records that fourteen white women married free colored men between 1781 and 1813 in Jamaica (1984, 13). It is a story that is yet to be explored.

12. "Subaltern or subordinate knowledges are composed not only of philosophies that have been assigned a nondisruptive place but also of ones that are unrecognizable according to institutionalized systems of meaning. Hence, even though subaltern groups think according to the terms of hegemonic discourse, their philosophy manifests itself in the *contradiction* between thought and action" (Sharpe 1993, 16).

13. Cooper explains this position as the singer's affectation of a "poor me gal" pose designed to gain sympathy (1995, 32).

14. See, for instance, "Arrival of the Snake-Woman," "The View from the Terrace," and "Lily Lily" (1989).

15. Prince's statement that the hut was separate from the room she had in Wood's yard gives a more complicated picture of domestic living arrangements than the opposition between the Great House and slave quarters would lead one to believe.

Bibliography

MANUSCRIPT SOURCES

James Ford Bell Library at the University of Minnesota, Minneapolis
Stedman, John Gabriel. Journal, diaries, and other papers. 1772–96.

University of the West Indies, Mona
Sistren Theatre Collective. *Nana-Yah.* 1980.

OFFICIAL DOCUMENTS

Parliamentary Papers, British Library, London
Accounts and Papers 92, no. 34 (1790–91).
Reports from Committees 20, no. 16 (1831–32).

Public Records Office, London
C.O. 137/21, folio 42, The further Examination of Sarra alias Ned taken by
    order of His Excellency, October 1, 1733.
C.O. 137/21/folio 207, Ayscough to Board of Trade, with enclosures.
Journals of the Assembly of Jamaica, vol. 3. Jamaica, 1733–34.

National Library of Jamaica, Kingston
Jamaica Exhibition Bulletin 1, no. 8, June 28, 1890.

SECONDARY SOURCES

Acholonu, Catherine Obianuju. 1989. *The Igbo Roots of Olaudah Equiano: An
    Anthropological Research.* Owerri, Nigeria: AFA Publications.

Agorsah, E. Kofi. 1994. "Archaeology of Maroon Settlements in Jamaica." In *Maroon Heritage: Archaeological, Ethnographic, and Historical Perspectives,* ed. E. K. Agorsah, 163–87. Barbados: Canoe Press.

Aidoo, Agnes Akosua. 1981. "Asante Queen Mothers in Government and Politics in the Nineteenth Century." In *The Black Woman Cross-Culturally,* ed. F. C. Steady, 65–77. Cambridge, Mass.: Schenkman.

Alpern, Stanley B. 1993. *Amazons of Black Sparta: The Women Warriors of Dahomey.* New York: New York University Press.

Anderson, Benedict R. 1983. *Imagined Communities: Reflections on the Origin and Spread of Nation.* London: Verso.

Andrews, Evangeline Walker, ed. 1939. *Journal of a Lady of Quality; Being the Narrative of a Journey from Scotland to the West Indies, North Carolina, and Portugal, in the Years 1774–1776.* New Haven: Yale University Press.

Andrews, William L. 1993. "The Changing Rhetoric of the Nineteenth-Century Slave Narrative of the United States." In *Slavery in the Americas,* ed. W. Binder, 471–86. Wurzberg, Germany: Königshausen & Neumann.

"The Anti-Slavery Society, and the West India Colonists." 1831. *Bermuda Royal Gazette* 4, no. 47 (November 22): 3.

Atwood, Thomas. 1791. *The History of the Island of Dominica.* London: J. Johnson.

Aub, Beth. 1989. "Nursing in Nannyland." *Sunday Gleaner,* April 4, 6.

Baker, Houston A., Jr. 1984. *Blues, Ideology, and Afro-American Literature: A Vernacular Theory.* Chicago: University of Chicago Press.

Barret, Leonard. 1976. *The Sun and the Drum.* Kingston, Jamaica: Sangster.

Barthes, Roland. 1989. "The Discourse of History." In *The Rustle of Language,* trans. Richard Howard, 127–40. Berkeley: University of California Press.

Beckles, Hilary. 1989. *Natural Rebels: A Social History of Enslaved Black Women in Barbados.* London: Zed Books.

———. 1999. *Centering Woman: Gender Discourses in Caribbean Slave Society.* Princeton, N.J.: Marcus Wiener.

Beckwith, Martha Warren. 1929. *Black Roadways: A Study of Jamaican Folk Life.* Chapel Hill: University of North Carolina Press.

Benedict, Barbara M. 1994. *Framing Feeling: Sentiment and Style in English Prose Fiction, 1745–1800.* New York: AMS.

Benoit, Paul Jacques. 1839. *Voyage à Surinam: Description des possessions Néerlandaises dans la Guyane.* Bruxelles: Société des Beaux-Arts.

Bhabha, Homi K. 1994. *The Location of Culture.* London: Routledge.

Bickell, Rev. Richard. 1825. *The West Indies As They Are; or A Real Picture of Slavery: But More Particularly As It Exists in the Island of Jamaica.* London: Hatchard.

Bilby, Kenneth M. 1984. "'Two Sister Pikni': A Historical Tradition of Dual Ethnogenesis in Eastern Jamaica." *Caribbean Quarterly* 30, nos. 3 and 4: 10–25.

Bilby, Kenneth, and Filomina Chioma Steady. 1981. "Black Women and Survival: A Maroon Case." In *The Black Woman Cross-Culturally,* ed. F. C. Steady, 451–67. Cambridge, Mass.: Schenkman.

Bolingbroke, Henry. 1807. *A Voyage to the Demerary.* London: Richard Phillips.

Booth, Karen. 1985. "When Jamaica Welcomed the World: The Great Exhibition of 1891." *Jamaica Journal* 18, no. 3: 39–51.

Brana-Shute, Rosemary. 1985. "The Manumission of Slaves in Suriname, 1760–1828." Ph.D. diss., University of Florida, Gainesville.

———. 1989. "Slave Manumission in Suriname, 1760–1828." *Slavery and Abolition* 10, no. 3: 40–63.

Brathwaite, Edward Kamau. 1971. *The Development of Creole Society in Jamaica, 1770–1820.* Oxford: Clarendon Press.

———. 1977. *Wars of Respect: Nanny, Sam Sharpe, and the Struggle for People's Liberation.* Kingston: Agency for Public Information.

———. 1984. "Caribbean Women During the Period of Slavery." *Caribbean Contact* (May 12): 2, 13.

———. 1994. "Nanny, Palmares and the Caribbean Maroon Connexion." In *Maroon Heritage: Archaeological, Ethnographic, and Historical Perspectives,* ed. E. K. Agorsah, 119–38. Barbados: Canoe Press.

Breeze, Jean "Binta." 1988. *Riddym Ravings and Other Poems.* Edited by M. Morris. London: Race Today Publications.

———. 1991. *Tracks.* Shanachie Records. CD 47008.

———. 1994. *Word Sound 'Ave Power: Dub Poets and Dub.* Notes. Heartbeat. CD H8 15.

Brodber, Erna. 1983. "Oral Sources and the Creation of a Social History of the Caribbean." *Jamaica Journal* 16, no. 4: 2–11.

Burnard, Trevor. 1998. "The Sexual Life of an Eighteenth-Century Jamaican Slave Overseer." In *Sex and Sexuality in Early America,* ed. M. D. Smith, 163–89. New York: New York University Press.

Bush, Barbara. 1990. *Slave Women in Caribbean Society, 1650–1838.* Bloomington: Indiana University Press.

Bush-Slimani, Barbara. 1993. "Hard Labour: Women, Childbirth and Resistance in British Caribbean Slave Societies." *History Workshop Journal* 36 (Autumn): 83–99.

Campbell, Mavis C. 1988. *The Maroons of Jamaica, 1655–1796: A History of Resistance, Collaboration and Betrayal.* Granby, Mass.: Bergin & Garvey.

Carey, Beverly. 1973. "The Maroons—Our Forgotten Heroes of History." *Sunday Gleaner,* September 23.

———. 1997. *The Maroon Story: The Authentic and Original History of the Maroons in the History of Jamaica, 1490–1880.* Gordon Town, Jamaica: Agouti Press.

Carmichael, Mrs. 1969 [1833]. *Domestic Manners and Social Condition of the*

White, Coloured, and Negro Population of the West Indies. Reprint ed. 2 vols. New York: Negro University Press.

Carretta, Vincent. 1999. "Olaudah Equiano or Gustavus Vassa? New Light on an Eighteenth-Century Question of Identity." *Slavery and Abolition* 20, no. 3: 96–105.

Child, Lydia Maria, ed. 1838. *Narrative of Joanna; An Emancipated Slave of Surinam.* Boston: Isaac Knapp.

———. 1996 [1833]. *An Appeal in Favor of That Class of Americans Called Africans.* Edited by C. L. Karcher. Amherst: University of Massachusetts Press.

Chin, Timothy S. 1997. "'Bullers' and 'Battymen': Contesting Homophobia in Black Popular Culture and Contemporary Caribbean Literature." *Callaloo* 20, no. 1: 127–41.

Cliff, Michelle. 1984. *Abeng.* New York: Penguin.

———. 1987. *No Telephone to Heaven.* New York: Dutton.

———. 1991. "Caliban's Daughter: The Tempest and the Teapot." *Frontiers* 12, no. 2: 36–51.

———. 1994. "History as Fiction, Fiction as History." *Ploughshares* 20, nos. 2–3: 196–202.

Condé, Maryse. 1999. *Land of Many Colors; and Nanna-ya.* Translated by Nicole Ball. Lincoln: University of Nebraska Press.

Cooper, Carolyn. 1994. "'Resistance Science': Afrocentric Ideology in Vic Reid's *Nanny Town*." In *Maroon Heritage: Archaeological, Ethnographic, and Historical Perspectives,* ed. E. K. Agorsah, 109–18. Barbados: Canoe Press.

———. 1995. *Noises in the Blood: Orality, Gender, and the "Vulgar" Body of Jamaican Popular Culture.* Durham, N.C.: Duke University Press.

Cooper, Helen M. 1996. "'Tracing the Route to England': Nineteenth-Century Caribbean Interventions into English Debates on Race and Slavery." In *The Victorians and Race,* ed. S. West, 194–212. Hants, U.K.: Scolar Press.

Cooper, Thomas. 1824. *Facts Illustrative of the Condition of the Negro Slaves in Jamaica.* London: J. Hatchard & Son.

Craton, Michael. 1982. *Testing the Chains: Resistance to Slavery in the British West Indies.* Ithaca, N.Y.: Cornell University Press.

Cundall, Frank, ed. 1907. *Lady Nugent's Journal: Jamaica One Hundred Years Ago.* London: Adam & Charles Black.

Dadzie, Stella. 1990. "Searching for the Invisible Woman: Slavery and Resistance in Jamaica." *Race and Class* 32, no. 2: 21–38.

Dalby, David. 1971. "Ashanti Survivals in the Language and Traditions of the Windward Maroons of Jamaica." *African Language Studies* 12: 31–51.

Davis, Angela Y. 1983. *Women, Race and Class.* New York: Vintage.

Davis, Charles T., and Henry Louis Gates Jr., eds. 1985. "Introduction: The Language of Slavery." In *The Slave's Narrative.* Oxford: Oxford University Press, xi–xxxiv.

de Certeau, Michel. 1984. *The Practice of Everyday Life*. Translated by Steven Rendall. Berkeley: University of California Press.

———. 1988. *The Writing of History*. Translated by Tom Conley. New York: Columbia University Press.

Defoe, Daniel. 1975 [1719]. *Robinson Crusoe*. Edited by M. Shinagel. New York: W. W. Norton.

Douglass, Frederick. 1962 [1892]. *Life and Times of Frederick Douglass, Written By Himself*. Reprint ed. London: Collier Books.

———. 1987 [1845]. *Narrative of the Life of Frederick Douglass, an African Slave, Written by Himself*. In *The Classic Slave Narratives*, ed. C. T. Davies and H. L. Gates Jr., 243–331. New York: Penguin.

Edwards, Bryan. 1807. *The History, Civil and Commercial, of the British Colonies in the West Indies*. 4th ed. 3 vols. London: J. Stockdale.

Edwards, Paul, ed. 1988. "Introduction" to *Equiano's Travels*, vii–xix. Portsmouth, N.H.: Heinemann.

Equiano, Olaudah. 1987 [1789]. *The Interesting Narrative of the Life of Olaudah Equiano, or Gustavus Vassa, The African*. In *The Classic Slave Narratives*, ed. C. T. Davies and H. L. Gates Jr., 3–182. New York: Penguin.

Fabian, Johannes. 1985. "Culture, Time, and the Object of Anthropology." *Berkshire Review* 20: 7–23.

Ferguson, Moira, ed. 1987. *The History of Mary Prince, a West Indian Slave, Related by Herself*. London: Pandora.

———. 1992. *Subject to Others: British Women Writers and Colonial Slavery, 1670–1834*. New York: Routledge.

Flannigan, Mrs. 1844. *Antigua and the Antiguans*. 2 vols. London: Saunders and Otley.

Ford-Smith, Honor. 1986. "Una Marson: Black Nationalist and Feminist Writer." Unpublished paper in the National Library of Jamaica, Kingston.

———. 1996. *My Mother's Last Dance*. Toronto: Sister Vision.

———. 1997. "Ring Ding in a Tight Corner: Sistren, Collective Democracy, and the Organization of Cultural Production." In *Feminist Genealogies, Colonial Legacies, Democratic Futures*, ed. M. J. Alexander and C. T. Mohanty, 213–58. New York: Routledge.

Foucault, Michel. 1980. *The History of Sexuality*, vol. 1: *An Introduction*. Translated by Robert Hurley. New York: Vintage.

———. 1989. "Film and Popular Memory." In *Foucault Live*, ed. J. Johnston, 89–106. New York: Semiotext(e).

Freud, Sigmund. 1963. "Screen Memories." In *Early Psychoanalytic Writings*, 229–50. New York: Collier.

Fryer, Peter. 1984. *Staying Power: The History of Black People in Britain*. London: Pluto.

Garrett, George. 1992. "Separate Prisons." *New York Times Book Review*, February 26, 1, 24–25.

Gates, Henry Louis, Jr. 1987. *Figures in Black: Words, Signs, and the "Racial" Self.* New York: Oxford University Press.

———. 1988. *The Signifying Monkey: A Theory of Afro-American Literary Criticism.* New York: Oxford University Press.

Gikandi, Simon. 1992. *Writing in Limbo: Modernism and Caribbean Literature.* Ithaca, N.Y.: Cornell University Press.

Gilroy, Beryl. 1991. *Stedman and Joanna—A Love in Bondage: Dedicated Love in the Eighteenth Century.* New York: Vantage.

———. 1998. *Leaves in the Wind: Collected Writings of Beryl Gilroy.* Edited by Joan Anim-Addo. London: Mango Publishing.

Gilroy, Paul. 1987. *There Ain't No Black in the Union Jack.* London: Hutchinson.

———. 1993. *The Black Atlantic: Modernity and Double Consciousness.* Cambridge: Harvard University Press.

Glave, Thomas. 1999. "Toward a Nobility of the Imagination: Jamaica's Shame." *Gay Community News* 24, nos. 3–4: 34–37.

Goodison, Lorna. 1986. *I Am Becoming My Mother.* London: New Beacon Books.

Gottlieb, Karla Lewis. 1994. "'The Mother of Us All': A History of Nanny, Leader of the Windward Jamaican Maroons." Master's thesis, Feminist Studies of Ethnicity, San Francisco State University, San Francisco.

Goveia, Elsa V. 1980. *Slave Society in the British Leeward Islands at the End of the Eighteenth Century.* Westport, Conn.: Greenwood.

Gray, Thomas R. 1975 [1881]. *The Confession, Trial and Execution of Nat Turner, the Negro Insurrectionist.* Reprint ed. New York: AMS Press.

Griffin, Farah Jasmine. 1996. "Textual Healing: Claiming Black Women's Bodies, the Erotic and Resistance in Contemporary Novels of Slavery." *Callaloo* 19, no. 2: 519–36.

Gronniosaw, James Albert Ukawsaw. 1774. *A Narrative of the Most Remarkable Particulars in the Life of James Albert Ukawsaw Gronniosaw, an African Prince.* Newport, R.I.: S. Southwick.

Guha, Ranajit. 1988. "The Prose of Counter-Insurgency." In *Selected Subaltern Studies,* ed. R. Guha and G. Spivak, 45–86. New York: Routledge.

Gunning, Sandra. 2001. "Traveling with Her Mother's Tastes: The Negotiation of Gender, Race, and Location in *Wonderful Adventures of Mrs. Seacole in Many Lands.*" *Signs* 26, no. 4: 949–81.

Gwilliam, Tassie. 1998. "'Scenes of Horror,' Scenes of Sensibility: Sentimentality and Slavery in John Gabriel Stedman's *Narrative of a Five Years' Expedition Against the Revolted Negroes of Surinam.*" *English Literary History* 65, no. 3: 653–73.

Hall, Douglas. 1989. *In Miserable Slavery: Thomas Thistlewood in Jamaica, 1750–86.* London: Macmillan.

Hall, Stuart. 1990. "Cultural Identity and Diaspora." In *Identity: Community,*

Culture, Difference, ed. J. Rutherford, 222–37. London: Lawrence & Wishart.

Handler, Jerome S. 1974. *The Unappropriated People: Freedmen in the Slave Society of Barbados.* Baltimore: Johns Hopkins University Press.

Harris, Col. C. L. G. 1951. "'Nanny,' the Maroon." *Gleaner,* November 8, 7.

———. 1967a. "The Maroons—Praised and Condemned." *Gleaner,* July 23, 7.

———. 1967b. "The 'Spirit of Nanny.'" *Sunday Gleaner,* August 6, 11–12, 28.

———. 1984. "History of the Moore Town Maroons." In *Jamaican Folk Tales and Oral Histories,* ed. L. Tanna, 19–20. Kingston: Institute of Jamaica.

Hart, Richard. 1950. "Cudjoe and the First Maroon War in Jamaica." *Caribbean Historical Review* 1: 46–79.

———. 1985. *Slaves Who Abolished Slavery,* vol. 2: *Blacks in Rebellion.* Kingston, Jamaica: University of the West Indies.

Hartman, Saidiya V. 1997. *Scenes of Subjection: Terror, Slavery, and Self-Making in Nineteenth-Century America, Race and American Culture.* New York: Oxford University Press.

Haselstein, Ulla. 1998. "Giving Her Self: Harriet Jacobs' *Incidents in the Life of a Slave Girl* and the Problem of Authenticity." In *(Trans)Formations of Cultural Identity in the English-Speaking World,* ed. J. Achilles and C. Birkle, 125–39. Heidelberg: Universitätsverlag C. Winter.

Hemings, Madison. 1999. "Madison Hemings's Memoir." In *Sally Hemings and Thomas Jefferson: History, Memory, and Civic Culture,* ed. J. Lewis and P. S. Onuf, 255–58. Charlottesville: University Press of Virginia.

Heuman, Gad, ed. 1986. *Out of the House of Bondage: Runaways, Resistance and Marronage in Africa and the New World.* London: Cass.

Higman, Barry W. 1984. *Slave Populations of the British Caribbean, 1807–1834.* Baltimore: Johns Hopkins University Press.

Hine, Darlene, and Kate Wittenstein. 1981. "Female Slave Resistance: The Economics of Sex." In *The Black Woman Cross-Culturally,* ed. F. C. Steady, 289–99. Cambridge, Mass.: Schenkman.

Hoogbergen, Wim. 1990. "The History of the Surinam Maroons." In *Resistance and Rebellion in Suriname: Old and New,* ed. G. Brana-Shute, 65–102. Williamsburg, Va.: College of William and Mary.

Hulme, Peter. 1992. *Colonial Encounters: Europe and the Native Caribbean, 1492–1797.* New York: Routledge.

Hutcheon, Linda. 1989. *The Politics of Postmodernism.* New York: Routledge.

Irigaray, Luce. 1985. *This Sex Which Is Not One.* Translated by Catherine Porter and Carolyn Burke. Ithaca, N.Y.: Cornell University Press.

Jackson, Gale. 1992. "mary prince bermuda. turks island. antigua. 1787." *Kenyon Review* 14, no. 1: 4–8.

Jackson, Gale, Kimiko Hahn, and Susan Sherman. 1992. *We Stand Our Ground: Three Women, Their Vision, Their Poems.* New York: Ikon.

Jacobs, Harriet. 1987 [1861]. *Incidents in the Life of A Slave Girl, Written by Herself.* In *The Classic Slave Narratives,* ed. C. T. Davies and H. L. Gates Jr., 333–515. New York: Penguin.

Kaplan, Carla. 1993. "Narrative Contracts and Emancipatory Readers: 'Incidents in the Life of a Slave Girl.'" *Yale Journal of Criticism* 6, no. 1: 93–119.

Kerr, Paulette A. 1995. "Victims or Strategists? Female Lodging-House Keepers in Jamaica." In *Engendering History: Caribbean Women in Historical Perspective,* ed. V. Shepherd, B. Brereton, and B. Bailey, 197–212. New York: St. Martin's Press.

Kopytoff, Barbara. 1973. "The Maroons of Jamaica: An Ethnohistorical Study of Incomplete Politics, 1655–1905." Ph.D. diss., University of Pennsylvania, Philadelphia.

———. 1976. "Jamaican Maroon Political Organization: The Effects of the Treaties." *Social and Economic Studies* 25, no. 2: 87–105.

L. M. S. Sept. 1796. "Stedman's Expedition to Surinam." *The Analytical Review* 24, no. 3: 225–37.

Lalla, Barbara. 1996. *Defining Jamaican Fiction: Marronage and the Discourse of Survival.* Tuscaloosa: University of Alabama Press.

Lamming, George. 1991. *In the Castle of My Skin.* Ann Arbor: University of Michigan Press.

Law, Robin. 1993. "The 'Amazons' of Dahomey." *Paideuma* 39: 245–60.

Lewis, M. G. [Matthew Gregory]. 1929 [1834]. *Journal of a West India Proprietor, 1815–17.* Edited by M. Wilson. Boston: Houghton Mifflin.

Long, Edward. 1774. *The History of Jamaica.* 3 vols. London: T. Lownudes.

Macqueen, James. 1831. "The Colonial Empire of Great Britain." *Blackwood's Magazine* 187 (November 30): 744–64.

"A Maroon Celebration." 1976. *Star* (Kingston, Jamaica), October 14, 1.

"Maroon Factions Clash, But Tribute Paid to Nanny." 1975. *Star,* October 31, 40.

Martin, Leann Thomas. 1973. "Maroon Identity: Processes of Persistence in Moore Town." Ph.D. diss., University of California, Riverside.

Mathurin, Lucille. 1974. "An Historical Study of Women in Jamaica from 1655 to 1844." Ph.D. diss., University of the West Indies, Mona, Jamaica.

———. 1975. *The Rebel Woman in the British West Indies during Slavery.* Kingston: Institute of Jamaica.

Mathurin Mair, Lucille. 1990. "Recollections of a Journey into a Rebel Past." In *Caribbean Women Writers: Essays from the First International Conference,* ed. S. R. Cudjoe, 51–60. Wellesley, Mass.: Calaloux Publications.

McDowell, Deborah E. 1989. "Witnessing Slavery after Freedom—Dessa Rose." In *Slavery and the Literary Imagination,* ed. D. E. McDowell and A. Rampersad, 144–63. Baltimore: Johns Hopkins University Press.

Midgley, Clare. 1992. *Women against Slavery: The British Campaigns, 1780–1870.* London: Routledge.

Miller, Jefferson. 1979. *Capital of Earth: The Maroons of Moore Town*. Rolling Calf Films. Videocassette.

Mintz, Sidney W. 1995. "Slave Life on Caribbean Sugar Plantations: Some Unanswered Questions." In *Slave Cultures and the Cultures of Slavery*, ed. S. Palmié, 12–22. Knoxville: University of Tennessee Press.

Mohammed, Patricia. 2000. "'But Most of All Mi Love Me Browning': The Emergence in Eighteenth- and Nineteenth-Century Jamaica of the Mulatto Woman as the Desired." *Feminist Review* 65 (Summer): 22–48.

Mordecai, Pamela, and Betty Wilson, eds. 1989. *Her True-True Name: An Anthology of Women's Writing from the Caribbean*. Portsmouth, N.H.: Heinemann.

Moreton, J. B. 1790. *Manners and Customs in the West India Islands*. London: W. Richardson.

Morgan, Philip D. 1995. "Slaves and Livestock in Eighteenth-Century Jamaica: Vineyard Pen, 1750–1751." *William and Mary Quarterly* 52, no. 1: 47–76.

———. 1999. "Interracial Sex in the Chesapeake and the British Atlantic World, c. 1700–1820." In *Sally Hemings and Thomas Jefferson: History, Memory, and Civic Culture*, ed. J. E. Lewis and P. S. Onuf, 52–84. Charlottesville: University Press of Virginia.

Morrison, Toni. 1987. "The Site of Memory." In *Inventing the Truth: The Art and Craft of Memoir*, ed. W. Zinsser, 101–24. Boston: Houghton Mifflin.

Morrissey, Marietta. 1989. *Slave Women in the New World: Gender Stratification in the Caribbean*. Lawrence: University Press of Kansas.

Mullen, Harryette. 1992. "Runaway Tongue: Resistance Orality in *Uncle Tom's Cabin, Our Nig, Incidents in the Life of a Slave Girl*, and *Beloved*." In *The Culture of Sentiment: Race, Gender and Sentimentality in Nineteenth-Century America*, ed. S. Samuels, 244–64. New York: Oxford University Press.

Murray, Reginald. 1951. "A Visit to Nanny Town." *Sunday Gleaner*, October 28.

Naipaul, V. S. 1962. *The Middle Passage: Impressions of Five Societies, British, French and Dutch, in the West Indies and South America*. London: A. Deutsch.

Naylor, Gloria, and Toni Morrison. 1985. "A Conversation." *Southern Review* 21, no. 3: 567–93.

Newson, A. S. 1993. "Stedman and Joanna: A Love in Bondage." *World Literature Today* 67, no. 1: 219.

Nichols, Grace. 1990. "The Battle with Language." In *Caribbean Women Writers: Essays from the First International Conference*, ed. S. R. Cudjoe, 283–89. Wellesley, Mass.: Calaloux Publications.

O'Callaghan, Evelyn. 1993. "Historical Fiction and Fictional History: Caryl Phillip's *Cambridge*." *Journal of Commonwealth Literature* 29, no. 2: 134–47.

Paquet, Sandra Pouchet. 1992. "The Heartbeat of a West Indian Slave: 'A History of Mary Prince.'" *African American Review* 26, no. 1: 131–45.

Patterson, Orlando. 1967. *The Sociology of Slavery: An Analysis of the Origins, Development and Structure of Negro Society in Jamaica.* Rutherford, N.J.: Farleigh Dickinson University Press.

———. 1982. *Slavery and Social Death: A Comparative Study.* Cambridge, Mass.: Harvard University Press.

Pfaff, Françoise, ed. 1996. *Conversations with Maryse Condé.* Lincoln: University of Nebraska Press.

Phillips, Caryl. 1991. *Cambridge.* New York: Vintage.

Pinckard, George. 1816. *Notes on the West Indies, Including Observations Relative to the Creoles and Slaves of the Western Colonies and the Indians of South America.* 2d ed. 2 vols. London: Baldwin, Cradock, and Joy.

Poovey, Mary. 1984. *The Proper Lady and the Woman Writer: Ideology as Style in the Works of Mary Wollstonecraft, Mary Shelley, and Jane Austen.* Chicago: University of Chicago Press.

Pratt, Mary Louise. 1992. *Imperial Eyes: Travel Writing and Transculturation.* New York: Routledge.

Price, Richard. 1973. "Introduction" to *Maroon Societies: Rebel Slave Communities in the Americas,* ed. R. Price, 1–30. Garden City, N.Y.: Anchor Press.

———. 1983. *First-Time: The Historical Vision of an Afro-American People.* Baltimore: Johns Hopkins University Press.

Price, Richard, and Sally Price, eds. 1988. *Narrative of a Five Years Expedition against the Revolted Negroes of Surinam: Transcribed for the First Time from the Original 1790 Manuscript.* Baltimore: Johns Hopkins University Press.

Prince, Mary. 1987 [1831]. *The History of Mary Prince, A West Indian Slave.* In *The Classic Slave Narratives,* ed. C. T. Davies and H. L. Gates Jr., 183–242. New York: Penguin.

Ragatz, Lowell J. 1970. *A Guide for the Study of British Caribbean History, 1763–1834.* New York: Da Capo Press.

Raiskin, Judith. 1993. "The Art of History: An Interview with Michelle Cliff." *Kenyon Review* 15, no. 1: 57–71.

Reid, Vic. 1983. *Nanny-Town.* Kingston: Jamaica Publishing House.

Riland, John. 1827. *Memoirs of a West-India Planter.* London: Hamilton, Adams, & Company.

Roberts, W. Adolphe. 1955. *Jamaica: The Portrait of an Island.* New York: Coward-McCann.

Rodney, Walter. 1972. *How Europe Underdeveloped Africa.* London: Bogle-L'Ouverture Publications.

Rushdie, Salman. 1984. *Shame.* New York: Vintage.

Rushdy, Ashraf H. A. 1997. "Neo-Slave Narrative." In *The Oxford Companion to African American Literature,* ed. W. L. Andrews, F. S. Foster, and T. Harris, 533–35. New York: Oxford University Press.

Samuels, Allison. 2002. "Angela's Fire." *Newsweek,* July 1, 54.

Saunders, D. Gail. 1985. *Slavery in the Bahamas, 1648–1838.* Nassau, Bahamas: The Nassau Guardian.

Schiller, Jacque Lynn. 2001. "Marc Forster Lets Silence Speak for Itself." IndieWIRE Webzine. URL: www.indiewire.com/film/interviews/int_Forster_Marc_011112.html.

Scott, James C. 1990. *Domination and the Arts of Resistance: Hidden Transcripts.* New Haven: Yale University Press.

Scott, Michael. 1833. *Tom Cringle's Log.* Edinburgh: W. Blackwood.

Senior, Olive. 1989. In *Arrival of the Snake-Woman and Other Stories,* 1–45. Burnt Mill, England: Longman.

————. 1991. *Working Miracles: Women's Lives in the English-Speaking Caribbean.* Bloomington: Indiana University Press.

Sharpe, Jenny. 1993. *Allegories of Empire: The Figure of Woman in the Colonial Text.* Minneapolis: University of Minnesota Press.

————. 1995a. "'Something Akin to Freedom': The Case of Mary Prince." *differences* 8, no. 1: 31–56.

————. 1995b. "Of This Time, Of That Place: A Conversation with Caryl Phillips." *Transition* 5, no. 4: 154–61.

Shyllon, Folarin. 1977. *Black People in Britain, 1555–1833.* London: Oxford University Press.

Silenieks, Juris. 1984. "The Maroon Figure in Caribbean Francophone Prose." In *Voices from Under: Black Narrative in Latin America and the Caribbean,* ed. W. Luis, 115–25. Westport, Conn.: Greenwood Press.

Simmonds, Lorna. 1987. "Slave Higglering in Jamaica 1780–1834." *Jamaica Journal* 20, no. 1: 31–38.

Smith, Liz. 2002. "Angela's Bashes." *Newsday* (New York). June 27, A15.

Smith, Valerie. 1987. *Self-Discovery and Authority in Afro-American Narrative.* Cambridge: Harvard University Press.

————. 1990. "'Loopholes of Retreat': Architecture and Ideology in Harriet Jacobs's *Incidents in the Life of a Slave Girl.*" In *Reading Black, Reading Feminist: A Critical Anthology,* ed. H. L. Gates Jr., 212–26. New York: Meridian.

Sollors, Werner. 1998. "A British Mercenary and American Abolitionists: Literary Retellings from 'Inkle and Yarico' and John Gabriel Stedman to Lydia Maria Child and William Wells Brown." In *(Trans)Formations of Cultural Identity in the English-Speaking World,* ed. J. Achilles and C. Birkle, 95–123. Heidelberg: Universitätsverlag C. Winter.

Spillers, Hortense J. 1987. "Mama's Baby, Papa's Maybe: An American Grammar Book." *Diacritics* 17, no. 2: 65–81.

Spivak, Gayatri Chakravorty. 1988. "Can the Subaltern Speak?" In *Marxism and the Interpretation of Culture,* ed. C. Nelson and L. Grossberg, 271–311. Urbana: University of Illinois Press.

————. 1999. *A Critique of Postcolonial Reason: Toward a History of the Vanishing Present.* Cambridge: Harvard University Press.

Stauder, Jack. 1974. "The 'Relevance' of Anthropology to Colonialism and Imperialism." *Race* 16, no. 1: 29–51.

Stedman, John Gabriel. 1806 [1796]. *Narrative of a Five Years' Expedition against the Revolted Negroes of Surinam.* 2d ed. 2 vols. London: J. Johnson & T. Payne.

————. 1824. *Joanna, Or, the Female Slave: A West Indian Tale.* London: L. Relfe.

"Stedman's Narrative of an Expedition to Surinam." 1796. *Critical Review* 19: 52–60.

"Stedman's Surinam." 1796. *British Critic,* November 8, 536–40.

Stewart, John. 1823. *A View of the Past and Present State of the Island of Jamaica; With Remarks on the Moral and Physical Condition of the Slaves, and on the Abolition of Slavery in the Colonies.* Edinburgh: Oliver & Boyd.

Sypher, Wylie. 1942. *Guinea's Captive Kings: British Anti-Slavery Literature of the Eighteenth Century.* Chapel Hill: University of North Carolina Press.

Thicknesse, Philip. 1790. *Memoirs and Anecdotes of Philip Thicknesse.* 3 vols. Dublin: William Jones.

Thomas, Herbert T. 1890. *Untrodden Jamaica.* Kingston: Aston W. Gardner.

Thompson, Stanbury, ed. 1962. *The Journal of John Gabriel Stedman, 1744–1797.* London: Mitre.

Trinh, T. Minh-Ha. 1989. *Woman, Native, Other: Writing Postcoloniality and Feminism.* Bloomington: Indiana University Press.

Tuelon, Alan. 1973. "Nanny—Maroon Chieftainess." *Caribbean Quarterly* 19, no. 4: 20–25.

Turner, Mary. 1982. *Slaves and Missionaries: The Disintegration of Jamaican Slave Society, 1787–1834.* Urbana: University of Illinois Press.

Tyrrell, William Blake. 1984. *Amazons: A Study in Athenian Mythmaking.* Baltimore: Johns Hopkins University Press.

Tyson, Gerald P. 1979. *Joseph Johnson: A Liberal Publisher.* Iowa City: University of Iowa Press.

van Leer, David. 1990. "Reading Slavery: The Anxiety of Ethnicity in Douglass's Narrative." In *Frederick Douglass: New Literary and Historical Essays,* ed. E. J. Sundquist, 118–40. Cambridge: Cambridge University Press.

Van Lier, R. A. J. 1971. *Frontier Society: A Social Analysis of the History of Surinam.* The Hague: Martinus Nijhoff.

Waller, John Augustine. 1820. *A Voyage in the West Indies: Containing Various Observations Made during a Residence in Barbadoes, and Several of the Leeward Islands.* London: Richard Phillips.

Ward, J. R. 1988. *British West Indian Slavery, 1750–1834: The Process of Amelioration.* Oxford: Clarendon Press.

Webb, Barbara J. 1992. *Myth and History in Caribbean Fiction: Alejo Carpentier, Wilson Harris, and Edouard Glissant.* Amherst: University of Massachusetts Press.

Williams, Joseph J. 1938. *The Maroons of Jamaica.* Chestnut Hill, Mass.: Boston College Press.

"Wood v. Pringle." 1833. *The Times,* March 1, 6–7.

Yellin, Jean Fagan. 1985. "Text and Contexts of Harriet Jacobs' *Incidents in the Life of a Slave Girl: Written by Herself.*" In *The Slave's Narrative,* ed. C. T. Davis and H. L. Gates Jr., 262–82. Oxford: Oxford University Press.

———. 1989. *Women and Sisters: The Antislavery Feminists in American Culture.* New Haven: Yale University Press.

Index

Jackson, Gale, 135–36, 166n. 8
Jacobs, Harriet, xviii–xxii, 25, 98,
 121–23, 146, 165n. 28, 166n. 3
Jamaican nation, xvi, 23

Kaplan, Carla, xx

Lady Nugent, 45, 62, 88, 107
Lewis, M. G., 51, 107, 109–11, 116

manumission, 59, 68, 74–76, 101,
 113, 120, 137–38, 163n.12, 13
maroon, 4–6, 18; Colonel C. L. G.
 Harris, 6–7, 158nn. 4, 7;
 maroon identity, xvi, 5; oral
 histories, xiii, xxv, 1–4, 8, 12,
 14, 22, 39; resistance, 34, 59.
 See also Nanny
Mathurin, Lucille, xiv, 1, 59, 141,
 145, 149–50
McDowell, Deborah E., xiv
memory, xii, xiii, 39, 87; collective
 xiii, 1, 14, 106, 115, 160n. 27;
 counter-memory, xxv
mimicry, xxii–xxiii, xxv–xxvi, 61–62,
 92, 99
Mohammed, Patricia, 162n. 4
Monster's Ball, 153–55
Moreton, J. B., 47, 51, 78, 107, 143,
 145
Morgan, Philip D., 4, 65, 164n. 19,
 n. 20
Morrison, Toni, xi–xii, 123
Morrissey, Marietta, xv, 58, 60
Mullen, Harryette, 141

Naipaul, V. S., 17, 159n. 11
Nanny, xvi–xvii, 1–2; maroon
 leader, 3–6, 9–12, 13–14,
 24–28; National Hero, 17–22,
 29–31, 159n. 13; ohemaa, 22–24,
 159n. 14; obeah woman, 2–3,

16, 24–25, 27, 35–36, 37–38;
 science woman, 3–4, 24, 37, 41;
 woman warrior, 7, 12–13, 31–35,
 37, 158nn. 6, 7. *See also* feminity,
 "wild femininity"
Nanny Town, 2, 5, 7–8, 15–16,
 25–27, 159n. 16
Nichols, Grace, 33–34
Noble Slave, xxv, 79

obeah, 3, 160n. 3; obeah woman,
 xii, xxv, 3, 24–25, 27, 35–38, 51,
 117
oral tradition, 9–12, 14, 16–18,
 158n.10
oral storytelling, 3, 6, 30–31, 136,
 147–48

Paquet, Sandra Pouchet, 133–34
Patterson, Orlando, 45, 163n. 13
Phillips, Caryl, xii; *Cambridge,* xxiv,
 88–90, 105–19, 123, 146–47
Pinckard, George, 164n. 26
Poovey, Mary, 52
postcolonialism, xxiii–xxiv, 97, 99,
 102
postmodernism, xi, 39, 105–6,
 116–18, 147
Pratt, Mary Louise: anticonquest,
 49–51, 101; contact zones,
 3–4; reciprocity, 49–51, 83,
 86, 101–2
Price, Richard,159n. 17; and Sally
 Price, 54, 73, 78, 162n. 2
Price, Sally. *See* Price, Richard
Prince, Mary: abolitionist, 115,
 146; author, 118–19, 121, 127,
 140, 151; Christian woman,
 132–33, 119, 142–43; domestic
 slave, 129–32; moral character of, 121–23, 126, 127–29,
 136–40, 140–42, 147–49;

trickster, 35–36, 57, 78, 117
Trinh T. Minh-Ha, 89–90
Trouillet, Michel-Rolph, xv
Turner, Nat, 113, 135–36

Van Lier, R. A. J., 58, 103–4,
  165n. 4

Williams, Joseph J., 158n. 6

Yellin, Jean Fagan, 164n. 24,
  165n. 28

Jenny Sharpe is professor of English and comparative literature at the University of California at Los Angeles. She is author of *Allegories of Empire: The Figure of Woman in the Colonial Text* (Minnesota, 1993).